Lead Generation

FOR DUMMIES®

A Wiley Brand

by Dayna Rothman

Foreword by Jon Miller
Cofounder of Marketo

FOR DUMMIES®
A Wiley Brand

Lead Generation For Dummies®

Published by: **John Wiley & Sons, Inc.,** 111 River Street, Hoboken, NJ 07030-5774, www.wiley.com

Copyright © 2014 by John Wiley & Sons, Inc., Hoboken, New Jersey

Published simultaneously in Canada

For general information on our other products and services, please contact our Customer Care Department within the U.S. at 877-762-2974, outside the U.S. at 317-572-3993, or fax 317-572-4002. For technical support, please visit www.wiley.com/techsupport.

Wiley publishes in a variety of print and electronic formats and by print-on-demand. Some material included with standard print versions of this book may not be included in e-books or in print-on-demand. If this book refers to media such as a CD or DVD that is not included in the version you purchased, you may download this material at http://booksupport.wiley.com. For more information about Wiley products, visit www.wiley.com.

Library of Congress Control Number: 2013954102

ISBN 978-1-118-81617-2 (pbk); ISBN 978-1-118-81589-2 (ebk); ISBN 978-1-118-81586-1 (ebk)

Manufactured in the United States of America

10 9 8 7 6 5 4 3 2 1

Table of Contents

Part II: Connecting Inbound Marketing and Lead Generation 71

Chapter 6: Generating Leads with Content Marketing 73

Chapter 7: Putting Your Best Foot Forward with Your Website 99

Chapter 23: Ten Powerful Lead-Generation Tactics 349

Foreword

* *

*B*ack in 1994, I had just graduated from college and was getting ready to buy my first car. I had some hopes and dreams about what I wanted, but I also needed to make sure I got the right car — one that was reliable enough, not too expensive, had the right options, and so on.

So what did I do? I spent a week going to various dealers, doing test drives, asking questions (and getting some high-pressure tactics to buy *right now*). Ultimately, I did pick the one I wanted. Of course, then I had to go figure out my financing options, which again required the painstaking process of talking with various sales reps and agents. I wasn't happy with the process, but I didn't have a choice.

Fast-forward to today. When I recently bought a car, I did all the research online over the course of a few weeks. I was able to compare models, search reviews, read forums, and see what my friends had to say. I was able to pick the exact model I wanted, with the exact features. And I was able to figure out exactly what I should pay for it. I negotiated the price and the financing online. The first — and only time — I actually spoke with a dealer was to sign the paperwork and take delivery.

Why the difference? Back in the 1990s, if a potential customer wanted to learn about your products or solutions, they found that information was scarce. They could not "just Google it," and the only route to the information was to talk to a representative of the company. This was true across many industries: technology sales, healthcare plans, industrial solvents, and so on — and as I found, automobile purchases.

Today, however, rise of the Internet has resulted in a quick transition from information scarcity to information abundance. Product information is now ubiquitous. The web provides consumers with instant information gratification. Mobile devices add a wherever/whenever dimension to every aspect of the experience. Consumers can access detailed specs, pricing, and reviews about goods and services 24/7 with a few flicks of their thumbs on their smartphones. Meanwhile, social media encourages consumers to share and compare. As a result, buyers today form brand perceptions and make significant purchasing decisions based on online research and prior to or without any direct contact with a salesperson.

This in turn is letting buyers seize control of their buying processes, and to delay engagement with the company until they are much further along. The power is shifting from the sellers to the buyer. According to Forrester research, buyers today are between two-thirds to 90 percent done with their buying cycle before they want to talk with a representative of the company. In the case of my car purchase, I did 99 percent of the process myself.

The shift in how buyers research and buy products and services is causing dramatic changes in how companies market and sell to them. Back in 1994, if someone heard that I was in the market for a new car, I would be defined as a "lead," and the right thing to do would have been to pass me to sales. I expected that I would need to talk to a sales person, and the sales person expected they would need to talk to a lot of early-stage buyers. At the time, that's what lead generation was all about.

But today, if a sales representative calls me while I'm still in my early research phase, it's just another unwanted sales call — an expensive, unproductive, cold call that's frustrating to me, and, I'm sure, to the poor sales person making that call.

This is redefining the art and science of lead generation. The old ways of generating leads are giving way to new, modern methods that embrace today's empowered, digital buyer. The new rules of lead generation are first, instead of pushing a message out to potential customers, attract buyers to you with relevant and valuable content. Second, instead of passing everyone immediately to sales, nurture leads over time by engaging them in a dialogue.

The abundance of information creates a scarcity of attention. Social scientist Herbert Simon first talked about attention economics when he wrote, "In an information-rich world, the wealth of information means a dearth of something else: a scarcity of whatever it is that information consumes. What information consumes is obvious: attention of its recipients."

This means it is harder and harder today to push a message out to buyers. Traditional lead generation tactics are, at the core, about renting the buyer's attention from someone else. Take television as an example; the network got the viewers to watch, and the advertiser literally interrupts the program to get their message across. At a tradeshow, the producer got the audience to the event; the marketer is renting some physical space on the show floor and is hoping to catch the attendee's attention as they walk by. These kinds of tactics worked in the era of information scarcity — and they still play a role today — but they are also becoming harder and harder to execute well in the era of information abundance.

Fortunately, there are times in every buying cycle when the customer is actively seeking information, just like I was as I did my recent car purchase. Forty-six percent of daily searches are for information about products and services (source: SRI, October 2010). From typing something into Google to putting together a short list to building an ROI justification, buyers want trusted information to help them — and they are seeking that information by searching online and asking their social networks. Here, the buyer is actively giving their attention, and the company that best provides the information they are seeking it is in the best position to earn their eventual business.

To replace outdated "renting attention" marketing tactics, companies are deploying new methods to build awareness and generate leads. They are helping prospects to find their company in the early stages of their decision-making process. Instead of finding leads; they are helping leads find them.

They are doing this by creating great content and then using that content as "bait" to attract potential buyers and build relationships. This content is not about the company or its products and services; it educates or entertains. For example, say you are a retailer of fashionable shoes. Instead of sending promotional offers to your customers (10 percent off! Free shipping! Buy now!), you become a trusted source of advice about fashion and trends. This makes content the perfect antidote to buyers who don't want to be sold to and will screen out anything they don't want. It's also the perfect alternative to "rented attention" because brands build "owned attention" when they publish their own content. Alec Baldwin got it wrong in *Glengarry Glen Ross*: Success today is not about "ABC: Always Be Closing." Today, it's "Always Be Helping."

When done right, this approach has dramatically better economics than traditional marketing techniques that rely on interrupting the customer. David Merman Scott writes that "Prior to the web, organizations had only two significant choices to attract attention: buy expensive advertising or get third-party ink from the media. But the web has changed the rules." Instead of renting buyer attention from third-parties, today's lead generation is about creating your own audience and attracting your own attention. It's brains, not budget.

Content that is educational or entertaining attracts potential customers before they are ready to engage with sales, perhaps while they are still doing research. This has created a gap between when a prospect is created and when she is ready to be a "lead." In fact, on average, less than 25 percent of the new prospects companies generate are actually ready to engage with sales when they first enter the funnel (source: RainToday). Some of the remaining prospects may be truly unqualified, but as many of 70 percent of them will eventually buy a product from you — or your competitors.

So what should you do with those leads?

If you send them to sales before they are ready, you risk annoying the prospect and exacerbating the problem of sales complaining about the quality of marketing leads. Also, because sales is focused on closing business, not developing it, those leads often end up in "limbo" and get dropped on the floor.

The answer is *lead nurturing*: the process of building relationships with qualified prospects regardless of their timing to buy, with the goal of earning their business when they are ready. Prospects may not want to be sold to, but they do want help and support with their education and research process.

Lead nurturing is not sending out an e-newsletter on a semi-regular basis, randomly calling leads every few weeks to see if they are ready to buy yet, blasting your entire database with a new case study, or pushing content that promotes your products and services but is not relevant to your prospects' interests or needs at their stage of buying. Lead nurturing is no different than building any long-term relationship — you need to be a good partner, foster respect and trust, be a good listener, and keep things interesting. You need to be consistent and relevant.

Another way to think of lead nurturing is that you are marketing to prospects you have already spent money to acquire. The Bridge Group found it takes an average of seven or eight marketing touches to convert a new name into a sales-ready lead, so lead nurturing should be about generating leads from your existing marketing database. Another way to think about the return on investment of lead nurturing is to examine the percentage of sales leads that come are "slow leads," defined as potential buyers who were not ready for sales when they first came in to the database, but are now. Most companies do a mediocre job of staying in touch with this kind of prospect; at these companies, slow leads make up less than 25 percent of all sales leads; but with a disciplined lead nurturing process in place, slow leads can make up 50 percent or more.

Of course, when you embrace the idea of not sending everything to sales, you must also be able to identify when leads that are being nurtured *should* be promoted to sales. That's why *lead scoring* is first cousin to lead nurturing. Lead scoring is a shared sales and marketing methodology for ranking leads in order to determine their sales-readiness. You score leads based on the interest they show in your business, their current place in the buying cycle, and their fit in regards to your business.

By helping sales focus on the hottest leads and opportunities, lead scoring can substantially improve sales effectiveness. According to CSO Insights, a sales consultancy, companies that say it's easy to get information about prioritizing sales efforts achieve an average of 97 percent of their revenue plan, whereas companies that say it is hard achieve an average of only 79 percent. When sales spends more of their time productively selling to the right people, you'll see higher win rates, shorter sales cycles, faster sales ramp times, and possible even a larger average selling prices.

Attracting buyers with relevant content and nurturing leads over time are just a few of the new rules of lead generation that are discussed in this guide. It's jam-packed with actionable tips and ideas that will help your business generate more and better quality sales leads, perhaps with less investment and effort. Get ready to learn about how content marketing, social media, your website, event marketing, other paid programs, and more can assist you in delivering the right leads to sales at the right time. So dive right in!

— Jon Miller, cofounder of Marketo

Introduction

As a marketer, you hear a lot about the "new marketing landscape." And most likely, you feel overwhelmed by all of the new marketing channels that you just *have* to be on to generate leads. But how do you weed through all of the information to know what lead generation strategies work for you and your business without pulling your hair out?

In this book, I do the footwork for you and present you with actionable information on what channels and strategies are available and how to assess them for your own unique business situation. And because lead generation should never end with lead acquisition, I present you with strategies to improve your lead nurturing and scoring techniques to make sure you send only the most qualified leads to sales, who then can close more deals. And because this book provides you with strategies to measure your efforts, *you* get to look like a rock-star marketer in front of your C-suite!

About This Book

To write this book, I did a ton of research in addition to calling upon my own personal experience as a marketer in the technology sector, where some of the most innovative marketing is occurring. Because I work as the senior content marketing manager for Marketo, one of the leading thought leaders in the lead generation and marketing automation space, I'm in the trenches every day working with our lead generation team to bring in revenue.

The information in this book is on the cutting edge of what is happening now in marketing, and it can (and will) help you and your teams be better marketers. But I'm not perfect, of course, and I undoubtedly missed something. So let me know! Your comments, questions, and compliments help improve future editions. You can contact me directly at daynaleighrothman@gmail.com.

Conventions Used in This Book

To help you navigate this book efficiently, I use a few style conventions:

- ✔ Website addresses, or URLs, are shown in a special monofont typeface, like `this`. If you're reading this in an ebook, those links are clickable.

- ✔ Numbered steps that you need to follow are set in **bold**.

- ✔ New terms are set in *italic* typeface.

- ✔ Sidebars present technical information that you don't have to know but that might interest those of you who want to understand the technology behind the function.

Foolish Assumptions

I made a few assumptions about you when writing this book. To make sure we're on the same page, I assume that

- ✔ You know something about marketing, but not necessarily a lot.

- ✔ You want to learn *at least* the basics of lead generation and maybe even want to delve into the advanced stuff, which I also write about.

- ✔ You have a general concept of what a website is, you know how to use social channels, and you understand the concept of email marketing.

- ✔ In fact, I assume that you have *sent* an email before.

- ✔ You know that technology is moving fast, and marketing needs to move just as fast.

- ✔ You are committed to improving your marketing and generating more (and better) leads for your sales team.

Icons Used in This Book

The Tip icon marks tips (duh!) and shortcuts that you can use to make life easier.

Remember icons mark the information that's especially important to know. To siphon off the most important information in each chapter, skim through these icons.

The Technical Stuff icon marks information of a highly technical nature that you can normally skip over.

The Warning icon tells you to watch out! It marks important information that may save you headaches.

How This Book Is Organized

This book is divided into parts, which are further divided into chapters. You can read it cover-to-cover, or you can skip around. At the very least, I recommend you familiarize yourself with Part I and II, so you know what lead generation is and how to go about defining your leads, and then skip around to what is most applicable to you and what you want to learn.

This book takes you from the basics to advanced techniques that are cutting edge in marketing, so feel free to skip around based on the level of your expertise!

Part I: Getting Started with Lead Generation

This part explains what lead generation is and why it matters. Lead generation helps you generate more leads, send better leads to sales, and grow your business in many ways. Lead generation also incorporates many channels and strategies. This part outlines the tactics, so you understand not only what to expect in the coming chapters of this book, but also how each tactic and channel relates to lead generation as a whole. You will also learn the foundation of lead generation: how to define your leads, define your goals and strategy, choose the right technology, and build a rock-star lead generation team.

Part II: Connecting Inbound Marketing and Lead Generation

This part is where the magic starts to happen! Learn about inbound marketing and some of the different tactics that you can employ to amplify your efforts. This part goes into detail to explore content marketing, your blog, website, search engine optimization, and social media. Because today's buyers are now searching for *you*, learn about how inbound marketing techniques can help you be found by your target audience.

Part III: Linking Outbound Marketing with Lead Generation

You can't rely on inbound marketing alone for your lead generation efforts. By putting some paid and outbound tactics to work in parallel with your inbound efforts, you can drive leads further down your funnel at a faster rate. This part discusses the importance of paid programs like pay-per-click ads, content syndication, direct mail, event marketing, and inside sales.

Part IV: The Middle of the Funnel

Lead generation is not done at lead acquisition, which is a common mistake that many marketers make. This part defines mid-funnel marketing techniques, like lead nurturing and scoring, and discusses why they are important. Because many of your leads will not be ready to buy right away, what are you doing to nurture them until they *are* ready to buy? Learn about email marketing to your database, lead nurturing, and lead scoring so your leads never dry up.

Part V: Measuring Your Lead Generation Efforts

Today's marketers need to test, optimize, and measure. No longer should marketers be seen as a cost center. Due to advances in testing and measurement, marketers can now have a seat at the revenue table. This Part goes into detail on how to test your lead generation campaigns and how to develop solid lead generation metrics so every program you create is measureable. Learn how to tie each and every lead generation program to revenue over the lead lifecycle.

Part VI: The Part of Tens

This part gives marketers some quick ideas and tips on how to improve lead generation strategy. Learn about the ten most common lead generation pitfalls, my top ten lead generation influencers to watch, and ten powerful lead generation tactics to consider (that I don't focus on in detail throughout the book).

Beyond the Book

- ✔ **Cheat Sheet:** This book's Cheat Sheet can be found online at www.dummies.com/cheatsheet/leadgeneration. See the Cheat Sheet for definitions of lead generation terms and a listing of useful, free lead-generation apps.

- ✔ **Dummies.com online articles:** Companion articles to this book's content can be found online at www.dummies.com/extras/leadgeneration. The topics range from content creation to sales enablement best practices, how to make sure your emails actually get to where they're going, top social media strategies, and top lead generation blogs to check out.

- ✔ **Updates:** If this book has any updates after printing, they will be posted to www.dummies.com/extras/leadgeneration.

Where to Go from Here

This book was not designed to be read cover-to-cover (unless you want to, of course). Each chapter provides practical marketing techniques and tactics you can use to promote your business and generate more leads. You can pick it up and choose what chapters to read at any time. For instance, maybe this week you want to learn about content marketing (Chapter 6), but next week you have a meeting with your executive team and need some tips on measuring and analytics (Chapter 20). You can pick the book up at either one of those chapters and be ready to execute without too much jumping around.

Part I
Getting Started with Lead Generation

In this part . . .

- Grow your business with lead generation
- Define what a lead means for you and your business
- Craft your lead-generation road map
- Choose the right technology and team to hit the ground running

Chapter 1

Beginning Your Lead Generation Journey

In This Chapter

▶ Getting started with lead generation

▶ Understanding the changing landscape of the marketer and buyer

▶ Amplifying your marketing with lead generation

▶ Forming a complete lead generation strategy

According to Google chairman Eric Schmidt, "There was 5 exabytes of information created between the dawn of civilization and 2003, but that much information is now created every two days, and the pace is rapidly increasing." It's incredible to think about the amount of information that your customers and prospects are seeing each and every day.

In fact, SuperProfile states that "on any given day, the average customer will be exposed to 2,904 media messages, will pay attention to 52, and will positively remember 4." The buying process has drastically changed too. No longer are buyers relying on Joe the local car salesman to help them make a decision. Instead they are doing their own research and educating themselves throughout the buying process: Think review sites, social channels, Google, and more. By the time a buyer walks into your business, she is armed with information and likely has already made a decision.

What's more, buyer expectations are much higher. If I get back to my desk at work and discover that Chipotle has messed up my order, I don't hesitate to send them a tweet to let them know. You would be surprised how quickly they respond. And if they don't, I send them another tweet to let them know I am disappointed at their lack of response. As a company, you need to learn to build trust and create relationships with your buyers. If you break that trust, your buyers won't come back. Or worse, they will tell everyone about their bad experience.

All of these factors put marketers in a complicated situation. How do you find these leads, break through the noise, and create relationships? How do you make sure *your* messages are heard and resonate with your audience? And how can you help your customers educate themselves through the buying process so that they ultimately choose you and your company? It's a lot to think about!

Lead generation is your answer. *Lead generation* describes the marketing process of engaging and capturing interest in a product or service for the purpose of developing a sales pipeline and ultimately gaining new customers.

Lead generation has become an increasingly popular strategy to create demand and help your marketing messages be heard across multiple different channels. Lead generation helps your company increase brand awareness, build relationships, drive more qualified leads into your sales funnel, and ultimately close deals. Sounds pretty great, right?

In this chapter I cover how lead generation can help your business grow by enabling you to find more leads, enhance prospect relationships, maximize your marketing spend, and ultimately, be a more strategic marketer. Plus, I go into detail on the ways lead generation connects with various marketing channels and strategies (some that you might be using today, and others that you might not have tried yet).

Growing Your Business

Whether you are a small five-person technology company just starting out, or a huge multibillion-dollar enterprise corporation, you want your business to grow. A lot. And as a marketer, you might be finding that it isn't enough anymore to purchase an ad in a print magazine, buy a list of leads, and have your sales teams sit in a room and call on a bunch of cold prospects. In today's multichannel world of mobile devices and social media, you need to do more than cold call to close a sale. Plus, having your sales teams call leads that are never going to buy is a huge waste of time and money.

Marketing has changed. In order to grow your business, you need to reach your buyers through many different marketing channels, such as social media, search engines, your website, events, and more. And by creating a well-thought-out lead generation strategy that maps to business priorities, you can effectively grow your business by generating more leads for your sales teams to call. The beauty of lead generation is that it covers a lot of ground if you incorporate multiple channels into your strategy.

And not only are you generating *more* leads, but you're generating *better* leads. By better leads, I mean warmer leads. What are *warm* leads? They are potential customers who are very close to purchasing by the time they reach your sales teams — which means happier sales executives, happier marketers, and more customers.

But how are you going to grow your business through lead generation? Stay tuned.

Finding more leads

Let me take a step back and talk about finding leads. Every business could use *more* leads. More leads mean more potential customers ready to buy your product or service. Finding an abundance of leads is hard — really hard. And it has become even harder and more complex due to the changing nature of the Internet and the rapid pace at which today's businesses are expected to grow.

Marketers of yore tried to generate leads through many outbound (and often aggressive tactics) such as cold calling, batch and blast email tactics, trade-shows, print and radio advertising, and list purchasing. Although outbound techniques certainly have their place and are indeed part of a well-rounded lead generation strategy (as I discuss later in this book), used alone, they can be a turnoff to many of today's buyers.

Modern marketers also need to employ tactics like social media, content marketing, SEO, and similar strategies to generate more (and warmer) leads for their sales teams.

In fact, the marketing team at Marketo (a leading marketing automation software provider that also happens to be my employer) generates about 80 percent of their sales pipeline. That's pretty impressive and certainly a stat that many companies aspire to. The marketing machine generates enough leads that the sales teams can focus more on selling and less on prospecting. To grow your business, this is what you want to do, and where lead generation can really make an impact.

Enhancing prospect relationships

Even more important than generating a ton of leads is generating a ton of *qualified* leads that are interested enough in your product or service that they could potentially become customers. Generating leads like they are going out of style won't matter if they are bad leads, so take care. As I mentioned earlier, today's buyer self-educates. And because of the open nature of the Internet, he has high expectations for customer service. Additionally, today's buyer values relationships and trust, and likes to interact with brands on a more personal level through social channels such as Facebook and Twitter. He wants to be spoken *with,* not spoken *at.*

Companies today need to focus on creating relationships with leads so that when a buyer is ready to purchase, your company is top-of-mind. This is done through engaging leads with educational content, being active on social channels to develop a following, face-to-face interactions at events, and other relationship-building lead generation tactics.

Remember, the days of the faceless corporation are over. Your buyers want to engage with you as they would engage with a friend. Consumer companies like Coca-Cola, Nike, and Apple do a great job creating relationships with customers through storytelling, great branding, and creative lead generation tactics. Appealing to your buyer creates brand ambassadors, ultimately helping you grow your company and generate more high-quality leads.

Maximizing your spending

Lead generation enables you to maximize your spending as a marketer and ultimately gain greater credibility within an organization. Marketing has been increasingly pressured to produce metrics and be accountable for a budget, and is often scrutinized for wasting expensive sales resources calling on bad leads that are not qualified in any way. Because lead generation provides you with the framework for measureable campaigns, return on investment (ROI) becomes easier to report on.

Lead generation helps you focus on program ROI, evaluate leads to determine sales-readiness, and nurture leads that are not quite yet ready to buy. By being focused and strategic with your lead generation strategy, you can truly begin to maximize your marketing spending while making sure you are focusing on sending qualified leads to sales.

Additionally, tactics like social media, blogging, content marketing, your website, and SEO give you a huge bang for your buck. Instead of renting attention, as you would in paid programs, you are owning your own attention. What is the difference? Well, *renting attention* is paying someone to borrow their audience — like an event or a paid ad. *Owning attention* is the ability to develop your *own* following through content marketing and social media. And when you combine these techniques with paid programs such as events, email marketing, and inside sales, you can truly maximize your spending.

Being more strategic

Creating an integrated lead generation strategy for your business enables you to capture and nurture leads in a more strategic way. Many companies lack a lead acquisition *strategy*. Marketing managers may place a few ads, start a Facebook page, or create a three-page ebook, but they think of lead generation as a tactical part of marketing. Instead, you need to think of lead generation holistically and strategically in order for it to be effective. Integrate many facets of your marketing department including events, email marketing, social media, paid programs, lead nurturing, and sales to thematically concentrate and maximize your overall efforts.

Tying It All Together

Lead generation strategy is a combination of many different tactics that are interconnected to create a multichannel plan of attack. To be successful and grow your business, you can't just focus on one tactic and ignore the rest. Budget is always a concern, so do what you can and be strategic in what you choose to focus on. But not doing that one webinar per year or creating a half-baked Facebook page and forgetting about it immediately aren't going to yield the results you are looking for.

This book takes an in-depth look at all of the different lead generation tactics you can employ for success, but before you embark on a journey towards lead generation awesomeness, it makes sense to get a lay of the land. What types of marketing channels exist and how do they relate to lead generation specifically? Read on.

Inbound marketing

According to Jon Miller, VP and cofounder of Marketo, *inbound marketing* is "the process of helping customers find your company — often before they are even looking to make a purchase — and then turning that early awareness into brand preference and, ultimately, into leads and revenue." Inbound marketing is a critical component to lead generation.

Why is inbound marketing important? According to Forrester Research, buyers seek out three pieces of content about a vendor for every one piece sent by a marketer, and for every one piece sent by sales. Therefore, you need to make sure those three pieces of content are from your company.

Inbound marketing tactics such as content marketing, social media, SEO, and website optimization are truly leading the pack when it comes to where marketers are spending their lead generation budgets, as you can see in Figure 1-1.

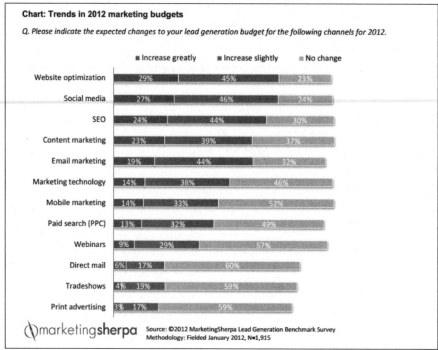

Figure 1-1: A MarketingSherpa lead generation benchmark survey for 2012.

Content marketing

Content, which often takes the form of an ebook, video, infographic, or slide deck, is the fuel for most (if not all) of your lead generation campaigns. No matter what channel you choose — whether it's your website, blog, or email marketing — you need a high-value offer to pique the interest of your lead. Quality content that shows a true understanding of the lead's business challenges is the perfect way to grab the customer's attention, begin building that needed brand awareness, and entice her to fill out a form at the same time.

Website

Your website is where you want to drive all of your lead generation efforts. It is your home base and where a lead can find everything he needs to know about your company. Your website is also where you house your contact information for leads that you want to contact you right away, and where you can attempt to capture lead information through forms. If it's done well, your website can really show your personality and attract the attention of your prospects.

Blog

Your company blog is where you get a chance to inject your personality and build credibility as the thought leader in your space. By leveraging subject matter experts from within your organization, your blog can be a destination spot for potential customers looking for best practices in your industry. Your blog is also a great place to capture lead information by prompting them to subscribe to an RSS (Really Simple Syndication) feed or engaging with them through the comment feature of your blog. Be careful though. If you have no subject matter experts on your team, don't try to fake it with a bunch of buzzwords. Instead, work to train them on becoming experts and encourage them to follow industry blogs and their own research. Remember, it's about establishing your company's expertise in the space.

Social media

Social media is a great platform for you to share your voice and spread the word. There are many channels to choose from, like Facebook, Twitter, LinkedIn, and Google+, and each one enables your business to build an organic following and attract brand ambassadors. Social channels are a great place to share your content, blogs, and other product or service-specific information, while also adding your brand's personality to the tone of the message. Paid advertising on social channels enables you to collect lead information and get your message seen by many, based on specific targeting criteria.

Search engine optimization

SEO (search engine optimization) plays a crucial role in attracting potential leads to your website through organic searches on search engines such as Google, Yahoo!, and Bing. By choosing to set up business-specific keywords, you can optimize and build your website so that when a lead searches for one of your keywords on a search engine, your website pops up on the first few pages of Google. This may help a lead find your company, but as I stated previously, you've got to present her with knowledgeable content in order for that visitor to go deeper into your website and keep coming back.

Outbound marketing

Although inbound marketing is getting a lot of buzz, the key to successful lead generation is a well-rounded marketing mix. This includes both inbound and outbound techniques. Through outbound marketing programs, you actively go out to find your customers, often via paid channels. Another distinction to make is that inbound marketing works for broad lead generation activities, but outbound is good to amplify your inbound efforts and target specific opportunities. And in many cases, outbound techniques can have that "wow" factor to make your company stand out since these strategies are often highly targeted with an obvious call-to-action. As a result, good outbound marketing can lead someone down your sales funnel, as discussed in more detail in the next chapter, at a faster rate, assuming he is a good lead.

PPC (pay-per-click) advertising

By paying to advertise on search engines such as Google, Yahoo!, and Bing, your message can be seen by leads searching for keywords specific to your business. Pay-per-click (PPC) ads show up on the side and top of the organic search results and use targeted ad copy to tempt leads to click a high-value offer such as a content piece that relates directly to a search term. PPC ads also take the form of banner advertising on many websites and can be found on social channels such as LinkedIn.

Content syndication

Content is the fuel for your lead generation efforts. But it's not enough to merely put content on your own website: You also want to make sure it is seen by thousands (or millions) of potential leads. Content syndication can take the form of both paid efforts, selecting websites that will host your content, and nonpaid efforts, like writing a guest blog post on an industry association's website, or sharing your content through RSS feeds and social media. Many content syndicators require that leads fill out a form asking for contact information such as email addresses, address, company, and so on, adding more qualified leads to the database.

Direct mail

Although there are many views on the effectiveness of direct mail, when combined with the other efforts listed here, direct mail can be a highly effective way to reach and engage your target audience. By focusing on sending creative and targeted communications, you can grab the attention of someone who has previously not responded to other lead generation efforts.

Event marketing

Event marketing is a fantastic way to generate leads, create lasting relationships, and engage with current customers for upsell and cross-sell opportunities. Events often take the form of webinars, conferences, tradeshows, or seminars and offer your company a chance to meet your leads face-to-face and form a lasting impression. This helps you cement relationships and top-of-mind when your lead is ready to make a purchase decision.

Inside sales

An important part of being successful with your lead generation efforts is the ability to turn marketing leads into sales pipeline. Your inside sales team can help you with this. Inside sales takes marketing-generated leads, calls and qualifies them, and then hands them off to an account executive or a more experienced sales person to close. The team is often considered part of the marketing function because without its help, marketing leads often don't get called and can dry up — you definitely don't want the fantastic leads you have worked so hard to generate sitting neglected in the dark.

Email marketing

Email marketing often uses leads already in your database or leads from a list. By creating emails to promote content pieces, events, new product launches, and so on, you can create additional buzz and demand for your company. Email marketing attracts leads to your website, blog, social channels, events, and webinars, making it a fantastic channel to move leads through your sales funnel.

Lead nurturing and lead scoring

Many marketers forget that lead generation is *not* finished after the lead has been acquired. Instead, it's just beginning. Many of the leads you have generated and brought into your database are not quite ready yet to buy. So through lead nurturing, systematically sending emails that move a lead closer to a purchase, you can help turn your lukewarm leads hot. And by assigning leads scores based on how closely they fit your buyer profile and where they are on their buyer journey, you know exactly when a lead needs to be sent to sales. You don't want a hot lead that is itching to make a purchase going cold because no one is calling him.

Chapter 2

Identifying Your Leads

*W*hat is a lead, anyway? And more importantly, what is a *good* lead? In searching for the perfect definition of a lead, I came across a blog post on the Marketo website that addressed this discussion exactly. Here is what the leading industry thought leaders had to say on the subject.

Jon Miller, cofounder of and VP of marketing for Marketo, says, "In Marketo's revenue cycle, a lead is a qualified prospect that is starting to exhibit buying behavior." Craig Rosenberg, sales and marketing expert and founder of the awesome blog *The Funneloholic*, states, "There are two elements to a lead — demographic and psychographic. When it comes to the psychographic element, your definition of a lead will depend on your company, where you're selling, and who you're selling to."

A pretty solid start, but ultimately your definition of a good lead is very particular to your own criteria — you need to ask yourself who historically has been buying your product or service.

Defining Your Leads

Not all leads are created equal. And it is critical before you embark on your lead generation journey to determine what your definition of a *good* lead is. And it's not just your definition that matters. What is your sales department's definition of a *good* lead? After all, salespeople are the ones who are following up and closing deals. So if marketing thinks a good lead is one thing and sales vehemently disagrees, you have a problem. Organizational alignment and a clear, spelled-out definition of a lead make for a good lead generation program.

Of course, there's no easy way to do this. A "good lead" can be just as objective as say, the best artist or musician. What if I think the best band is Led Zeppelin and you're more of a Pink Floyd person? Everyone has an opinion. And you can bet on the fact that the CEO, CMO, and VP of sales all have a unique definition of what they think the "best lead" is. Remember to be realistic and compromise. After you have set up your lead definitions, you can put lead scoring into place, which I go more into detail about in Chapter 18.

The first step to coming up with an agreed-upon lead definition is having a meeting with all stakeholders, and then opening the discussion up to both your sales and marketing teams. Create a list, diagram your lead flow on a whiteboard, and then come up with "the one lead definition to rule them all."

Assessing demographic fit

First, look at some basic demographics. Who is your buyer? Use demographic information (ideally from your customer relationship management program or marketing automation software) to begin creating a profile of the individual or group who most often purchases your product or service. Demographics become more important for B2C (business-to-consumer) companies as the demographic attributes of individuals work fairly well to determine how to segment your marketing campaigns. Demographics are also extremely useful for B2B (business-to-business) companies and can be used quite effectively to develop your lead generation strategy.

Typical demographic attributes can consist of

- ✔ Gender
- ✔ Title
- ✔ Age
- ✔ Education (degrees and certifications)
- ✔ Years of experience
- ✔ Income
- ✔ Specialties

You can add many more demographic attributes to this list, depending on what is important to your marketing efforts. The more detailed your demographic list is, the closer you can get to really defining what a good lead means to your company.

Demographic profiling is an attempt to generalize and create a profile of your target buyers and leads. Often, your leads will be very different from your developed profiles. Remember to always reassess your demographic lead profile frequently as your business needs and priorities change.

Applying firmographic profiles

Just as demographics apply to people, *firmographics* help you narrow down what sort of organizations buy your product or service. This is highly important, particularly to a B2B organization. Firmographics look at information such as location, company size, and industry.

Most companies sell products or services within particular verticals, like high tech, healthcare, financial services, and so on, to certain-sized companies. For instance, an enterprise application firm whose software costs upwards of $500,000 per year would not want to bother with leads from a company that could only afford to spend about $15,000 per year. This is where firmographics becomes very important to your lead generation segmentation.

When looking at firmographics, you often measure

- Company size
- Company location
- Revenue
- Number of divisions
- Industry
- Number of products/services sold
- Geographic markets served
- Rankings/stock indexes (Fortune 500, Inc. 500, and so on)

Qualifying leads with BANT

BANT stands for Budget, Authority, Need, and Time, and is a more advanced lead qualification practice than demographics and firmographics. BANT takes into consideration the ability to secure facts about the prospect before moving forward, and therefore these are questions often asked by the sales rep to further qualify the lead.

Although you can ask some of these questions up front on a website form, my philosophy is that your forms should always be short and leave the tough questions to your sales teams. Research shows that the longer the form, the more drop-off you have.

So let's dig into the specifics and further define BANT:

- **Budget:** Budget is a big one. Make sure the lead can afford your product or service. This is often one of the first questions that your sales rep asks in order to determine whether the lead is good or not. Both B2B and B2C companies care about the answer to the budget question: "How much do you have budgeted for this project/item?"

   Your lead will likely not give you a specific answer, so expect a range, and be ready to ask some other questions (like what she's currently using today) to indirectly deduce a conclusion. And also remember that budgets are flexible and can change. However, don't spend time trying to sell a $3,500 handbag to someone who only really has the money to spend $350.

- **Authority:** After you have determined that a lead has the dough to spend on your product or service, find out whether he has the authority to make the decision. Can he sign that dotted line? If so, you are truly in luck. But most likely, the first contact you speak to will be a "gatekeeper" of sorts, or an "influencer," as I like to call them. Your first contact, even if she is not the decision-maker, is most likely *crucial* to the decision-making process. She has either been tasked to find a solution, or is the one experiencing the pain that your product can rectify.

   If you determine that the lead is an influencer, your sales team needs to dig deep to find out who the decision-maker is because that is someone you *need* on your lead list.

- **Need:** Your lead has to *need* your product or service. Simple as that. It never works out if the lead wants your product or service but doesn't really need it. But remember, your leads may not *know* that they have a problem, so it's up to your sales team to show it to them. If your lead fits all of your other criteria, a good sales executive can help her find that pain (or future pain) and solve it — with your product or service, of course!

- **Time:** What is your lead's purchasing timeframe? It needs to map pretty closely to your delivery process so that you are aligned with what your lead needs. For instance, say you run an office furniture supply store and you get a call from a company 1,000 miles away that needs an order for 100 chairs that you have currently back-ordered. The customer wants them delivered in three days. You obviously can't get the chairs shipped on time. Therefore, the timeframe in which your prospect needs your product does not align with your capabilities. Of course, you want to try and sell her another chair that you *do* have in stock, but be wary when expectations and reality don't line up. You want to be careful to set realistic expectations.

Defining Your Sales Funnel

After you have a good idea who your best leads are, the next step to defining your lead generation process is to define your sales funnel — knowing where a prospect is in his buying journey so that you can align it directly to your marketing and sales processes. Mapping your lead generation efforts to your funnel is extremely important as it dictates your campaigns, messaging, and expected metrics.

Many companies typically define the sales process as a funnel. (The top of the funnel is where you get the broadest amount of leads and the bottom of the funnel is where a lead turns into a customer.) Take a look at Figure 2-1 as an example of a typical sales funnel.

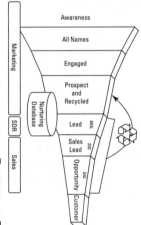

Figure 2-1:
A typical
sales funnel.

By tailoring programs and messages to this process, you can move leads down the funnel starting from the top of the funnel (early awareness) to the bottom of the funnel (late-stage buyers).

Understanding your funnel stages

Every company has a different funnel depending on its sales processes. However, for the sake of simplicity, I talk about a funnel that I'm familiar with — Marketo's. Marketo defines the sales and marketing process in stages:

  ✔ **Awareness and Friend:** This stage covers all leads who might know who Marketo is but that are not known in their database. Marketo understands that a lead might be visiting their website or downloading an ebook, but has not formally identified himself. These leads are curious about who Marketo is; they are often brought in through inbound marketing efforts such as social media and content.

- ✔ **Name:** This is when an individual has officially entered Marketo's database. To Marketo, a name is just a name; it is not yet a lead at all. Why? Because names have not yet *engaged* with the company. Remember, just because someone gets scanned at your tradeshow booth doesn't mean she wants to communicate with your company in a meaningful way. Therefore, she is not yet considered a lead.

- ✔ **Engaged:** Marketo doesn't move names to the next stage in the funnel until they have had some sort of meaningful conversation with the client. An engaged individual knows he is in the database, he has maybe attended a webinar or downloaded an ebook, and he expects Marketo to email and communicate with him.

- ✔ **Target:** Once an individual has engaged with Marketo in some way, Marketo uses lead scoring (more on that in Chapter 18) to determine whether that person is a qualified buyer. That means she is a fit for their ideal demographic and behavioral criteria.

- ✔ **Lead:** Finally! A target becomes a lead. Not until this moment does marketing pass a lead to sales. To become a lead, a person has to show sufficient interest in Marketo. Maybe she has downloaded a few whitepapers, attended a few events, and responded to a direct mail campaign. This person has a high lead score.

- ✔ **Recycled:** Sometimes a prospect won't actually become a lead yet. She may have downloaded a few ebooks, but when she's called by sales, she is not ready to buy. Instead of leaving that potential future lead in a black hole to dry out and die, you want to make sure she is recycled into your lead nurturing database. That way, you can continue sending your prospect relevant and educational materials in hopes that one day soon she will indeed become a viable lead.

- ✔ **Sales lead:** If the lead is truly qualified and he has had a good conversation with the inside sales team, he is passed on to an Account Executive (AE). The AE also speaks directly with the lead and has seven days to either turn the lead into a true sales lead, or send him back to marketing for lead nurturing, where marketing adds that lead into a campaign to re-engage him over time.

- ✔ **Opportunity:** From there, a lead becomes an opportunity when sales has qualified the lead and it is an active selling opportunity. To give you some insight, at Marketo, about a quarter of leads generated become opportunities.

- ✔ **Customer:** Woot! You now have a full-blown customer and your lead has converted to a sale.

Always remember that every company's sales funnel is going to be different, so take some time to speak with your internal sales and marketing teams to come up with your own definitions (or feel free to use Marketo's as a model).

After you have mapped out your sales funnel and have a good idea of what happens to leads when they come into your system, spend time mapping your lead generation efforts to buying stages. You can define a buying stage by how close a lead is to making a buying decision — and it's critical to create lead generation programs that resonate to where buyers are in their purchasing decisions.

Most companies typically define their buyer stages as *early*, *mid*, and *late* or top-of-funnel (TOFU), middle-of-funnel (MOFU), and bottom-of-funnel (BOFU). Take a look in Figure 2-2, which shows you how a sales funnel can map to buying stages.

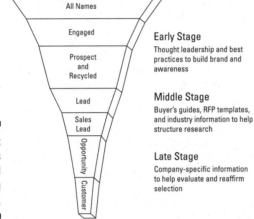

Figure 2-2:
A sales funnel and buying stage map.

Early-stage buyers

Early-stage buyers often map to the awareness/friend, name, engaged, and target stages in your sales funnel. Early-stage buyers have either never heard about your company or have very little brand awareness. The goal of early-stage content assets and lead generation campaigns is to bring leads into your funnel and get them interested enough in what you are all about, so they want to stick around, consume more content through your lead nurture channels, and ultimately become customers.

The important thing to note at this stage when it comes to your lead generation campaigns is that you want to make sure you are tailoring your messaging for early-stage buyers. Someone who just learned about your company probably doesn't want to watch a customer testimonial. Instead, he is more interested in learning who you are and consuming thought leadership in the form of best practices.

Typically during this stage, buyers are either looking for general industry best practices and haven't realized they have a problem yet, or they realize they have a problem and are just starting their research. Your campaign messaging and offers must align with what a buyer is looking for in this stage. The idea is that through proper targeting and appropriate messaging, you can bring early-stage buyers into your funnel and help them move through their educational journey to become mid-stage buyers.

Mid-stage buyers

A buyer becomes mid-stage after she has shown some interest in your business's core competencies. That lead has displayed some sort of buying behavior and is potentially a true sales lead. A mid-stage buyer should map to the lead and sales lead stage of your sales funnel.

Whereas your early-stage offers and messaging often align to industry best practices and actionable tips, and have a focus on creating a relationship and trust with your buyer, your mid-stage offers are meant to direct your lead's focus towards your product.

If a lead sticks around, subscribes to your blog, downloads a variety of ebooks, and even attends a webinar, she is likely in the middle stages of your funnel. She has shown a real interest in your company and is ready to receive more targeted messaging and offers that tie in nicely with what your company can offer.

For example, consider a company that sells budgeting software to the enterprise. Maybe your early-stage offers discuss budgeting best practices, common budgeting pitfalls, how to optimize your budget, and so on. Then after a lead has shown interest, she is ready to receive offers that talk specifically about budgeting software. Notice how a buyer is moving from broad to specific interest in your product or service.

Late-stage buyers

Late-stage buyers are generally in the opportunity category and are getting pretty hyped up on your company's goods. They have successfully made it through your early-stage offers, have gone through the mid-stage gauntlet, and are now downloading very product-centric information such as pricing sheets, customer testimonial videos, and datasheets. Your early- and mid-stage offers have set the stage, and your leads now have a good understanding of how your product or service can cure their pain. Late-stage is a good time to be engaged with a sales person, as late-stage buyers are clear hand-raisers and have shown a solid interest in your company.

Chapter 3

Setting Your Lead Generation Goals

In This Chapter

▶ Making all programs measureable

▶ Organizing your lead generation plan

▶ Getting key stakeholders on board

▶ Partnering with sales for a closed-loop lead lifecycle

As a marketing team, have you ever been called the "arts and crafts" table? I have! At a company I used to work for, the sales reps used to tease us and call us the "arts and crafts" table and jokingly ask us what we were going to put glitter on next. It was all in good fun, but it was the symptom of a problem that many marketers are faced with: They have trouble proving to their organization that they are accountable for their actions. The term "arts and crafts" conveys that marketers are thought of as a bunch of people sitting around a table creating paintings and doing fun projects, but making no meaningful contribution to the business.

We do fun projects, of course, but times have changed. And thanks to the measurability of most lead generation programs, efforts are now planned and measurable. Particularly with the advent of marketing automation technologies that enable marketers to track program successes and return on investment (ROI), marketers are now able to finally have a seat at the revenue table. There is much more involved in marketing for lead generation than simply creating a crafts project.

So, in order to maintain (or prove) that marketing can be accountable, impactful, metrics-minded, and meticulous, it's important to set your lead generation goals up front before you embark on creating specific campaigns. How are you going to plan your roadmap and what metrics are you going to set?

This chapter goes into detail to help you define your lead generation goals, craft your lead generation road map, build a business case for lead generation to key stakeholders, and align your sales and marketing teams.

Defining Your Key Metrics

Before you even start creating your lead generation blueprint and building your business case, you need to define your key metrics. What are you looking to get out of lead generation? How will lead generation affect your organization and what are you trying to achieve?

You then need to determine where you are now, what your sales and marketing teams have historically been doing, and whether it has been effective.

Why is this important? Well, your key metrics and what is important to you and your organization will be the driving forces behind your lead generation plan. They will also help you accurately plan resources and allocate dollars.

Asking important questions

Get your team in a room, sit down, and get ready to answer some important baseline questions to guide your goal-setting. I call this the *discovery phase*. By determining what you are doing now, you can set an initial benchmark for where you are today and where you want to be a month from now, six months from now, and so on. It might be helpful to have both sales and marketing in this meeting to get a closed-loop look at your sales process.

Ask yourself a selection of the following questions broken down into a sales and marketing process category:

✔ **Sales processes**

- What is your average sales price?

- What is your average sales cycle?

- What are your revenue goals per quarter?

- What is your *win rate* — the percentage of leads that turn into sales?

- How do you define an opportunity and what are the steps involved to move an opportunity to a sale?

- How many "influencers" usually influence a sale?

- What does your sales team look like? Do you have inside sales reps and account executives, or do you only have an outside sales team?

- What do sales reps do with leads that do not turn into opportunities?

- What percentage of marketing generated leads would your sales teams define as good leads?

- Where does your sales team look to find leads without the help of marketing?

✔ **Marketing processes**

- What lead generation programs are you currently participating in?

- Do you have a content plan? Do you have a company blog?

- Is your company active on social media channels?

- What happens to new leads when they enter your customer relationship management (CRM) system?

- What happens to new leads that don't convert right away?

- What is the ROI of your lead spending? What is your cost per lead?

- Do you have a marketing automation platform (a software solution that helps marketers deploy — and automate — marketing programs and lead generation activities to increase revenue)? For more on this, see Chapter 4.

- Do you have a lead scoring and lead nurturing program?

- How are you tracking metrics currently?

- What is the conversion rate from leads to opportunities?

- What is your success/win rate?

- What is marketing's contribution to the sales pipeline?

- What is marketing's contribution to closed revenue?

- What is your current cost per lead?

The answers to these questions are not only good benchmarks for when you move forward, but they also show you where you might need improvement.

Establishing your goals

Everyone reading this book works for a company that is at one level or another involved with a lead generation strategy. Some of your companies may be brand new and not yet active on social channels; others might have some lead generation campaigns in place, but not a complete strategy. Your wish list very much depends on where you are currently in your lead generation journey.

Take a look at your answers to the questions that I asked in the previous section. What stuck out to you? What are you trying to accomplish? It might be increased brand awareness, more activity on social channels, higher conversion rates, more leads, and so on.

One important thing to note before you start mapping out your plan is to think big, start small, and act quickly! Consider your best-case scenario, your ultimate wish list, and then just start chipping away at it. Move quickly. Don't sit around waiting for everything to be aligned perfectly. You need to try each lead generation tactic and strategy in order to iterate and be successful.

It is critical to establish your goals and ROI estimates up front for each lead generation campaign. All too often, marketers plan programs and commit their budgets without establishing any concrete set of expectations for the program outcome. This becomes extremely problematic and is another reason that the usefulness of marketing often gets questioned. The solution to this issue is to set upfront goals for each of your campaigns. Setting goals for individual programs and channels enables you to establish targets to compare results, in addition to creating "what if" scenarios to see how changing your parameters may vary the results. Remember: Design *all* programs to be measureable.

The best way to lay out your goal metrics is to create a worksheet listing overall goals for lead generation and then goals for each individual channel for which you intend to spend time developing a strategy.

Here are some common conversion metrics that lead generation marketers often track:

- ✔ **Marketing percentage of contribution to sales pipeline:** This is the percentage of revenue in the sales pipeline (opportunities) that originated from marketing efforts.

- ✔ **Marketing percentage of contribution to closed revenue:** This metric is the percentage of closed and won deals that originated from marketing efforts — who becomes a customer?

✔ **Quantity of sales-qualified leads (SQLs):** This number signifies the amount of SQLs that your marketing team sends over to sales. These are leads that sales deems good and potentially sales-ready. In some places, this means when the sales department moves an opportunity to a next stage along the funnel.

✔ **Quality of SQLs:** This is the total percentage of SQLs not rejected by sales. Remember the focus on quality over quantity because this metric is an important one.

✔ **Cost per inquiry:** This number is the total lead acquisition cost divided by the total number of inquiries.

✔ **Cost per lead:** This is determined by dividing your total campaign cost by quantity of leads acquired through that campaign.

✔ **Inquiry to marketing qualified lead (MQL):** This is the percentage of conversion from initial inquiry to MQL. A MQL is defined by a lead that marketing deems qualified to push to the inside sales team, based on specific, predetermined criteria.

✔ **MQL to sales accepted lead (SAL):** This is the conversion from MQL to SAL. A SAL is defined by a lead that sales accepts but may not have qualified that lead yet.

✔ **SQL to opportunity:** This defines how many SQLs move to opportunities, which are defined by leads that are sales-ready and being actively pursued by sales.

There are of course a whole slew of additional metrics you might want to track, including website traffic increase, follower increases on social channels, form fill-out and subscriber opt-in rates, and so on. I go into metrics in *much* more detail in Chapter 20.

Take a look at Figure 3-1 for a chart from a recent survey that IDG Enterprises and the B2B Technology Marketing Community conducted on marketing trends in lead generation to see some of the most common metrics that lead generation marketers are looking at today.

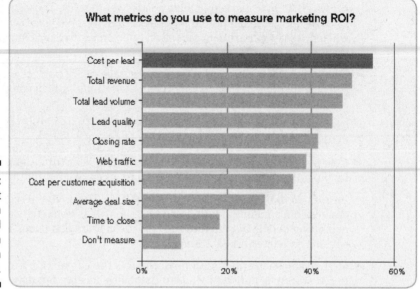

Figure 3-1:
The most
common
lead
generation
metrics in
2013.

After you have determined what overall goals you plan on measuring, you can dig deeper into each channel to define what some of your high-level metrics might be in each area. For instance, you might lay out your goals for social media as an increased number of followers, more social shares, more re-tweets, and so on. This will be very specific based on your business priorities.

As part of the planning process when you determine your strategy, answer the following three questions:

- ✔ What will you measure?
- ✔ When will you measure it?
- ✔ How will you measure it?

You need to take specific steps to make all of your programs measureable. This might also include setting up various test and control groups to measure impact and iterate based on results. I go into more detail on testing strategies in Chapter 19.

Crafting Your Road Map

Now that you have a sense of what you might want to measure and are beginning to flesh that out, it's time to create your road map. Where are you now and where do you want to be in six months, one year, or two years? It's important to develop your milestones and create a plan of attack.

Ask yourself the following four questions:

- ✔ What are your marketing objectives for the next few years?
- ✔ Where do you think you have gaps in your current marketing mixture?
- ✔ What new channels have you been dying to try?
- ✔ What is your budget?

The next step is prioritizing your objectives. I recently downloaded this very handy slide deck from a company called Brainrider Knowledge Marketing Group on creating your lead generation objectives. They break down your lead generation objectives into four categories:

- ✔ Generating awareness
- ✔ Acquiring prospects
- ✔ Nurturing prospects
- ✔ Qualifying sales readiness

You want to spend time to prioritize these goals. Take a look at the example in Figure 3-2 based on the Brainrider system for prioritizing your lead generation objectives.

Priority			How many qualified customers...
☐	Generating Awareness and	VISITOR	Find you and your expertise
☐	Acquiring Prospects	PROSPECT	Identify themselves and give you permission for contact
☐	Nurturing Prospects	ACTIVE PROSPECTS	Are actively engaging with your content
☐	Qualifying Sales Readiness	MQL/SAL	Meet a Marketing Qualified Lead definition Signal sales readiness

Figure 3-2: Prioritizing your lead generation objectives.

After you have determined your priorities, you can begin choosing what lead generation channels make sense for your marketing mix. Just to give you a sampling of what you might want to choose from, consider creating your strategy around the following tactics:

- ✔ Content marketing
- ✔ Website
- ✔ Blog
- ✔ Social media
- ✔ Search engine optimization (SEO)
- ✔ Email marketing
- ✔ Pay-per-click advertising (PPC)
- ✔ Content syndication
- ✔ Direct mail
- ✔ Event marketing
- ✔ Inside sales
- ✔ Lead nurturing and scoring

After you have determined your priorities, objectives, marketing mix, and budget, you can begin crafting your ultimate road map to lead generation awesomeness!

Setting up your plan

Now you have to set up your plan to make it accessible and actionable. Your initial setup plan can be in any form that makes it easily understandable for you, your team, and other stakeholders and executives. My initial advice is to chronicle your objectives and channel strategy in either an Excel or Google Spreadsheet. The great part about Google Spreadsheets is that everyone on your team can access the plan at any given time, even simultaneously, which is great if you have team members that work from home or who work out of a different office. Having your plan on a regular Excel spreadsheet might cause version control issues, and people might be left with outdated data and information. Another option is using a service like Box or Dropbox to house your spreadsheet. Because it is stored in the cloud and has lock and unlock functionalities, you can also share your latest plan amongst the team.

Next, start matching lead generation tactics to overall priorities (which should map nicely to your sales funnel that you created in the last chapter). For instance, one of the top channels you want to get more exposure in might be content marketing, which maps very nicely to generating awareness for your brand at the top of your funnel.

Figure 3-3 based on Brainrider's plan illustrates this concept and gives you a mapping template to fill in.

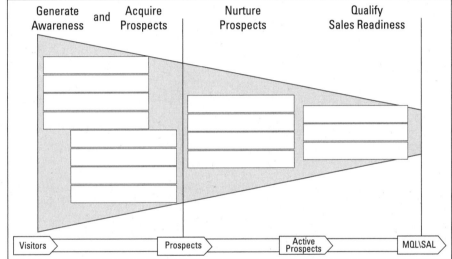

Figure 3-3:
Listing programs and mapping to objectives.

Then you can dive down even deeper into all of your programs by creating a list of strategic channels and tactics you intend to employ to be successful attaining your goals. Figure 3-4 shows an example of a programs pick list that you can create for this purpose. Of course, your program list and objectives are going to be different, but this gives you a good example of how to set one up.

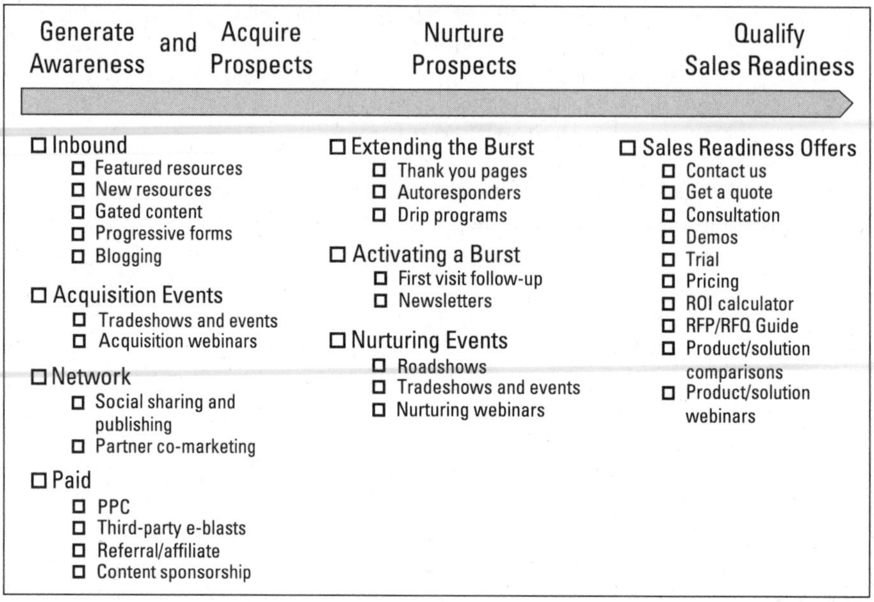

Generate and Acquire Awareness Prospects	Nurture Prospects	Qualify Sales Readiness

☐ Inbound
   ☐ Featured resources
   ☐ New resources
   ☐ Gated content
   ☐ Progressive forms
   ☐ Blogging

☐ Acquisition Events
   ☐ Tradeshows and events
   ☐ Acquisition webinars

☐ Network
   ☐ Social sharing and publishing
   ☐ Partner co-marketing

☐ Paid
   ☐ PPC
   ☐ Third-party e-blasts
   ☐ Referral/affiliate
   ☐ Content sponsorship

☐ Extending the Burst
   ☐ Thank you pages
   ☐ Autoresponders
   ☐ Drip programs

☐ Activating a Burst
   ☐ First visit follow-up
   ☐ Newsletters

☐ Nurturing Events
   ☐ Roadshows
   ☐ Tradeshows and events
   ☐ Nurturing webinars

☐ Sales Readiness Offers
   ☐ Contact us
   ☐ Get a quote
   ☐ Consultation
   ☐ Demos
   ☐ Trial
   ☐ Pricing
   ☐ ROI calculator
   ☐ RFP/RFQ Guide
   ☐ Product/solution comparisons
   ☐ Product/solution webinars

Figure 3-4:
An example program pick list.

The final step to your initial planning process is to create a detailed, actionable plan that your marketing team can follow and execute on. Creating a spreadsheet that maps each program to the chosen priority is a great way to stay organized. Also make sure you have date ranges and columns to input your ROI metrics.

Creating a timeline to hit objectives

I have seen so many marketers create amazing plans, get their teams excited about the possibilities, and then fall flat because they don't create a proper timeline to hit objectives. Think big, start small, act fast. This is critical. After you've done all of this fantastic planning, it would be a real bummer if nothing was executed on. Be realistic about what you can accomplish and in what timeframe.

For example, maybe one of your goals is to get 3,000 followers on Twitter. Great goal, but make sure you have set realistic and attainable expectations. Be sure to find the happy medium between too-high and too-low expectations. If you tell your poor social media manager that you need her to execute on this goal and attract 3,000 Twitter followers in three weeks, that's pretty unreasonable. It takes a lot of time to attract followers on Twitter. However, telling her that you need it to happen within the next year is too broad of a goal. A more realistic goal would be to get 3,000 Twitter followers over the course of four to six months, depending on your existing social media presence. And then make sure to have specific key performance indicators (KPIs) in place for every month. Maybe you want your social media manager to work on attaining 400–600 followers each month, for example.

Use a spreadsheet as a place to track monthly goals and develop quarterly and yearly milestones to hit. By communicating them with your team, you will have accountability to make sure that all goals are attained in the allocated timeframe.

Building a Business Case

You are armed with your goals and your lead generation plan, but now you need stakeholder buy-in. For many of you, this is the tough part. Close your eyes, take a deep breath, and know that you will have a huge accomplishment under your belt when you get your executive stakeholders to applaud your strategic and tactical planning efforts and give you all of the dollars you need to get this thing done! But I recognize this takes a lot of planning (and courage).

So what is stakeholder buy-in, anyway? You need the support of your executive team to make your dreams a reality. Your stakeholders give you budget, help you staff, and support your program efforts. They are also the people who very carefully watch your successes.

In order to build a successful business case, you need the following tools for success:

- ✔ **Your lead generation plan:** Hopefully you've created your lead generation plan using the techniques given in this chapter. Make sure you have your well-organized project plan, which channels you intend to participate in, and your priorities listed and mapped.

- ✔ **Your success metrics:** How are you planning on measuring your success and what are you planning on measuring? Maybe you are planning to implement a marketing automation tool to help with tracking, or maybe you just plan to start on a spreadsheet for now. Either way, you need to have a clear idea of how success will be measured.

- ✔ **Your budget:** Your key stakeholders want to know how much budget you need to implement your lead generation plan. Be sure to include any additional marketing staff headcount dollars in this budget estimate. You might not have an exact number now, but try and get an estimate of needed funds. Review your costs from last year to get a baseline.

✔ **Your timeline:** What is the timeline in which you intend to attain your goals? What can your stakeholders expect in one month, six months, or one year?

✔ **Your presentation:** I go into more detail about your stakeholder presentation in the next few pages, but you want to create a well-thought-out PowerPoint or Keynote presentation to give the team. Remember, they might not know what lead generation is, so be sure to describe the benefits.

Choosing your stakeholders

Ask yourself the question, who in your organization needs to know about your program and give it their blessing? Chances are you have a handful or more of people who need to know about your program and who have a say in how things should be carried out. These are your *program stakeholders.* These are the people you need to present your plan to. How do you choose who these people are?

In my experience, there are a variety of people in different departments who you need support from. They may include but aren't limited to the following:

✔ **The CMO (chief marketing officer):** This could be your direct boss or your boss's boss, or maybe it's even you! But the CMO needs ultimate signoff on your proposal because he will be providing the budget. He is also most likely the person to whom you need to be reporting metrics and outcomes.

✔ **The VP of Sales or GM (general manager):** Your sales executives are the next on your list who need to buy into your plan: They are affected by it just as much as you are. Sales and marketing need to be aligned for your programs to work, so the VP of Sales or your GM is a critical component for success.

✔ **The CTO/CIO (chief technology/information officer):** If you are planning on implementing any technology, whether it is a marketing automation platform or even a program like HootSuite to run your Twitter profiles, your CTO needs to be in-the-know. She has to provide resources and help you determine which applications would be the best fit.

✔ **The CFO (chief financial officer):** You definitely need budget. And your CFO wants to know how much you need and what you need it for. Sometimes you won't need the CFO to sign off on your projects if your CMO is signing off, but every company is different.

✔ **The CEO:** Depending on program size and your company size, the CEO may want to be involved in your decision-making process. Make sure you keep him in the loop and invite him to meetings when appropriate.

Coming up with your list of needs

Now that you have a clear understanding of *who* needs to sign off on your program, you need to determine what you need from them and why they should care. Think of stakeholder buy-in as a strong lead generation program in itself: Always have a clear call-to-action (CTA) and show what's in it for them. What do you want to ask them for?

If you go into the meeting, present your plan, and don't ask for anything, you will probably hear crickets from your stakeholder team as they try to figure out why you invited them to your meeting in the first place.

So have an ask (or several) and make sure to include all of your asks in your presentation. Your needs depend of course on your own unique business case, but here is an example of what you might want to cover:

✔ Needed budget for all programs

✔ Needed headcount for program execution and success

✔ Needed technology for metrics measurement and project planning

✔ Needed internal resources for support and planning

✔ Needed SLAs (service-level agreements) that you might want to put in place to ensure follow-through from different teams

Also make sure that you have a timeline for when you need the final decisions from your stakeholders. Particularly, let them know if you have any programs planned that have deadlines or that are time-specific like an event. This helps to move the process along.

 You also want to schedule regular check-in meetings with your stakeholder groups. Schedule a follow-up meeting after your initial presentation so that you can discuss with them further questions or concerns and understand when your stakeholders intend to give you the answers to some of your questions about budgets and headcount. Then make sure you set ongoing check-in meetings with them to report on progress.

Developing your presentation slide deck

I believe the key part of presenting to your stakeholders is making sure you present the details of your plan in a clear and concise manner. I find that the most effective way to do this is through a Microsoft PowerPoint presentation. You can set the scene, give background on your topic, present your plan, and then ask final questions at the end. A PowerPoint gives your presentation structure and gives you an outline to follow.

Consider the following outline for your slides:

- ✔ **Slide 1:** Title Page: *[Insert company name] Lead Generation Plan*. Also include the definition of lead generation on this slide.

- ✔ **Slide 2:** Agenda: Include what you are going to speak about in your presentation so that your stakeholders know the meeting roadmap.

- ✔ **Slide 3:** Executive summary: You may want to have an executive summary here that reviews what you are going to talk about and some of your key points.

- ✔ **Slides 4–6:** Background: You may want to set the scene for your stakeholders. Talk about the changing marketing landscape, the new buyer, and so on. Also discuss where your marketing is now. It is here that you want to build a compelling case as to why a lead generation program is needed.

- ✔ **Slides 7–10:** WIIFM: These are the WIIFM (What's in It for Me) slides. Meaning, this is where you define lead generation and show your stakeholders all of the benefits of implementing a lead generation strategy.

- ✔ **Slides 11–12:** Plan: In these slides, you want to discuss and show what your actual plan is and why. Show them your project plan and walk them through each step.

- ✔ **Slide 13:** Metrics: Show how you plan on measuring your success.

- ✔ **Slide 14:** Getting started: How do you plan on getting started with your lead generation efforts? Include a timeline that shows step-by-step where you plan on being in three months to a year.

- ✔ **Slide 15:** Summary: Before you go into your Calls to Action (CTAs), show them a quick summary of what you discussed. Make sure your best key talking points are there.

- ✔ **Slide 16:** CTAs: What do you need from your stakeholder group and when do you need it by?

- ✔ **Slide 17:** Next steps: Take this time to set up those meetings that I discussed earlier in this section.

- ✔ **Slide 18:** Thank you and Q&A: Never forget to thank your stakeholders for attending. Then open the meeting up for Q&A. No doubt there will be plenty of questions you might need to answer.

Aligning Your Sales and Marketing Teams

Alignment between sales and marketing during the lead generation process is critical for success. The two teams have an extremely symbiotic relationship, and companies that understand this are ahead of the game. Traditionally, sales and marketing haven't had the greatest relationship with one another. Sales thinks marketing doesn't give them good leads, and marketing thinks sales doesn't follow up on its perfectly good leads. That's just the tip of the iceberg. For many organizations, sales and marketing just don't speak the same language.

This lack of alignment can be detrimental to the success of both sales and marketing. Therefore, it is really important to work on creating a strong relationship that benefits both parties.

For lead generation specifically, alignment becomes critical as marketing relies on sales for its programs to be a success. No matter how fantastic your lead generation programs might be, if sales doesn't call your leads, none of them will turn into customers. Good alignment creates happy marketers, happy sales teams, and happy customers overall. Without good alignment, everyone loses in the end.

For alignment to occur, eliminate the blame game and start working toward considering both sales and marketing as one team. This is tough, but by consistent communication, service-level agreements (SLAs), and an understanding between the two teams, sales and marketing alignment can happen.

Crafting a sales and marketing workshop

The first step to communication and common definitions is a joint sales and marketing workshop. I discuss this briefly in the previous chapters, but it's a critical step to aligning the sales and marketing function, which is absolutely necessary for successful lead generation strategies. And it is certainly not easy. In the famous words from the movie *Cool Hand Luke*, "What we've got here is failure to communicate."

You also want to inject some team camaraderie into your sales and marketing alignment workshop, so schedule a full day, with half of the time dedicated to a team-building activity like a barbecue or bowling — something to align your marketers and sales executives in a more casual environment.

During the first half of your workshop, you need to address the following needs:

✔ Come up with shared definitions for leads, opportunities, qualified leads, and so on.

✔ Come up with a clear profile of buyers and customers.

✔ Determine what technology you need/have to enable a closed-loop lead generation solution.

✔ Determine how to hold your teams accountable.

✔ Figure out what type and frequency of communication you need to be successful.

You also need to make sure you are informing your sales team of your lead generation strategy and plans. Consider using your stakeholder presentation deck and updating it to be applicable to your sales team. The sales team also needs to know the definition of lead generation, what channels you intend on being active on, and how your success is measured. Also let them know what you expect from them throughout the process.

Managing your service-level agreements

One of the most important items you need to create during your sales and marketing alignment meeting is your service-level agreements (SLAs). This is where you can put some muscle behind your alignment. It is certainly great to have a meeting, discuss definitions, and shake hands at the end, but both sales and marketing need some reassurance that there is a formal system in place.

In the past, SLAs were typically used in technical support, where tickets prioritized, followed up on, and escalated in case a technical support associate did not follow up on the issue in the allotted time. This technique has become increasingly popular in the sales and marketing world to prevent either team from dropping the ball.

The easiest way to keep track of these SLAs is in a customer relationship management (CRM) system or a marketing automation tool because you need a way to determine when a lead gets passed from marketing to sales and when that lead has received a follow-up call.

After you have that agreed-upon criteria between sales and marketing on the definition of a good lead, you can use the SLA process to ensure that marketing isn't wasting the sales team's time with poor leads, and you can ensure that sales follows up with marketing's leads in an agreed-upon amount of time. And because you are tracking it in a CRM or marketing automation tool, there is tangible proof of what exactly is going on.

Marketo does a fantastic job of implementing SLAs, so I have been fortunate to have first-hand experience here. Bill Binch, senior vice president of sales at Marketo, states, "In our early days, we built our first SLA based around a marketing-to-sales SLA: When a sales rep received a lead that met the defined criteria, he or she had 24 hours to reach out to that lead. If they didn't reach out, they got a reminder 24 hours later telling them that the lead is getting stale. At 48 hours, the rep and their boss got an email and eek, at 72 hours, that alert went to our CEO. No bueno if you're a sales rep working in a marketing automation company."

Pretty intense, but very powerful. Marketo also began extending SLA to include what happens after the rep has followed up with a lead. After a rep reached out, an entirely new SLA started. The rep now had seven days to qualify the lead and convert him. The rep generally had three options. He could turn the lead into an opportunity, he could defer the lead, saying there was no opportunity at this time, or he could recycle the lead back to marketing through lead nurturing. Pretty neat, right?

SLAs are a great way to get very specific about your various needs, requirements, and expectations.

When you draft your SLA, make sure you include the following sections:

- ✔ **Summary:** A brief explanation of what your SLA is and why it is being implemented.

- ✔ **Common terminology and definitions:** List all common terminology and definitions. Examples are: Sales Qualified Lead, Marketing Qualified Lead, Sales Accepted Lead, and so on, in addition to any metrics and measurements that need to be defined.

- ✔ **Marketing accountability:** What SLAs have you put in place for marketing? This may include lead quality, lead quantity, and so on.

- ✔ **Sales accountability:** What SLAs have you put in place for sales? This usually aligns to follow-up timing, but could also include mandatory data fields in your CRM tool (what a sales rep has to put into your CRM after she has a call with the lead), minimum close ratios of marketing leads, and so on.

- ✔ **Plan of action:** What steps are needed in place to get this done? How often are your groups communicating and when? What is to be covered in the meetings?

Make your SLA easily accessible via Google Drive, Box, Dropbox, or your CRM tool. Take a look at Figure 3-5 to see a sample of a sales and marketing SLA developed by Carlos Hidalgo, the CEO of ANNUITAS.

Funnel Stage	Team	Action	Timeframe
MQL	Marketing	Send MQl to AM	3 Hours
MQL	Account Management	Follow Up on MQL	48 Hours
MQL	Account Management	Report on Disposition	5 Business Days
SAL	Account Management	Convert to Contact (SAL) once Accepted	24 Hours
SAL	Account Management	Report on Disposition	5 Business Days from time of Conversion
SQL	Account Management	Convert to SQL (Opportunity) once Qualified	24 Hours
SQL	Account Management	Report on Pipeline Value	10 Business Days from time of Opp Creation
Closed Won/Lost	Account Management	Report on Close and Reason	24 Hours from time of Win/Loss

Figure 3-5:
A sample sales and marketing SLA.

Chapter 4

Choosing the Right Technology

. . . .

In This Chapter

▶ Navigating the complex marketing technology landscape

▶ Determining the right mix of solutions for your business

▶ Embracing change management as part of your implementation process

▶ Assigning resources and user roles

. . . .

A fully-baked lead generation strategy enables you to attract leads from multiple different channels and have numerous programs running at the same time. It's extremely difficult to manage and track your efforts without the help of one (or more) technology platforms.

There is a huge upside to making a technology investment. Even though you are spending money upfront, you save money in the long run due to fewer human resource needs, enabling you to do more in-house. Technology also helps you measure and optimize your investments so you know exactly what is working and what isn't. And finally, investing in technology helps you grow your lead generation practice faster, which in turn helps your company grow faster. You can't argue with that!

But there are so many options to choose from that it can be overwhelming. Just look at Figure 4-1, which shows the marketing technology LUMAscape — the choices are endless. (A LUMAscape, created by Luma Partners, shows a visual representation of the marketing technology landscape broken down by use-case and channel.)

The key is narrowing down your choices by determining what is best for your organization based on needs, lead generation channels, lead generation metrics, and budget.

Another key factor to keep in mind when choosing the right technology is future growth. If you are a smaller company with a rapid growth trajectory, choosing a platform that scales is critical for future success. You don't want to spend time and money vetting a technology solution only to find out that it just can't get you to where you want *or need* to be.

Figure 4-1:
The marketing technology LUMAscape.

You waste precious time, money, and resources when you make a rash technology choice. So be sure to think about where you are today and where you want to be one year, five years, and in some cases even ten years from today.

You're probably about to shut this book because your head hurts after looking at that marketing technology LUMAscape, but never fear. In this chapter, I'm going to take some time to go through available technologies and the top vendors in each space to help you narrow down your choices.

Defining Your Options

You don't need a tool for every single channel and tactic within a lead generation strategy. It all depends upon your plan and your specific goals. And of course, it also depends on what budget you might have available for a technology implementation. Many of these technology solutions can be quite pricey, so prioritize based on need. For instance, if you have strong goals in social media, you might consider purchasing a social media management tool, and saving money by using a free version of Google Analytics to track website activity instead of purchasing a whole suite of analytics tools.

Here are some of the technology solution categories that are available for lead generation activities:

- ✔ Customer relationship management (CRM)
- ✔ Marketing automation
- ✔ Email service providers
- ✔ Social media trackers
- ✔ Social media management tool
- ✔ Website analytics

Note that there is no way I can cover every single software category or vendor in this book, so this *not* an exhaustive list. Plan on doing your own research based upon what you are focusing most of your energy on. The following selection of technologies and vendors are meant to help you begin *thinking* about technology solutions and how they fit into your overall marketing strategy. When you've made your decision, find the right *For Dummies*-related title to complement your information gathering.

Discovering Customer Relationship Management (CRM)

I start with customer relationship management (CRM) software because you most likely already have this in place. This is the technology your sales team uses to track leads, opportunities, and deals. Additionally, some marketing departments might also be using a CRM currently to track programs and send emails.

However, note that a CRM tool was *not* made exclusively for marketers, and thus is not an ideal solution for your lead generating efforts. The solution you should choose to track your campaigns should primarily target the needs of marketers, like a marketing automation-specific application or an email service provider.

If you do have a CRM, it is important to know what you are using, how things are currently tracked, and how that system might integrate with other technology solutions you plan on implementing. Most CRM systems integrate quite nicely with a suite of marketing technologies.

No matter what software you as a marketer decide to use for your own lead generation efforts, leads should ultimately be transferred to your CRM so that your sales team can eventually take over the sales process when a lead is ready to buy.

Having a CRM in place ensures a closed-loop lead generation strategy with maximum sales and marketing alignment.

- ✔ **Salesforce CRM (www.salesforce.com):** Salesforce is arguably the most well-known CRM software on the market today. It is cloud-based, which makes it accessible and cost-effective for businesses of all sizes. It is also built to be incredibly scalable. Salesforce excels by having a robust functionality and the ability to customize the application to fit your business needs. The user interface is also easy to understand, and you can access data from mobile and tablet devices. Another great thing about Salesforce is that it integrates with many different partners and other technology providers quickly and easily.

- ✔ **Microsoft Dynamics CRM (www.crm.ms):** The benefit to implementing a solution like Microsoft Dynamics CRM is that it integrates nicely with other Microsoft solutions such as Office and SharePoint. As a result, you get a consistent user experience across multiple Microsoft platforms. Dynamics is also easy to use and has powerful reporting capabilities that integrate with Microsoft Excel. Dynamics also backs up its software with a service-level agreement (SLA) that promises 99.9 percent uptime, which is more than what many of the other CRM providers offer.

- ✔ **SugarCRM (www.sugarcrm.com):** This is a great solution for the business on a budget. SugarCRM provides an excellent user interface and really easy drag-and-drop features. It also has an out-of-the-box integration with Google and Microsoft products. Another great feature is that you can choose to deploy your instance in the cloud or on-premise. A wide range of social functionalities are also built in, such as the ability to gather intelligence on how leads are interacting with you on social channels.

Looking into Marketing Automation

Now on to the exciting stuff! Marketing technology! Marketing automation is a software platform made specifically for marketers, so they can run the business of marketing. It's pretty cool. In the past, marketers had to piece-meal together a variety of different software tools to create a hodgepodge of functionality.

But what is marketing automation? According to Marketo, marketing automation is "the technology that allows companies to streamline, automate, and measure marketing tasks and create workflows so they can increase operational efficiency and grow revenue faster."

Features of marketing automation platforms include

- Email marketing
- Landing pages
- Campaign management
- Marketing programs
- Lead generation
- Prediction/lead scoring
- CRM integrations
- Social marketing
- Marketing resource management
- Marketing analytics

Most companies could benefit from implementing a marketing automation tool, but take a look at Table 4-1 and do this quick worksheet, based on research from Gleanster, to find out if you are ready for marketing automation.

Table 4-1	Worksheet: Are You Ready for Marketing Automation?				
Factor	**Disagree** 1	2	3	**Agree** 4	5
Our revenue process is complicated. It involves multiple touches from marketing and sales.					
We target sophisticated buyers who do a lot of research before they engage with us.					
Our company requires more insight into the exact value that our marketing programs deliver, so we can quantify our investment.					
Our customer base out-sizes our sales team, so we lack direct personal relationships with all of our customers and prospects.					
It would be impossible to personally call every potential customer or new lead that we generate.					
Many of our new leads aren't yet ready to buy from us. They require nurturing.					

(continued)

Table 4-1 *(continued)*					
Factor	**Disagree**				**Agree**
	1	**2**	**3**	**4**	**5**
We would improve our sales results if marketing played a bigger role in our revenue process, particularly as it applies to nurturing relationships with targeted early-stage prospects.					
We already use most, or all, of the capabilities of our current email marketing service provider.					
Data drives almost every decision that our marketing team makes.					
Our marketing team is generating (or has specific plans to generate) significant amounts of personalized content for our target prospects.					

For each category, select the appropriate number. If you strongly disagree, choose 1. If you strongly agree, choose 5. Choose 2 if you somewhat disagree, 3 if you're neutral, and 4 if you somewhat agree. Tally your score when you're finished. If you scored higher than 35, you're ready for marketing automation. If you scored between 20 and 35, you're approaching readiness and should consider making a move soon. If you scored below 20, you may not be ready for marketing automation yet.

Now take a look at some of the top vendors in the space:

- ✓ **Marketo (www.marketo.com):** Marketo is one of the big names in the marketing automation space. Marketo was founded in 2006, and as of this writing, has more than 2,300 customers and 100,000 users worldwide. Marketo is known for having a combination of robust features paired with an easy-to-learn user interface. It can handle a broad range of functions such as engagement-based lead nurturing, social marketing, and email. It also has a rich suite of analytics and reporting capabilities, and its own third-party vendor marketplace for add-on functionality. Marketo is cloud-based and integrates with some of the top technology platforms available to marketers.

- ✓ **Eloqua (www.eloqua.com):** Eloqua, another player in the marketing automation space, was recently purchased by Oracle and is now part of Oracle's marketing cloud. Eloqua was founded in 1999 and has more than 1,100 customers and 70,000 users worldwide. Eloqua has extensive functionality to help marketers do very specific targeting of the right buyers and to execute on multiple campaigns. The platform also offers dynamic lead scoring and social marketing functionality. The integration with Oracle makes it a perfect choice for anyone using that platform. Eloqua also integrates with other CRM solutions.

✔ **HubSpot (www.hubspot.com):** Founded in 2006, HubSpot's sweet spot is smaller companies and marketing departments. In addition to some traditional marketing automation technologies, HubSpot also includes functionality for blogging, SEO, and website pages. The platform is a great option for smaller businesses looking to automate more of their inbound marketing processes; however, it lacks some of the complexity that Marketo or Eloqua provides.

Exploring Email Service Providers (ESP)

An email service provider inherently has less functionality than marketing automation. The main function of an email service provider (ESP) is to send emails. Mostly batch-and-blast, ESPs are good if your business is highly focused on email communications. They also provide basic metrics attached to your email efforts. However, note that they do not provide functionality for lead management (lead nurturing and lead scoring), and they do not provide the depth of metrics that marketing automation platforms can provide.

If you are a small business or on a budget, an ESP could be a good choice because many low-cost providers are available to fit all levels of need. ESPs are also a popular choice amongst business-to-consumer (B2C) businesses who aren't looking for the depth of functionality that a marketing automation system can provide, and who are primarily focused on large email sends.

✔ **ExactTarget (www.exacttarget.com):** ExactTarget is one of the largest ESPs on the market today. Founded in December 2000, ExactTarget is the ESP of choice for many of today's top consumer brands. In June 2013, it was purchased by Salesforce to form the core of its new marketing cloud. ExactTarget provides functionality to connect with customers through email, integrated text messaging, voice messaging, and social channels.

✔ **Responsys (www.responsys.com):** Responsys uses customer demographics and behavior to tailor messages to individual audiences. Like ExactTarget, Responsys helps users manage email campaigns with calendars and automated scheduling. Responsys is recommended mostly for enterprise companies.

✔ **MailChimp (http://mailchimp.com/):** Praised for its user-friendly interface and easy setup, MailChimp offers both monthly pricing plans and pay-as-you-go, which is unique in the ESP space and is ideal for smaller companies. For parties and events, MailChimp provides mobile signup forms, which can be used in conjunction with event planning apps. MailChimp also integrates with Google Analytics so that email campaigns can be monitored against real-time sales.

Investigating Social Media Tracking Tools

If you have a social strategy for lead generation (which you absolutely should), you need a social media tracking tool so you can measure and analyze your social interactions. Social media tracking tools enable you to listen and respond to customer and prospect interactions on all of your social channels.

Through deep analytics and reporting, social media tracking tools can help you engage with your audience and provide them with relevant content based on their actions.

Note that many marketing automation tools are now including social analytics in their suite, but there are also many stand-alone vendors you can use to enhance social interactions.

- ✔ **Radian6** (`www.salesforcemarketingcloud.com`): Radian6 is a social media tracker that works in real time, using customized keywords, phrases, and filters to provide analysis and guidelines for tracking and engaging your audience through social channels. Radian6 is now part of the Salesforce Marketing Cloud, so its integration with Salesforce.com is improving with each release. Radian6 excels at lead generation, crisis management, and competitive analysis.

- ✔ **Sysomos** (`www.sysomos.com/`): Sysomos not only collects and stores data from customer and prospect interactions on social channels, but it also helps to score potential influencers — the people who engage the most with your content. Sysomos offers two tools — Sysomos MAP, which is focused mostly on analytics, and Sysomos Heartbeat, which includes the ability to collaborate and engage with bloggers and other influencers.

- ✔ **Lithium** (`www.lithium.com/`): Lithium Social Marketing tracks customer and prospect engagements across multiple social media platforms. Because Lithium tracks social campaigns in real time, marketers can quickly iterate their strategy to reflect the new information Lithium provides. Lithium also enables companies to create unlimited user profiles and up to 50 preset searches — far more than any other social trackers do.

Looking at Social Media Management Tools

In addition to a social media monitoring tool, your business should consider having a social media management tool. A social media management tool enables your social media manager and team to effectively keep track of and post on all of the social channels your company participates in.

You can have multiple social channels open at the same time in one dashboard, and you can post and create lists all in one place. A social media management tool becomes increasingly necessary as you scale.

✔ **HootSuite (`https://hootsuite.com/`):** HootSuite's management tools allow users to launch and monitor social media campaigns from a single dashboard to track and manage social engagement. HootSuite is a big player in the space with more than seven million users, and offers three solution levels — free, pro, and enterprise — all of which can orchestrate social campaigns and schedule messaging across multiple platforms.

✔ **Crowdbooster (`http://crowdbooster.com/`):** Crowdbooster offers different levels of solutions, from a simple metric reporter and social scheduler to real-time measurement of engagement. Crowdbooster focuses on Facebook and Twitter and can give targeted recommendations based on customer and prospect interactions. Crowdbooster can provide you with instant feedback about your performance on social channels and enables you to manage multiple social accounts in one place.

✔ **Argyle Social (`http://argylesocial.com/`):** Argyle Social excels mostly in the B2B (business-to-business) space, and enables users to create and assign custom tags and segments to potential customers. Argyle Social has a consolidated dashboard that monitors Facebook, Twitter, Google+, and LinkedIn.

Discovering Website Tracking Tools

When you are running lead generation campaigns to drive traffic to your website, you need a way to track your results. By implementing a website traffic tool, you can determine traffic increases and decreases, conversions, content engagement, social interactions, and more. Leveraging these tools and solutions is a great way to get a complete picture of how your lead generation campaigns are affecting website traffic.

✔ **Google Analytics (`www.google.com/analytics`):** Google Analytics, truly a must-have, is used by an estimated 10 million websites. That is huge! And it is the only major analytics solution that offers a free version. While premium users can enjoy enhanced support, additional customization options, and increased data security, all users can build out customized, segmented reports that are easy to view and share. The tool can measure content analytics, website traffic, and social interactions. Google Analytics can also measure and track visits from a smartphone or iPad.

✔ **Clicky (`www.clicky.com`):** Clicky has a user-friendly interface that provides easy-to-read-and-understand charts and graphics, along with real-time views of visits to your site. Clicky enables the user to sort by geographic location, referring link, and keyword search terms. The solution also shows real-time site data so you can see who is visiting each page of your website at any given time. Clicky is a large player in the space and is used by 650,000 websites.

✔ **Woopra (www.woopra.com):** Featuring a unique WordPress plugin, Woopra allows users to track blog authors, categories, comments, and searches. The solution also enables customer tagging, custom event tracking, and website retention reports. Well-suited for retail sites, Woopra can also generate revenue reports based on time period, categories, and SKUs (stock keeping units).

Making the Right Choice

It's incredibly tough to decide which technology solution is right for your business and your lead generation efforts. And you need to remember that you can't have them all, nor do you need them all. So beware of software sales reps trying to awe you with their platforms, and stay true to what you need as a business.

My advice? Start out small by choosing one or two platforms (at the most) that offer you the largest amount of functionality for your lead generation plans. If you intend on spending a lot of time on email campaigns, events, and social media, think about choosing a marketing automation platform coupled with a social media management tool. Or if you are thinking about mostly dabbling in PPC ads and website tracking, you might consider another set of tools. Know before shopping what sort of reports you envision running to get to that very-targeted segment of your audience. Don't assume that the vendor will be able to make that query.

And remember, there is more than just the implementation involved in ramping up a new technology solution. You also need to pay close attention to resource planning, training, and measuring ROI. If you don't have a proper plan in place to ensure success with your new tools, you will likely fall flat on your face and waste time and money.

Throughout the time I have worked in technology, I have seen failed implementation attempts time and time again. When you have decided on the right solution for your company, make sure you have a plan for rolling it out.

Planning your resource investment

As with any new software purchase, it is important to keep in mind resource planning. You need a team to learn and run your new technology, so be sure to include this as part of the budgeting process when determining how much you have spent. Depending on what platform you decide to go with, your resource investment could be smaller or more substantial. However, no matter what solutions you decide on, plan on having the following key resources in place for success:

- ✔ **A dedicated platform owner:** Someone needs to own everything pertaining to your new platform. Whether it is you or the person who will become the power user, you need someone who owns roll-out and is the point of contact for the rest of the organization. By assigning a dedicated resource to your project, you ensure that someone has ownership and success metrics surrounding implementation and usage.

- ✔ **Platform users:** Depending on your organization and chosen technology solutions, make sure you have assigned people the role of user. These users may be primary users; people who are in the platform constantly, or secondary users; people who are in the platform from time to time. Either way, make sure you assign roles to members of your team and outline who is using the technology, how they are using it, and when they are using it.

- ✔ **External agency:** Some companies outsource the management of their technology platform to external agencies. This can be common if you have a smaller team and don't have the bandwidth to train experts. External agencies are becoming more and more involved in including marketing technology services in their offerings mix. For example, many external marketing agencies are now offering marketing automation services. And agencies have historically also offered expertise in social media, SEO, and PPC.

- ✔ **Professional services team:** Many technology platforms offer professional services to help you get up and running with your solution. You can also contract with an outside consultancy for their expertise. A professional services team can help implement your solution in addition to working on training and change management for the rest of your organization. Make sure they have proven, prior expertise with both the marketing automation tool that you purchase, as well as the CRM system that you'll probably be integrating with.

Training your team

After you have the resources in place for success, you need to make sure your team is properly trained and ready to hit the ground running. This is a step that I often see companies glossing over. They have spent so much money on their new technology and their teams aren't trained. And what happens when your teams aren't trained? The software doesn't get used. Your team reverts back to the way they have always been doing things. The technology is there to make you effective and successful at lead generation, so enable your teams to achieve.

Here are a few steps you want in place for your training efforts:

- ✔ **Group training sessions:** Most software vendors include training as part of their service offering. They either come on-site or run training sessions remotely for your teams. Typical training sessions can last anywhere from two hours to three to four days, depending on the complexity of the application you are implementing. One key thing here is to make sure your teams are relatively freed from work obligations. You want them to be ready to learn and not stressed out by what is going on back in the office. This is certainly something we all fall victim to — listening with one ear while responding to an email. If your attendees are worrying constantly about the work they're falling behind on, they just won't suck up as much information as they need.

- ✔ **Frequent check-ins:** Invite your vendor to come back or check in remotely with your team on a weekly basis. Even if the check-in is only for 15 minutes, by putting something on the calendar, you can make sure your new software is top-of-mind. I would recommend weekly check-ins for the first three months, then cutting down to semi-monthly check-ins, and so on.

- ✔ **Assign study groups:** If you are planning to roll a piece of technology out to your entire team, you may want to assign study groups of two or more people. Collaboration and teamwork are great ways to learn something and learn it well. Have your groups work on homework assignments and encourage them to rely on each other to answer questions and provide suggestions.

- ✔ **Provide study materials:** Many companies provide study and training materials after a piece of software has been implemented. Sometimes this comes in the form of a Playbook, and sometimes these materials come in the form of a few blog posts or articles. Make sure you know what is available and you know how to use the materials. Pass them off to your team in case they have any questions while training.

- ✔ **Avoid the after-implementation doldrums:** After every implementation, the excitement dies down and reality sets in. In order to maintain a high level of usage and success from your chosen solutions, you need to keep the momentum up. This can come in the form of contests or prizes for power users, gamification within your system, or frequent check-ins to determine progress and milestones reached.

Chapter 5

Building a Rock-Star Team

You are close to getting your hands dirty in the nitty-gritty of lead generation, but you have one more hurdle to tackle. How do you set up your team? Who do you need to hire and how do you go about getting the right people?

In my experience as a marketer, having been on many teams and hiring many team members, this might be the most difficult and arguably the most important task that you have in front of you. In order for your lead generation efforts to be effective and your marketing to really stand out, you need a stellar team of A-players. These are going to be the people on the front lines working tirelessly to make this lead generation thing work.

And in fact, just to really stress how important good hires are, according to LinkedIn in a June 2013 article, "The U.S. Department of Labor currently estimates that the average cost of a bad hiring decision can equal 30 percent of the individual's first-year potential earnings. That means a single bad hire with an annual income of $50,000 can equal a potential $15,000 loss for the employer." That's a significant amount. And don't forget the cost of lost time and bad leads!

Identifying Who You Need for Success

So who do you need for lead generation success? It varies, based on your company size and how large your marketing team is. And in fact, you may already have many of these people employed already. But for the sake of being thorough, I am going to talk about all of the different potential hires you could make for a very robust lead generation team. And even if you decide you only want to hire one or two additional people, at least make sure that they have some of the skillsets I am about to outline.

But why do you need to hire additional headcount? Well, you need not only expertise in different areas of marketing, but also more bodies to monitor results and fine-tune tactics as you decide to run more lead generation campaigns. It's simple math. And many of the lead generation strategies that I outline in this book require a specific skillset that not every marketer has.

You might not find people out-of-the-box with all of these skillsets. Disciplines such as content marketing or marketing automation are fairly new, so be prepared to look for those with potential and be open to training them.

Marketing programs manager

The marketing programs manager is a key function for lead generation. This person manages all elements of your marketing programs including program selection, program deployment, budgeting, planning, and reporting. He should also be a jack-of-all-trades and understand many aspects of marketing such as events, webinars, email, online ads, and so on. Ideally, this hire should also be comfortable with technology, particularly marketing automation or email marketing, or you should be willing to train her.

If you decide to make only one additional hire, this should be the one, as the marketing programs manager typically runs many of your lead generation programs and is measured on program success.

Here is an example of the required skills or experience you might want to look for in your marketing programs manager:

- ✔ Bachelor's degree or MBA

- ✔ Experience with demand generation or lead generation

- ✔ Established record of managing events, email, online ads, sponsorships, and other lead generation campaigns

- ✔ Great communication skills, including writing and speaking

- ✔ Experience with customer relationship management (CRM) and marketing automation (or a desire to learn)

- ✔ A natural organizer who can demonstrate masterful handling of multiple projects at once

- ✔ Knowledge of Microsoft Office — Excel and PowerPoint especially

Social media manager

Your social media manager is another very important hire because social media has a key role in lead generation. This person should have a passion for creating programs on social sites such as Facebook, Twitter, LinkedIn, Google+, and others. He runs all your social programs and knows how to leverage social networks to enhance lead generation campaign performance and measure results. Ideally, this person should be extremely high-energy and enjoy interacting with prospects, customers, and influencers on social channels. You want to look for born networkers.

Here is an example of the required skills or experience you want to look for:

- ✔ Bachelor's degree
- ✔ Experience in or desire to learn how to manage social channels like Facebook, Twitter, LinkedIn, Google+, and so on
- ✔ Track record of establishing relationships with bloggers and the social press
- ✔ Knowledge of how to leverage social media for lead generation using paid ad programs
- ✔ Experience in (or a desire to learn) content development
- ✔ A highly creative nature with an understanding of what works for lead generation on social channels
- ✔ Experience with social monitoring tools
- ✔ Strong communication and writing skills
- ✔ Knowledge of Microsoft Office

Content marketing manager

Your content marketing manager is your dedicated headcount for content creation. She is instrumental in creating ebooks, infographics, videos, and other content assets that you will use in all your lead generation campaigns. The content manager also is instrumental in your lead generation campaign's core messaging and how that maps back to business priorities. This person must be highly creative, a thought leader, and an excellent communicator.

Here is an example of the required skills or experience you might want to look for in your content marketing manager:

- ✔ Bachelor's degree or MBA
- ✔ Passion for writing and excellent communication skills

✔ Project management experience for all content creation, including ebooks, infographics, slide decks, videos, and more

✔ Blog and webinar management

✔ Ability to ensure all content promotion is coordinated across multiple channels including social promotion, email, website, and events

✔ Ability to accurately report on all content marketing activities

✔ Knowledge of your industry and desire to be a thought leader

✔ Knowledge of Word, PowerPoint and Excel

Marketing operations manager

The marketing operations manager role is particularly important if you decide to invest in multiple technologies such as marketing automation and CRM. The marketing operations manager generates reports and conducts an analysis of your lead generation return on investment. This role also ensures activities are aligned between sales and marketing — like watching to make sure service-level agreements (SLAs) are being followed and that definitions remain consistent. The marketing operations manager also helps guide strategy iteration by knowing what works and what doesn't.

Here is an example of the required skills and experience you might want to look for:

✔ Bachelor's degree or MBA a plus

✔ Experience as a business analyst or in sales or marketing operations

✔ An extremely analytical nature and a love of numbers — this person will be running a lot of reports and reviewing data to measure marketing program ROI

✔ Ability to identify opportunities for program improvement and iteration based on collected data

✔ Experience with configuring CRM platforms, or at least running complex reports out of them

✔ Very strong quantitative skills and the know-how to create and translate data sets into business recommendations

✔ Marketing automation power user or shows a desire to learn a new technology

✔ Excellent project manager with proven success in driving initiatives forward

Online marketing manager

The online marketing manager can also be a key hire as his specialty is search engine optimization (SEO), pay-per-click (PPC), display advertising, and other paid program management — which is a large part of any lead generation strategy. The online marketing manager executes all online marketing plans to drive leads and company goals. She has strong analytical skills to create metrics-driven reporting and is a great project manager who can run many programs concurrently.

Here is an example of the required skills and experience you might want to look for in your online marketing manager:

- Bachelor's degree
- Ability to develop and implement strategy for SEO, PPC, display ads, social media advertising, and other paid programs — you want someone who can both think *and* do
- Ability to manage vendor relationships and evaluate effectiveness of each channel
- Ability to analyze website activity resulting from programs and make recommendations for improvements
- Ability to produce monthly reporting for each channel and identify and interpret trends
- Strong experience in media planning and familiarity with web-based lead generation activities
- Track record of success achieving and exceeding ambitious online marketing goals
- Strong communication skills, including excellent written skills
- Knowledge of Microsoft Office — Excel and PowerPoint especially

Creative design manager

The creative design manager is the person who creates the visual graphics for all of your lead generation campaigns. Whether it is design for an ebook, a banner for an email, or a brochure for an event, you need a graphic designer on staff, or you need to vet design agencies. I personally recommend you have at least one designer on staff: Design is central to marketing efforts. Your creative design manager focuses on visual branding, collateral design, web design, and event design.

Here is an example of the required skills and experience you might want to look for:

- ✔ Experience designing in a corporate environment
- ✔ Experience using Adobe Photoshop, Illustrator, and InDesign
- ✔ HTML/CSS, Flash, and video experience
- ✔ Desire to tie creative visuals for campaigns to overall business objectives
- ✔ Flexibility to work under tight deadlines when needed
- ✔ A diverse portfolio of creative designs for different mediums using different platforms

Event marketing manager

Events are also a large part of your lead generation strategy, and your event marketing manager is responsible for creating and executing your event programs. He focuses on program and agenda planning, administrative duties around event planning, creative execution, speaker management, sponsor management, and onsite execution — all with the ultimate goal of generating qualified leads for your business, which justifies the costs of putting on or attending that event. Your event marketing manager should be highly organized and an excellent project manager.

Here is an example of the required skills and experience you might want to look for:

- ✔ Bachelor's degree
- ✔ Great event-planning skills with an emphasis on strategic deal-making
- ✔ Passion for events and drive for creative planning
- ✔ Excellent communication and networking skills
- ✔ Negotiation skills
- ✔ Ability to problem-solve issues and quickly find solutions, often at the last minute (the show must go on!)
- ✔ Desire to interface with customers, partners, and employees
- ✔ Advanced knowledge of Microsoft Office — PowerPoint and Excel in particular

Recognizing the Right Traits for Success

When recruiting for a rock-star lead generation team, there are specific personality traits or soft skills that you should be looking for. Beyond just looking at years of experience and degrees, you need to assess a candidate's ability to thrive in today's technology-driven marketing environment. And based on my experience working on many innovative marketing teams, I look for very specific personality traits in my hiring. No matter what industry you are in, whether it is hotel management, construction, or anything else, lead generation is largely done online, so you must have your finger on the pulse of the ways consumers are researching in order to know where your customers are.

In fact, an inbound marketing software platform called HubSpot describes hiring marketers according to the DARC principle — Digitally fluent, Analytical, Influential social reach, and Content creators. I do not believe all of your marketing team has to abide by the DARC methodology to hiring, but there are very specific traits you should look for as you build your lead generation team.

Having a solid understanding of technology

This is one of the most important skills to look for when hiring for a lead generation role in today's marketing environment. You need to leverage many technologies in lead generation including CRM tools, marketing automation, social media, Google Analytics, and more. You need a team of people who not only understand why technology is critical to lead generation, but can also learn at an accelerated pace as new technology is released.

Many methodologies of hiring refer to this trait as being a *digital native*, *digitally fluent*, or a *digital citizen*. According to HubSpot, these are the people who "really get technology and are naturally curious about it." Here are some signs that the person you are about to hire is digitally fluent:

- ✔ He reads multiple different industry blogs.
- ✔ She uses Facebook, Twitter, LinkedIn, Google+, Pinterest, and so on, for her own enjoyment.
- ✔ He writes for different industry blogs or has a desire to do so.
- ✔ She is fluent in multiple different marketing technologies or has a desire to learn.

You may interview many people who are in varying stages of being a digital native, but most importantly, look for examples of a desire to learn new technology platforms. Curiosity is an important trait to focus on in your hiring decisions.

Possessing fantastic communication skills

All of your marketers should be content creators. And by that, I mean your team should have excellent writing skills that can be leveraged in all aspects of your lead generation strategy including ebook creation, blog writing, online ad writing, email crafting, social media updates, and so on. And each member of your team should be able to be called on at any given time to help create content. Particularly with your blog, you want diversity in voice, so each member of your marketing team should have a desire and passion to contribute to content in some way. According to HubSpot, "creating remarkable content that spreads virally in the social mediasphere attracts links from other sites and drives up your rankings in Google. This remarkable content turns your website from a small town like Wellesley, Massachusetts (one highway), to a large metropolis like New York City (many highways, many airports, many train stations, many bus depots)."

I particularly like this quote because I think it says it all. The more your team can create remarkable and useful content, the bigger your presence can be and the more leads you can generate.

Here are some signs that the person you are about to hire possesses fantastic communication and writing skills:

✔ He submits a well-organized and structured resume and cover letter, with no typos or bad grammar.

✔ She is able to give well-thought-out, linear answers in your interview questions.

✔ He reads multiple industry blogs and has written blog posts in the past.

✔ She might have an English degree or journalism background.

✔ He has a passion for writing and can excel at any writing exercise.

✔ She can sum up your core business differentiator in two or three sentences.

✔ He is active on social media channels and frequently uses them to search for content.

Owning analytics

You have probably noticed that I have been talking a lot about analytics. Measuring lead generation performance and being able to iterate programs in order to improve what you are doing is absolutely critical to successful lead generation. And analytical skills, as a marketer, are a fairly new need for businesses. But as marketing continues to get more sophisticated, you need people on your team who understand and have a natural passion for measurement. That means people who love numbers and tying efforts to outcomes, coupled with an intense love for spreadsheets and all things data.

Here are some signs that the person you are about to hire possesses the right amount of analytical skills:

✔ She loves data in all forms and particularly gets a kick out of creating spreadsheets, VLOOKUPS, statistics, and pivot tables.

✔ He is a master of project management and loves the details.

✔ She gets a kick out of experimenting with data-based what-if scenarios and problem-solving.

✔ He is not afraid to dig deeper into an issue or bottleneck to find out what went wrong.

Hiring and interviewing for analytical thinking is harder than it sounds. Many people say that they are analytical without truly knowing what you mean by "data-driven." Consider giving them a data-set or a problem to solve that demonstrates what you mean by analytical thinking within your own organization. Listen to how they would approach answering a question like, "How many phone booths are there in the United States?"

Looking at Recruiting Options

Now that you have an exhaustive list of nice-to-have lead generation team members, how do you find the perfect A-players? Whether you decide to hire every role on my list or just one or two people to do it all, making the right hire is the difference between a lead generation strategy that outshines the competition and one that can't even get out the door.

Finding the right talent is very difficult. Why? The skillsets that you need for lead generation are very specific and hard to find. Not all marketers are rooted in technology or understand the need for a robust analytics program. Plus, many of these skills are new — such as content marketing, social media, and marketing automation — so your talent pool is much smaller. Classic marketers that haven't kept up with advancements in technology might be able to use certain big-picture buzzwords, but know nothing of the way those concepts translate into a living, breathing, lead-generation machine. Therefore, don't be afraid to think outside of the box when it comes to your hiring options. If you don't, you likely won't find the type of candidate you need.

Personally, I've found it difficult to find the exact combination of traits that I am looking for in my own teammates and hires, so be prepared to train. There is nothing more exciting to a new hire than having a fantastic mentor. If you find the right person otherwise but he isn't analytical or digitally inclined, take the time to give that person the resources he needs to succeed.

Leveraging LinkedIn

I have found LinkedIn to be a great way to find incredible marketing talent. It's not enough to post your job opening on a career site and expect the right candidates to come flooding through your door. You need to use a mix of tactics to be truly effective. LinkedIn, essentially a social network site where people have their resumes up for everyone to view, is a great way to recruit the best of the best through your own network.

In fact, according to a 2013 study by the Society for Human Resource Management, 77 percent of employers use social networks to recruit. And among the recruiters using social tools, 94 percent say they used LinkedIn. With numbers like that, you can't afford to ignore LinkedIn.

Here are a few techniques to help with your LinkedIn recruiting efforts:

✔ **Upgrade your account to Business or Business Plus:** One of the first things you should do if you decide to use LinkedIn for your recruiting purposes is to invest the money to upgrade your account. The primary reason here is that you can use LinkedIn's Inmail and Introduction features. Inmail enables you to send direct messages to anyone on LinkedIn, and Introductions enables you to get introduced to inside sources at companies through your LinkedIn connections. Premium Search is also a key benefit of upgrading your account. You can see more profiles when you search and get more advanced filtering.

Figure 5-1 shows you the feature breakdown of each LinkedIn Premium account so you can decide what suits your needs.

Compare Plans	Free *Your Current Plan*	Sales Basic	Sales Plus	Sales Executive
Pricing: Annual | Monthly ↖ Save up to 25%		**US$15.95**/MO[1] *Billed annually* [Start Now]	**US$39.95**/MO[1] *Billed annually* [Start Now]	**US$74.95**/MO[1] *Billed annually* [Start Now]
Find Prospects				
Sales Alerts Stay on top of new leads.	3 weekly	5 weekly	7 weekly	10 daily
Lead Builder Manage your pipeline to source and close deals.		✓	✓	✓
Premium Search Pinpoint the right leads.[2]		4	4	8
Relate with Insight				
Full Profiles See full profiles of everyone in your network - 1st, 2nd and 3rd degree.	Limited Up to 2nd Degree	✓	✓	✓
Who's Viewed Your Profile Proactively manage inbound queries and interest in your profile.	Limited	✓	✓	✓
Full Name Visibility See full names of 3rd degree and group connections.				✓
Engage with Confidence				
Introductions Get warm introductions to inside sources at companies you're interested in.	5	15	25	35
InMail Messages Gain access to decision-makers. Response guaranteed.[3]			10 per month	25 per month
		[Start Now]	[Start Now]	[Start Now]

Figure 5-1:
The feature
breakdown
for LinkedIn
Premium
accounts.

✔ **Advanced People Search:** LinkedIn offers a variety of advanced search features. Advanced People Search enables you to search for people based on current company, location, and industry. However, if you have a Premium account, you can also search for years of experience, seniority, function, and company size, which is far better, particularly if you are looking for a very specific role, such as a content marketing manager who has been in the healthcare industry for three years.

Figure 5-2 shows a screenshot of LinkedIn's Advanced People Search. You can see what is available to regular LinkedIn accounts versus Premium accounts.

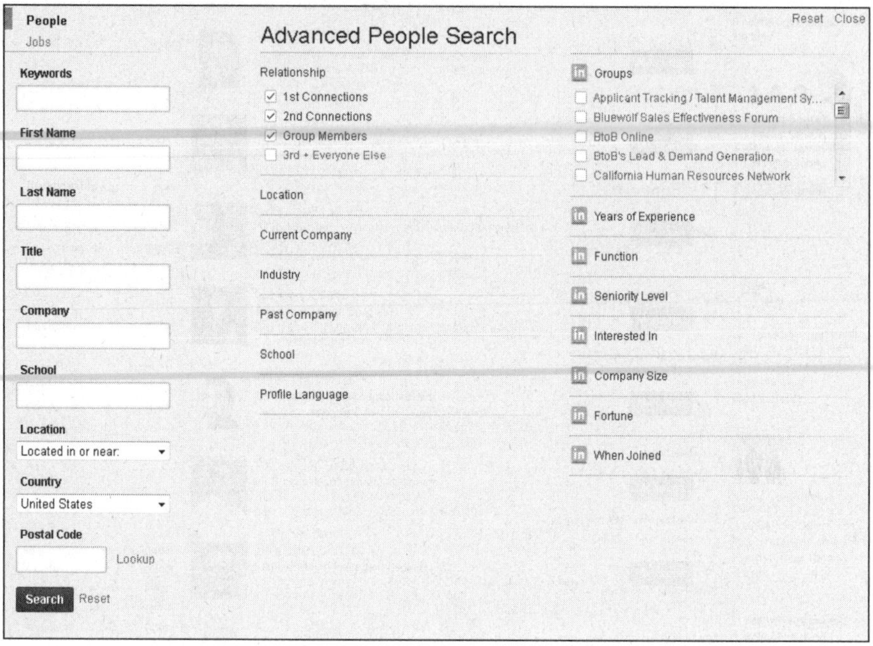

Figure 5-2:
A LinkedIn
Advanced
People
Search.

✔ **Inmail and Introductions:** After you have found your ideal pool of candidates, you want to contact them. The best way to do this in LinkedIn is via Inmail and Introductions. Inmail is truly the best option if you have a Premium account. This enables you to directly contact a person you might not be connected with through a message. Note that many of the Premium accounts have limited numbers of these, so use them with caution. The other way to contact a candidate is through Introductions. If you know someone who is connected to the candidate, ask your connection to introduce you.

If you are sending an Inmail, be sure to personalize your message, tell the candidate what stuck out in his profile, and also explain details about the job.

Figure 5-3 shows an example of what an Inmail sent to a candidate looks like.

✔ **Connect with a candidate:** If you decide you do not want to upgrade your LinkedIn account, you can always use the good old-fashioned Connect button. Ask your desired candidate to connect. You can either include your job description in your initial Connect message, or you can message her after she has accepted your request. I find this is a good tactic if you simply can't upgrade; however, it's certainly not as effective as using Inmail. Approach your outreach as your own mini-lead generation campaign. Think about what sort of qualified job candidates you want replying to your query.

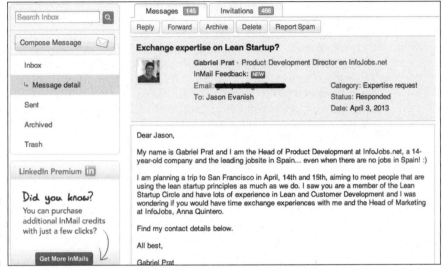

Figure 5-3:
LinkedIn
Inmail.

Contracting an outside recruiting firm

Some of the roles you have open for your marketing team might be very difficult to fill. Maybe you have spent time on LinkedIn, have gone through countless resume submissions, and still you haven't found anyone. Another option is to contract with an outside recruiting firm who knows your space or who recruits for creative/marketing-specific roles.

Make sure you spend time with your recruiting firm to go over job details, specific experience and traits you are looking for in your new hire, the budget for the role, and your organization's interview process. Find out up front how the recruiting firm chooses to be compensated so that your incentives to deliver qualified candidates are aligned.

Posting a job listing

This of course is the most basic and common way to find a new hire for your lead generation team — posting a job listing. After you craft your job description based on the different criteria that I outlined earlier, go ahead and post your listing on different job sites. Marketers frequent LinkedIn, Craigslist, TheLadders, and sometimes Monster and CareerBuilder. Also make sure you have your job listing posted on your company's own Careers page on its website.

Most likely, when you post your listing, you will get a large response, so make sure you have someone going through each resume and selecting only the best. Your first line of defense can be the keyword checker in your Applicant Tracking System, if your HR department has one. A *keyword checker* can go through each resume to search for specific keywords you deem as important to your job listing. As an example, for your content marketing role you might want to search for English, journalism, MBA, writing, communication, project management, Microsoft Office, and so on. A keyword checker can automate this process and send you only resumes that pass a certain keyword threshold.

Part II

Connecting Inbound Marketing and Lead Generation

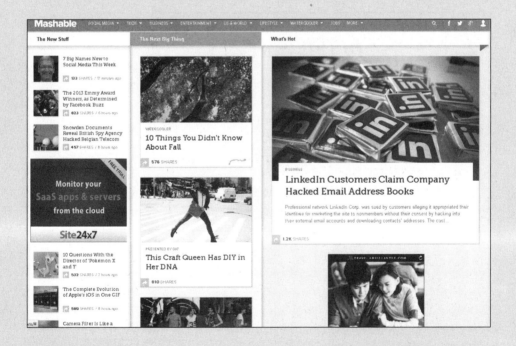

Visit www.dummies.com/extras/leadgeneration for more on how to create a big content piece from start to finish.

In this part . . .

- ✔ Fuel your inbound lead-generation campaigns with content marketing
- ✔ Optimize your website and search engine marketing for maximum lead conversion
- ✔ Create a blog that positions your company as an industry thought leader
- ✔ Use social media channels to generate viable leads for your business

Chapter 6

Generating Leads with Content Marketing

*E*veryone is talking about content marketing. If you've been to any marketing conferences in the past two years, you've probably noticed that content marketing is the new social media. It's a hot topic on every marketer's mind and is proving to be a large part of any successful lead generation effort.

Content marketing can be defined many ways, but I like C.C. Chapman's the best, from the book *Content Rules:*

"Content marketing is anything a company creates and shares to tell their story. It is conversational, human, and doesn't try to constantly sell to you. It also isn't a tactic that you can just turn on and off and hope that it will be successful. It has to be a mindset that is embraced and encouraged. You've got to start thinking like a publisher and use that to plan and execute your entire marketing plan, which content of any variety should be a part of."

Content marketing isn't new. Brands have been using the concept of content marketing to tell their story for decades. In 1895, John Deere released a customer magazine that now has 1,500,000 subscribers worldwide. In 1904, Jell-O created a recipe book that contributed to $1,000,000 in sales by 1906.

Consider even early cave paintings. Engaging an audience through a story has always been a primary way humans communicate with one another. Brands need to integrate this tactic into their lead generation efforts. Content marketing becomes particularly important as the new buyer self-educates through the buying journey via online channels. And because the new buyer represents a fundamental shift in how we as marketers reach audiences, creating valuable content has become a primary focus.

According to Heidi Cohen, content marketing expert and blogger, content marketing's major attributes include the following:

- ✔ Embodies the product or firm's core brand elements
- ✔ Uses a variety of media formats such as text, video, photos, audio, ebooks, and infographics to tell a brand story
- ✔ Can be consumed on a variety of devices such as computers, smartphones, and tablets
- ✔ Is distributed through your owned properties like your website and blog, through third-party contacts and vendors, and social media platforms
- ✔ Provides measureable results through the use of appropriate calls-to-action

In this chapter, you discover how to create a content marketing machine to fuel your lead generation efforts.

Exploring Content

Content helps you build trust and become a thought leader in your space. Content makes a buyer say, "Eureka! That's *just* the information I'm looking for!" and earns you a special place in his heart. Content is the Thelma to your Louise, the Sonny to your Cher. Content and lead generation truly create the perfect pair. Without quality content, you won't have a comprehensive lead generation plan.

Content is the basis of many (if not all) of your lead generation campaigns. When you send an email blast, host an event, or launch a social campaign or pay-per-click (PPC) ad, you're providing relevant (and hopefully insightful) content.

Rather than offering a boring datasheet that goes on and on about your product or service, create an ebook of actionable tips on how to fix a problem that causes potential buyers to pull out their hair. When you help a buyer with a problem, you become top-of-mind. After you gain a buyer's trust because you've helped him so many times, convincing a buyer that your product or service is the best becomes much easier.

Being a thought leader

When prospects discover your company, most likely, they don't yet have trust in your brand and they aren't ready to make a purchase. An overly promotional lead generation campaign can be a huge turnoff. A critical concept to understand is the difference between thought leadership and promotional content.

What is thought leadership? According to Jon Miller, VP of marketing and cofounder of Marketo, *thought leadership* "consists of ideas that require attention, that offer guidance or clarity. Thought leadership needs to be educational and ideally provocative." Instead of merely creating content that beats your company's chest, try to provide your audience with something that they can ponder. Thought leadership in content marketing helps you:

- ✔ Create relationships with customers and prospects by engaging in relevant conversations

- ✔ Differentiate yourself as a source for research and best practices across your industry

- ✔ Build trust with prospects so that when they are ready to make a purchase, they automatically go to the industry leader

Purely promotional content produced for the sole intent of closing a deal and sent to a prospect at the wrong time can come across as yelling. The key here is to make sure you are sending the *right* message at the *right* time in a lead's buying cycle.

Imagine you're a marketer working in a small company interested in best practices for email marketing. You search Twitter and find an interesting blog post on optimizing email for mobile technology. You click the blog post, read it, find it useful, and subscribe to the blog. If the first email you get from the company, which just happens to be a marketing automation software firm, is a datasheet about their product, you will most likely trash it.

However, if the first email you get from that company is an ebook of best practices for optimizing email for mobile channels, you will probably open it, read it, and look forward to additional educational content. And when you're ready to buy a marketing automation platform, the first brand that comes to mind might be the one who's been sending helpful content over a period of time. Marketo's downloadable ebook *The Definitive Guide to Marketing Automation* is an example of thought leadership content. (The guide covers best practices for marketing automation, not just Marketo. In fact, if you are using a competitor, this guide is just as helpful because it's platform-neutral.) Your audience can read your asset and educate themselves versus being sold to.

Leveraging promotional content

Promotional content is an asset that delivers a hard sell. Think of a datasheet, pricing sheet, or even an ebook that goes into more detail regarding product or service information. This content is considered late-stage (late in the buying process) and should be used when a lead is very close to making a purchase. In fact, when a lead downloads a piece of promotional, late-stage content, he is considered a hand-raiser, and should be contacted by sales immediately. When a potential customer downloads a pricing or product sheet, it's a key indicator of positive buying behavior.

Promotional content has its place later in the buying cycle, but for the purpose of lead generation, you will mostly be using content that can be considered thought leadership in nature because you are trying to create relationships.

Considering different forms of content

You can tell a story in many ways. Customers and prospects consume stories in many ways, too. Some may enjoy reading an ebook cover to cover; others might consume information visually through an infographic or a slide deck. If you only create ebooks, you'll reach *some* of your potential buyers, but never those who delete ebooks whenever they appear in their email.

To make sure you're reaching every potential buyer, use a variety of content types. Here are a few to consider:

- ✔ **Ebook:** An ebook is a digital book that consists of text and images. Ebooks can be easily consumed on computers and mobile devices. They can be a few pages, hundreds of pages long, or anywhere in between. The great part about an ebook is that you can base many of your additional assets off the written content.

- ✔ **Whitepapers and reports:** Many people think of whitepapers and reports as being interchangeable with ebooks. However, I think of a whitepaper more as a long-form authoritative report or manual. Whitepapers often take the form of benchmarks and industry reports.

- ✔ **One-pager/cheat sheet:** A one-pager or cheat sheet is a short piece of content that informs a reader about a product, service, or concept in an extremely digestible way. These are always one page, but copy can also be on the back.

- ✔ **Activity book/worksheet:** An activity book is a great way to get interactive with your content. Instead of just telling your audience what to do, walk them through it! Think check lists, questionnaires, and templates. Even consider something fun like a coloring book, word scramble, or crossword puzzle.

✔ **Video:** Marketing videos come in many forms. Think 60–90-second demo videos, animated shorts, live action commercials, webinar recordings, and presentation recordings, to name a few.

✔ **Infographic:** Visual content is a great way to reach your audience in a fun and interesting way. An infographic takes a complex story, often including stats and quotes, and uses graphical elements to bring it to life in a more concise manner. Infographics are typically short and are scrollable on a computer screen or mobile phone.

✔ **Slide Decks:** Visual slide decks are a great way to present longer form information in an engaging way. You can create a special visual slide deck using creative visuals from an infographic, or you can upload a webinar presentation slide deck. Slide decks should present information in an easy-to-digest format, and also tell a compelling story at the same time in order to engage your reader.

✔ **Podcasts:** Never underestimate the power of a podcast. A _podcast_ is a vocal recording of a presentation, webinar, or speech. A person can listen to a podcast on the go — in her car, on her headphones, and so on.

Delving into Content Planning

One of the most important aspects to content marketing for successful lead generation is the planning process. The best way to start planning your content is to conduct your own discovery session. Ask yourself, your marketing team, your salespeople, and your customer service representatives the following questions:

✔ Why are you creating content?

✔ What are your areas of expertise?

✔ What are the common concerns and pain points of your target audience?

✔ What are the topics you could write about that would address those pain points?

✔ Do you have any product/service offerings or announcements that you want to tie your content efforts to?

✔ Where do you want your content to live? In a content resource section? On your website home page? On your blog?

Hold meetings with members within your organization that you consider key stakeholders. And make sure to spend time with some of the people who are on the front lines everyday talking to customers.

Developing buyer personas

Once you get a good sense of your content marketing and organizational landscape through your discovery, you are ready to create your *buyer personas*. A buyer persona is a representation of your various buyers and influencers. Basically, who is buying your product or service? Understanding these buyer definitions is critical not only to your content creation, but to your lead generation efforts as a whole.

A persona uses data to help everyone that is creating content to focus on a *tangible* representation of a buyer, versus a nebulous, formless one. If a buyer persona is created without research and based on outdated assumptions and hunches, you can have a biased and incomplete view of who you are actually marketing to. I have seen many marketing teams that don't back up their hunches with measurable evidence. Personas then take on the attributes of whatever the most important person in the room thinks they should be.

The bottom line is the more you know about your *actual* buyers, the more you can focus your messaging and effectively target and speak to your audience.

How do you find out who your buyers are? Research, research, research. Set up time to speak with the following groups:

- ✔ **Sales:** Your sales team understands better than most in your organization who buys your product or service. They speak to prospects day in and day out and know buyer pain points, objections, and what gets them excited. And they not only understand who your primary buyer is, but they also understand the influencers — those who may not make a purchasing decision, but who heavily influence your purchasers.

- ✔ **Customers:** Current customers are a fantastic resource. They have already purchased your product or service and can tell you a lot about why they purchased, what their pain points are, and what a day in their life looks like. You might consider offering an incentive like a gift card or T-shirt to the customers who participate in your survey. One thing to note is that you want to experience the good, the bad, and the ugly, so make sure you interview customers who have had a wide variety of experiences with your company.

- ✔ **Prospects:** You also want to focus on those that are considering your product or service. Who are they? What attracted them to you? It may be tough to speak directly to prospects because they aren't customers yet, so use the data that you may already have in your customer relationship management (CRM) or marketing automation platform to determine who they are and what they do.

Not sure what questions to ask? Try asking your buyers these questions to get the information you need:

- ✔ What is your job title?
- ✔ What industry do you currently work in?
- ✔ What are your core job responsibilities?
- ✔ What do you love most about your job?
- ✔ What do you dislike most about your job?
- ✔ What interested you about our solution?
- ✔ What are the pain points relevant to our solution?
- ✔ Which needs might our solution address?
- ✔ What are you looking for in a solution?
- ✔ What is your preferred buying process?
- ✔ How are you researching product/solution information?
- ✔ What is your role in the decision-making process?
- ✔ How do you typically choose to consume information?
- ✔ How often are you on a mobile device or tablet?

Don't have the time to do this type of research? You can always bring in a third-party consulting firm to do this for you. Invest the time upfront before you risk wasting time creating content that doesn't make sense to or isn't even noticed by your intended audience.

After you have all of the information needed, you can begin building your personas. List them and start building your profiles. Figure 6-1 outlines a sample buyer persona worksheet, but make sure you include the following fields when you create your own worksheet:

- ✔ **Who:** Provide a detailed explanation of who the buyer is and include demographic information. To aid in your storytelling, consider adding real-life characteristics and descriptions to your worksheet. Even give your persona a name!
- ✔ **What:** Include a detailed explanation of job responsibilities and day-to-day life.
- ✔ **Pain points:** List each pain point that you collected from your interviews. What are the issues facing this persona — what makes this person pull his hair out every day? Addressing these pain points will be great topics for your content pieces.

✔ **Goals:** What are your persona's 2–10 year goals? How can your product help her get there?

✔ **Wish lists:** What does this person wish for? What are aspects of your product that can help your persona achieve his wishes?

✔ **Buying profile:** Describe how this person buys. Can you often find her on Twitter searching for reviews? Or maybe this person asks his friends for advice.

Buying Roles

Insert Buyer Roles. Let's use the roles suggested by SiriusDecisions.

Stages:	1. Loosening the status quo	2. Committing to Change	3. Exploring Possible Solutions	4. Committing to a Solution	5. Justifying the Decision	6. Making the Selection
Champion						
User						
CXO						
IT						

Your Turn

Insert the buyer roles of your company here, adding or deleting as necessary.

Stages:	1.	2.	3.	4.	5.	6.
A						
B						
C						
D						

Content

Finally, let's map your content into the cells of the matrix. For each grid box be as specific as you can about your content and list as many resources as you can that would be relevant for each person and buying stage.

Stages:	1.	2.	3.	4.	5.	6.
A						
B						
C						
D						

Figure 6-1:
A sample
buyer
persona.

After you have developed your buyer personas, you can start writing content that is applicable to their needs and profiles. Keep your buyer personas in mind as you create your content marketing plan.

Mapping buying stages

The next step in your planning process is mapping your buying stages. What kind of content do you want to send to your persona and when? It is crucial to send the right piece of content at the right time. Someone who is just learning about your company isn't ready for a case study, so don't send him one. Conversely, a prospect may not want another educational asset if they are ready to buy. The idea is to move each prospect down your buying funnel with content.

Typically, most companies have buying stages that look similar to the following list:

✔ **Early stage:** Your prospect has not yet indicated any buying intent or preference for your company. He most likely has just started the research phase. The content you send your prospect in this stage must be educational in nature and relevant to your prospect's interest.

✔ **Mid stage:** Your prospect may have indicated some interest in either your company or your product/service. The content you offer at this stage is geared toward helping your buyer differentiate your product from the competition so the right purchasing decision can be made. For instance, you want to offer buying guides, ROI calculators, and other content very closely related to your core product or service.

✔ **Late stage:** Your prospect has indicated strong interest for your product or service. She is well on her way to purchasing, and you should offer her pricing sheets, datasheets, and customer case studies. This is where you include your product-specific content assets. Sales may also be engaged at this time.

Figure 6-2 shows an example of content that is mapped closely to each buying stage. As the buyer gets closer and closer to purchasing, the content narrows to become more specific.

Depending on how many personas you created, you may want to create separate buying stages for each persona. For instance, if you have a CMO and a practitioner persona, they might have two completely different buying processes. Consider documenting each. This can help you segment and target even further.

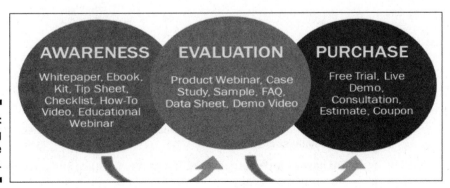

Figure 6-2:
Buying
stage
mapping.

AWARENESS

Whitepaper, Ebook,
Kit, Tip Sheet,
Checklist, How-To
Video, Educational
Webinar

EVALUATION

Product Webinar, Case
Study, Sample, FAQ,
Data Sheet, Demo Video

PURCHASE

Free Trial, Live
Demo,
Consultation,
Estimate, Coupon

Working with a content grid

After you have mapped both your buying stages and personas, you can create what is called a *content grid*. In this grid, you list out each persona, each buying stage, and then you insert applicable content in each cell.

For instance, say you are a marketer working for a professional services consulting firm. You have four total personas and one of them is the Chief Operating Officer (COO). You also have mapped your buying stages, so you know how to identify the COO buyer journey. In your grid, you want to make sure you have content that is applicable to the COO persona in all of your buying stages.

Figure 6-3 shows you an example of a content grid. Create your own in a spreadsheet or a PowerPoint slide and keep it handy throughout your planning efforts.

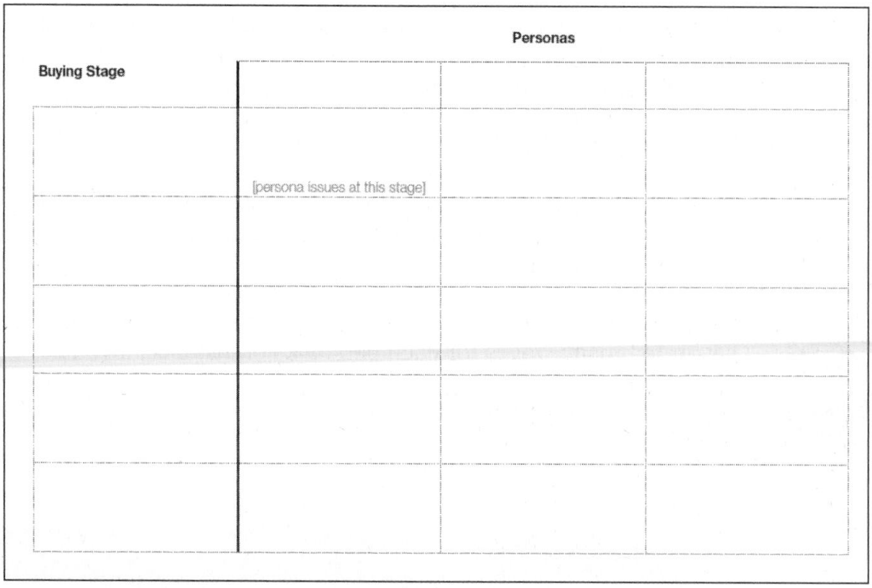

Figure 6-3: A sample content grid.

The key is to make sure you fill your content grid in for each stage of your funnel and each of your buying stages. This ensures that

- ✔ You fully understand each persona and what he experiences throughout the buying stages.
- ✔ You have mapped out each different buying stage and are close to your sales process.
- ✔ You know what content you already have and where you have holes.

Creating content arcs and themes

The next step to creating an awesome content marketing plan is to plan what content you are going to create. You have your buyer personas, you have a sense of what type of content you can create, so now what are you going to write about? No doubt it's a tall order.

You want to support business initiatives with your content, so the best place to start is to consider and map out the following topics as you create your content themes:

✔ Large product or service launches

✔ Large company announcements

✔ Hot topics and industry themes

✔ Search engine optimization (SEO) keyword needs

For product/service launches and company announcements, create a calendar at least six months in advance so you have a full view of what your company wants to promote. Then on the side, list at least four trending topics in your industry and at least four of the top keywords you want your website to rank for.

After you create your initial calendar setup, you will likely find that many of your product/service launches or announcements match up with both industry trends and your keyword needs (if you are focusing on the right topics). These consistent topics are your *themes* or *arcs*. Create an outline for each potential content arc and assign potential content types to each arc.

As an example, say you work for a natural food manufacturer. One of your arcs might look like the following:

Trend and Product Launches: Gluten-Free Natural Foods (April–June)

✔ Product launch: Gluten-free cookies (April)

✔ Service launch: Gluten-free shopper service (May)

✔ Product launch: Gluten-free frozen meals (June)

✔ Potential content ideas:

- Ebook on gluten-free living

- Video series on gluten-free recipes

- Cheat sheets on ingredients that contain gluten

- Infographic on the gluten-free alternative

- Buying guide to gluten-free products

- Blog posts on living healthier by going gluten-free

Start by trying one arc per quarter — four content arcs per year. After you have chosen your two (if you are planning for the next six months) or four (if you are planning for the next year), map your arcs to a calendar with approximate dates.

Take a look at Figure 6-4, which illustrates what your calendar might look like.

ROGER C. PARKER'S *PUBLISHED & PROFITABLE*

Weekly Editorial Calendar

Writing Success Cycle

QUARTER, YEAR   **3rd Quarter 2012**

	MEDIA & TITLE	DATE	DUE	RESULTS
MONTH **July 2012** **TOPIC OR THEME** **Choosing a book topic**	P&P blog, Where do Book Ideas Come From?	July 5	July 2	3 comments, 117 RTs
	Free webinar, Does Your Book Topic Make Sense?	July 10	July 6	
	CMI guest post, Topic Trends for Premium Books	July 18	July 13	
	P&P blog, Selecting Topics for Self-Published Books	July 23	July 20	
MONTH **August 2012** **TOPIC OR THEME** **Selecting a Title for Your Book**	P&P blog, 10 Keys to Book Title Success	Aug 1	July 27	
	Free webinar, Choosing the Right Book Title	Aug 7	Aug 3	
	CMI guest post, Title Suggestions for Premium Books	August 15	Aug 10	
	P&P blog, Testing Your Book Title Idea Before It's Too Late	Aug 20	Aug 17	
MONTH **Sept. 2012** **TOPIC OR THEME** **Creating a Table of Contents**	P&P blog, 12 Tools to Organize Your Ideas Into Chapters	Sept 5	Aug 31	
	Free webinar, Getting Started Harvesting Your Ideas	Sept 11	Sept 6'	
	CMI guest post, Finding Content Gold on Your Hard Drive	Sept 12	Sept 7	
	P&P blog, Using Mind Maps to Create a Table of Contents	Sept 17	Sept 14	

© 2012 Roger C. Parker | www.publishedandprofitable.com

Figure 6-4:
A content arc calendar.

Having a visual representation of what your content looks like for the next six months to a year helps you flesh out your lead generation programs and integrate your marketing to obtain goals that align to each core business priority.

One thing that is important to note here is that you want to maintain a steady drumbeat of interesting content. Your arcs should be the foundation of your content efforts, but don't be afraid to stray a bit if you see something else pop up that you are passionate about and want to create lead generation campaigns around. You never know what might be new and exciting in your industry that you have to comment on. The key is to look to your arcs and your calendar as a guideline, but always think outside of the box and don't be afraid to put efforts into something else that might also create buzz and drive revenue.

Doing More with Less in Your Content Marketing

Say you have a content plan that is tightly aligned with organizational objectives as well as industry trends and top keywords. Take a minute to sit down and take a few breaths. You have a good chunk of your foundation planning out of the way, and getting organized is half the battle.

But after you have your plan together, where do you start? This is a question I get constantly. "We have our plan, and we have some great pieces planned, but how do we get started and how do we do more with less?"

Even if you come from a large company where you have a large marketing budget and content marketing has been proven, you can always learn new ways to stretch your dollars and increase your return on investment. By being smart, thrifty, and understanding how your audience consumes content, you can quickly create a content marketing empire to be reckoned with!

Coming up with your big rock content pieces

The first step to creating a robust content library is thinking about your "big rock content piece." Your *big rock content piece* is a large piece of content (ideally 20 or more pages) that maps to each content arc. Your big rock is the big kahuna — the fire that ignites many of your lead generation campaigns.

Your big rock content piece fulfills the following goals:

- ✔ Showcases your thought leadership around your arc
- ✔ Shows off creative writing and design prowess
- ✔ Is dynamic enough to be the basis for other content pieces (more on that later in this chapter)
- ✔ Contains best practices, tips, and actionable insights

Your big rock piece is the basis for many additional content pieces such as ebooks, videos, webinars, and so on, so make sure that you keep this in mind during your planning phase, and think creatively about what to include in the piece to bring additional value.

Don't be afraid to make your big rock content piece long. Remember, you want to be recognized as a publisher, so the more value you add, the more your audience views you as a true authority. Be authentic, and people will notice.

I helped create several big rock content pieces at Marketo. Each one of these pieces aligns to one of their content arcs. For example, *The Definitive Guide to Social Marketing* aligned to a social marketing content arc and contains 81 pages of worksheets, tips, tricks, and best practices. Another example is *The Definitive Guide to Events*. Again, it's aligned to an event marketing content arc.

Follow this ten-step plan to organize your big rock content piece creation process:

1. **Meet with stakeholders.**

   Assuming that your big rock content piece aligns with business priorities and drives many lead generation campaigns, meet with internal stakeholders such as your CMO, VP of marketing, director of demand generation, your customer team, and so on, to get a sense of messaging, and to align timing and scheduling.

2. **Create a messaging document.**

   After your stakeholder meeting, take notes and create a messaging document to send out. This messaging drives both the core content for your ebook and your lead generation campaign messaging.

3. **Create an outline.**

   This is a crucial step to creating any content piece. A solid outline helps you flesh out details and align with stakeholders.

4. **Write your first draft.**

   Use internal resources or work with external writers to create your initial draft.

5. **Review.**

   Depending on your internal review process, this draft might go through multiple reviews with many people. Make sure it is viewed by as many eyes as possible.

6. **Write your second draft.**

   Incorporate the feedback and create your second draft. This is likely the one you send to your design team.

7. **Send to design.**

   After you have your second draft completed, send your copy to either your in-house creative team or an outsourced agency. Require that your team send you back two to three design options to choose from and make sure they understand ebook layout concepts.

8. **Look over the first design draft.**

   Your design team sends you back a templated, illustrated version of your ebook. Make sure you edit it for copy, consistency, and design. You might also want to send this version off to stakeholders for additional input.

9. **Look over the final design draft.**

   Hopefully you will only have two sets of edits to send to design. But regardless of how many rounds are necessary, make sure to go over the final draft with a fine-toothed comb.

10. **Promote!**

    You are at the finish line — of the content creation process, at least. Now you want to get promoting and start collecting those leads.

Slicing and dicing

Here comes the fun part: slicing and dicing your content pieces. Think of slicing and dicing like a turkey dinner. This concept was introduced by content marketing expert and Altimeter Group analyst, Rebecca Lieb, and it's a fantastic way to explain what you are going to do next.

According to Rebecca, "You start with the turkey dinner at Thanksgiving and that's the main event, and everybody knows that after Thanksgiving you're eating turkey sandwiches, you have turkey on your salad, maybe turkey and eggs for breakfast."

Basically, think of your big rock pieces as the main event, the turkey dinner, if you will, but then you slice and dice your amazing turkey into many different dishes that feed you and your family for some time to come.

Check out Figure 6-5, which illustrates the turkey analogy.

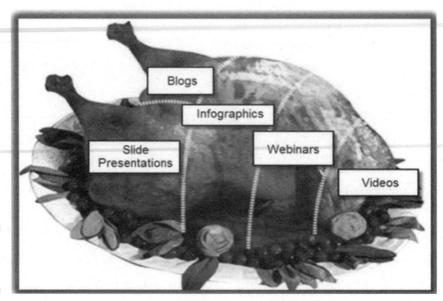

Now that you are thinking of your content as a tasty delicious Thanksgiving meal, what will your leftovers look like? Remember all of the content types I discussed in the beginning of this chapter? Think about which ones you might be able to create from your big rock piece. Here is an example of what I mean. From your big rock content piece (50 pages of content), you could create

- ✔ **Four ebooks:** Created from four separate chapters

- ✔ **Two checklists:** Created from existing checklists that you included in your initial ebook

- ✔ **One to two webinars:** Content created using content directly from your ebook

- ✔ **One to two podcasts:** Taken from your webinar recording

- ✔ **One to two slide decks:** Created from webinar slide deck

- ✔ **One video:** Created from your ebook messaging document

- ✔ **One infographic:** Created from some of the great stats you included in your ebook

- ✔ **Four to five blog posts:** Created from content taken directly out of your ebook

These examples alone constitute at least 15 additional pieces of lead generation fodder for you to use in email, social, paid programs, content syndication,
and so much more. Basically, from that one effort, you can create so many
valuable pieces, and that is why I love the tactic of creating the big rock content piece first. It can be easier and more streamlined than focusing your
efforts on five different ebooks when you are first starting out.

To illustrate this even further, Figure 6-6 shows slicing and dicing in action
with real content pieces.

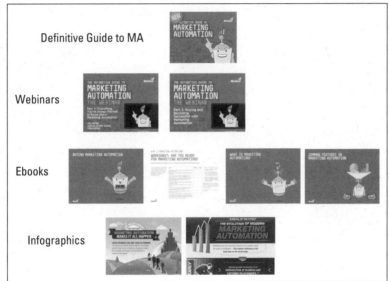

Figure 6-6:
Slicing
and dicing
content.

Repurposing

Big rock content is great and the turkey dinner idea is economical and efficient, but what if you just don't have the resources available to do either,
or you need something done in a short period of time? Repurposing is a
fantastic alternative if you are a small team or do not yet have the budget
you need to create a robust content marketing plan. Repurposing is also an
attractive content creation strategy for everyone else because even if you
have a large marketing team, you can always learn new techniques.

The concept of *repurposing* is taking something you created and putting a
new spin on it. The content you need already exists. Just think creatively
about where to find it.

Here are a few examples:

- ✓ **Blogs:** Most businesses have a blog (I cover that more in Chapter 8). Take a blog post you wrote and create an ebook out of it. Stretch the content as far as you can by having your design team provide engaging visuals throughout. You might be surprised to learn you can easily take a 500-word blog post and turn it into a five- to six-page ebook! And voilà! You have a content asset for an email blast. Take a look at what I mean in Figure 6-7.

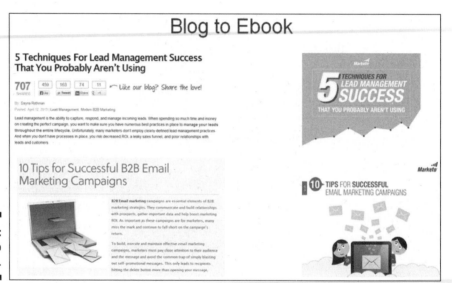

Figure 6-7:
Blog to
ebook.

- ✓ **Webinars and presentations:** Many businesses are starting to include webinars as a regular part of the lead generation mix (see more about creating webinars in Chapter 14). When you produce a webinar, make sure to have a writer on hand to create a transcript of what the speaker says in his presentation. From there, take the transcript, reorganize it if needed, and create an ebook or report from it.

- ✓ **Reports/ebooks:** Take a report or an ebook you create and turn it into a visual asset such as an infographic or a visual slide deck using the same content. Reports lend themselves well to visual content because they tend to have a lot of great data points. Ebooks should tell a story, so take that story and craft a visual slide deck. Figure 6-8 shows an example of how something like this can be approached.

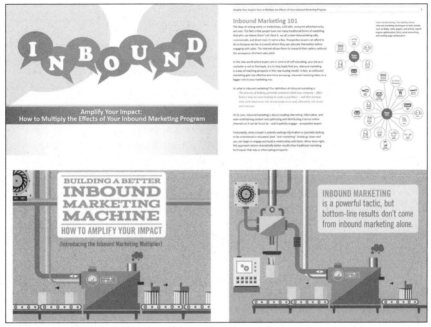

Figure 6-8:
From ebook
to visual
slide deck.

Rewriting and redesigning

Maybe you have some old content that you created a few years ago and aren't sure whether to toss or save it. You know it looks old and dated, but the information in there is still good.

What can you do to bring it up to date? Here are some simple steps you can follow:

1. **Do a content inventory.**

   Look through what you already have and create a list or a spreadsheet listing content types, subjects, and dates published.

2. **Do a read-through on older content.**

   Read through each content piece that is more than a year old. Note: If you are in technology, this time frame may be more like six months if your space is rapidly changing.

3. **Ask yourself key questions.**

   After you read through the content, ask yourself what you would need to do in order to get it updated. Is the content still relevant? Do your leads and customers still talk about this subject? Are the stats included in the piece up-to-date?

4. **Decide whether to keep or toss.**

   Based on your read-through, you can determine whether you should keep or toss each piece. There are two good rules of thumb here. If your content piece is about an event in the past, toss it. If your content piece is a report from a previous year, toss it as well.

5. **Rewrite as needed.**

   Go through each asset and update copy related to industry trends, making sure you update all of the outdated stats and your company boiler (the About Us content that should appear on the last page and tells readers of your ebook who you are and what you do).

6. **Consider a redesign:** One of the best ways for a content piece to look fresh enough to perform well in lead generation campaigns is for it to look modern. A simple redesign works wonders.

For an example of how a content overhaul can improve an old and outdated piece of content, see Figure 6-9.

Before   After

Figure 6-9:
A content redesign and rewrite.

A word of caution. If you do decide to retire a content place and scrap it, check to see whether it is active in any paid programs, and always set up a redirect to route readers to a current page. After something is posted on the Internet, there are most likely live links out there, and you want to make sure everything gets redirected. You don't want a lead who clicks on an old ebook to get an error page — make sure your lead always gets to your website.

Defining Content's Relationship with Other Lead Generation Efforts

Many of your lead generation campaigns are fueled by promoting your content. Although this book goes into great detail on how to create campaigns using various lead generation tactics, it's important to first lay out the foundation and define content's relationship with other lead generation efforts.

Email

Email is a great way to promote your content to your database. Consider creating email campaigns whenever you write an important new piece of content. Depending on your content cadence (how often you create and publish content), you may not want to send an email out for each piece of new content you develop, but you want to make sure you create dedicated campaigns to all of your larger pieces, particularly your big rock content pieces.

Figure 6-10 gives an example of what a content-specific email looks like.

Social media

Social media is a great place to promote all of your content, the big and the small pieces. Social media is also where you want to promote your visual pieces like infographics and visual slide decks. Videos also perform exceptionally well on social channels.

Schedule promotions spanning a few weeks for each piece of content. Make sure to create a custom image for Facebook, Google+, LinkedIn, and Pinterest. And the more creative your messaging, the more people will want to share and download your asset. Take a look at a few sample social promotions focusing on new content assets in Figure 6-11.

Develop a Flawless Event Strategy for 2013

Hi Dayna,

If you need to ensure your event marketing is successful from planning to promotion to follow-up, check out our brand new 120-page **Definitive Guide to Event Marketing**.

You'll get worksheets, checklists, and templates to help with:

- Multi-touch promotion planning - including email, social, and PR
- Staffing and executing top-notch events (online <u>and</u> offline)
- Measuring attendance, engagement, and revenue generated
- Designing event follow-ups that engage and convert prospects

Achieve record-breaking attendance and dramatic ROI for your 2013 events. **Download the Definitive Guide to Event Marketing** now.

Figure 6-10:
An email promoting a new content piece.

HubSpot
37 minutes ago

This blog editorial template is designed to keep you on track as you develop awesome content that your prospects, customers, and readers will love.

Download it here >> http://hub.am/1a3ZTb0

[Free template]:
BLOG EDITORIAL CALENDAR

Use this template to:

Organize your content authors & topics

Track keyword and call-to-action use

Develop content that is on time and on target

ATTRACT. Convert. Close. Delight.

Figure 6-11:
Social media posts for new content pieces.

Website

Your website is the home base for all content pieces. Consider hosting all of your content in a resource section (I dive more into that in Chapter 7). Also, make sure you add new content pieces to your home page and on all applicable product or service pages. For home page promotion ideas, refer to Figure 6-12, which shows how new content can be merchandised for optimal conversion.

Figure 6-12:
Home page showcases for content.

Blog

Each content piece should have at least one blog post created for lead generation purposes. Don't be afraid to take content directly out of the ebook and include a few links and calls-to-action (CTAs) within the body of the blog. Also include a few images that reflect the content piece design. Figure 6-13 shows how a blog can be used to promote downloads for a new content piece. The CTA at the end asks the reader to download the content asset.

Webinars and presentations

After a new content piece is created, always consider a webinar, particularly for your big rock content pieces. Have a thought leader in your organization speak to the key points and create a deck. Often people who haven't downloaded your asset will sign up for your webinar. From the webinar, you can get some nice qualified leads and promote additional downloads of your asset. Figure 6-14 shows an example of a larger content piece that was turned into a webinar and has done nicely as an additional asset.

Figure 6-14:
A webinar
created
from a
content
piece.

Paid programs

You can choose among many paid programs to promote your content asset and drive new leads. With a paid program, you pay a third party to show your content piece to a targeted audience in the hopes of capturing more leads. Paid programs are a great way to get new leads into your database, as long as the cost of getting noticed is offset by the interest that is generated. Paid programs typically ask for names on a form in exchange for a download of something that intrigues the target audience. Include content assets in pay-per-click (PPC) campaigns, banner ads, paid email programs, content syndication, and paid social campaigns.

Chapter 7

Putting Your Best Foot Forward with Your Website

In This Chapter

▶ Discovering website usability and design

▶ Forming calls-to-action that get results

▶ Constructing landing pages that work

▶ Verifying and optimizing website conversion points

*I*f you have to absolutely nail one thing for lead generation success, it is your website. Your website tells a lead who you are, what you do, and why she should care. It is your calling card, and if you don't get it right, your lead is going to shrug, turn around, and leave. As Kissmetrics, a blog about website analytics and testing, puts it, "Your leads are only as good as the website that produces them." Powerful words, and so true.

In order for your lead generation strategy to be effective, your website needs to be the ultimate lead generation tool because that is where you are going to be driving the majority of your traffic.

A good lead generation website should have great copy, clear calls-to-action (CTAs), efficient forms, and attention-grabbing content. But the trick is creating a healthy balance between good lead generation tactics and a well-designed and usable website for ultimate conversion.

You have many different goals for your website, and you don't want it to end up looking like a crazy lead generation website from 2006, like in Figure 7-1.

The trick is to make sure your viewers know exactly what to do and where to do it. And if you can clean up a cluttered website, your conversion numbers will steadily move upwards.

Figure 7-1:
A lead
generation
website
design to
avoid.

Here are some convincing statistics from Kissmetrics on website viewers and conversions:

✔ You have zero to eight seconds to reach users with a compelling headline and landing page. After eight seconds, the majority of visitors leave.

✔ Approximately 96 percent of visitors who come to your website are not ready to buy.

✔ The more landing pages you have, the more leads you are likely to get.

Exploring Website Usability and Design

Think of your website's utility and usability as the baseline for your website lead generation strategy. A website that looks great can only get you so far. You need your website to be *functional*. By functional, I mean that your website has to be logical to the buying personas visiting it, must do what you intend it to do (inform visitors and move them along the lead lifecycle), and should provide clear conversion paths for your viewers. To be truly effective with your website design, you need to take a user-centric approach to your thinking — how does a viewer consume information, where is she most likely to click, and how does he want to navigate your site? (If you haven't yet read Chapter 6, which discusses creating buyer personas, now's the time to do it.)

If you are only thinking in terms of raw lead generation and bombarding your viewers with a million calls-to-action in hopes of throwing some spaghetti at a wall and seeing what sticks, you will likely find that your website isn't very effective at actually generating qualified leads.

Instead, think about how *you* view a website. Where do you navigate to? What are some examples of where you have bounced off of the site due to poor usability? Also, think of some websites that you really admire. Who does a good job at telling you exactly what to do and how to do it?

Making your site scannable

If you understand how your visitors think about navigating a website, you can make smarter choices. According to *Smashing Magazine*, "Basically, users' habits on the web aren't that different from customers' habits in a store. Visitors glance at a new page, scan some of the text, and click on the first link that catches their interest or vaguely resembles something they are looking for. In fact, there are large parts of the page they don't even look at."

The key takeaway here is to make sure that your calls-to-action (CTAs) are clear and your content concise.

A recent usability study conducted by Jakob Nielson, principal analyst at Nielson Norman Group, claims that website viewers only read about 28 percent of the text on a web page. Therefore, you need to make your point as quickly and concisely as possible. For instance, if you want to include a tagline on your home page, make sure that it illustrates what your company does. Also, be sure to break up the text with headings and subheadings to optimize for website skimming.

Figure 7-2 shows an example from a Mashable article illustrating two different versions of their website copy — one with headings and one without headings. The one with headings is easier to skim, making it more digestible for a website visitor.

Version 1	Version 2
Mashable (Mashable Inc.) is an American news website and Internet news blog founded by Pete Cashmore. The website's primary focus is social media news, but also covers news and developments in mobile, entertainment, online video, business, web development, technology, memes and gadgets.	**Overview** Mashable (Mashable Inc.) is an American news website and Internet news blog founded by Pete Cashmore. The website's primary focus is social media news, but also covers news and developments in mobile, entertainment, online video, business, web development, technology, memes and gadgets.
On November 27, 2007, Mashable launched the 1st International Open Web Awards to recognize the best online communities and services. Voting was conducted online through Mashable and its 24 blog partners. On January 10, 2008 at the Palace Hotel, San Francisco, Mashable announced the winners of the first Open Web Awards. Winners included Digg, Facebook, Google, Twitter, YouTube, ESPN, Cafemom and Pandora.	**Mashable Awards** On November 27, 2007, Mashable launched the 1st International Open Web Awards to recognize the best online communities and services. Voting was conducted online through Mashable and its 24 blog partners. On January 10, 2008 at the Palace Hotel, San Francisco, Mashable announced the winners of the first Open Web Awards. Winners included Digg, Facebook, Google, Twitter, YouTube, ESPN, Cafemom and Pandora.
The 2nd Annual Open Web Awards was an online international competition that took place between November and December 2008. Among the winners in the 'People's Choice' component were Encyclopedia Dramatica in the wiki category, Digg in the 'Social News and Social Bookmarking' category, Netlog in the 'Mainstream and Large Social Networks' category and MySpace in the 'Places and Events' category.	The 2nd Annual Open Web Awards was an online international competition that took place between November and December 2008. Among the winners in the 'People's Choice' component were Encyclopedia Dramatica in the wiki category, Digg in the 'Social News and Social Bookmarking' category, Netlog in the 'Mainstream and Large Social Networks' category and MySpace in the 'Places and Events' category.
Mashable Connect is an annual invite-only conference. It was held on May 12 – May 14, 2011, with 300 attendees. Speakers included Scott Belsky, Founder & CEO, Behance Rohit Bhargava, SVP, Global Strategy & Marketing, Ogilvy. Sabrina Caluori, Director of Social Media & Marketing, HBO, and Greg Clayman, Publisher, The Daily.	**Mashable Connect Conference** Mashable Connect is an annual invite-only conference. It was held on May 12 – May 14, 2011, with 300 attendees. Speakers included Scott Belsky, Founder & CEO, Behance Rohit Bhargava, SVP, Global Strategy & Marketing, Ogilvy. Sabrina Caluori, Director of Social Media & Marketing, HBO, and Greg Clayman, Publisher, The Daily.
Themes discussed included content curation, the democratisation of content, social media, social television, and helping consumers deal with content overload.	Themes discussed included content curation, the democratisation of content, social media, social television, and helping consumers deal with content overload.

Figure 7-2:
Mashable's
scannable
website
copy.

You can also implement a heat mapping technology such as Crazy Egg to get a better visualization of where people click, where they scroll, and how they interact and read your website. This can help you make better decisions when it comes to how you lay out your text and where you put your CTAs. Figure 7-3 shows an example of Crazy Egg heat mapping — the darker areas on the heat map show where a visitor clicks, scrolls, or interacts with the page in some way.

Implementing clear conversion paths

In order for a website visitor to become a lead, you have to tell him where to go and what you want him to do. This sounds easy, but in reality can be quite difficult, especially if multiple groups within your company have input into what goes on your website. *Smashing Magazine* explains, "If the navigation and site architecture aren't intuitive, the number of question marks grows and makes it harder for users to comprehend how the system works and how to get from point A to point B. A clear structure, moderate visual cues, and easily recognizable links can help users find their path and aim."

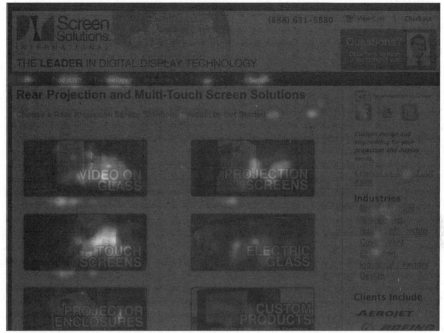

Figure 7-3:
A Crazy Egg
heat map.

Remember that crazy website in Figure 7-1? That is an example of a site with extremely poor conversion paths. Too many conflicting messages and not enough direction. Most likely, when a viewer comes to your site, she knows what she is looking for. Whether it is your latest content asset, or a product demo, show her where to go so that she can download that asset or fill out a form for that demo, quickly.

Take a look at Figure 7-4, which illustrates Salesforce's (www.salesforce.com) home page navigation. If I am looking for information about one of their products, I can easily head to the Products tab, where they give a breakdown of each product they offer and a brief descriptor. Or if I am looking for information on what industries they serve, I can easily navigate to the Industries page for a clear breakdown. Their navigation is intuitive and easy.

Many marketers attempt to put a creative spin on navigation verbiage — thinking that it looks more creative and appealing to the viewer. However, nothing beats good old-fashioned simplicity when dealing with the equivalent of virtual signposts on your website. Cute or witty synonyms for navigation verbiage only serve to puff up a marketer's ego at the cost of leads that leave your site because they're confused about where to go. Remember, you're a click away from being abandoned, so keep it simple.

After a viewer successfully finds the information he needs, make it easy for him to click on the correct CTA or fill out the right download form.

Figure 7-4:
Salesforce's
website
has intuitive
navigation.

Still using the Salesforce example, say I want information on their sales product, Sales Cloud. I click the corresponding navigation, and the first screen I get is a concise description of Sales Cloud and a CTA to view a demo. Check out what I mean in Figure 7-5. Their demo CTA is visual, appealing, and very large. There is no question what they want me to do.

Figure 7-5:
Salesforce's
website
has a clear
demo
request.

Improving website readability

The other key item to keep in mind is your website readability. As I pointed out earlier, viewers like to scan, so your copy must be clear, concise, and readable. In fact, according to the usability study conducted by Jakob Nielson, "A 58 percent increase in website usability can be achieved simply by cutting roughly half of the words on a website page."

Using too many fancy words that take up room but leave the visitor uninformed as to what your business does helps no one. Make sure your vocabulary is appropriate for someone at a more junior reading level. I've read suggestions to target an eighth-grade reading level, and I've also seen suggestions for fifth- to sixth-grade. This is not to say your viewers are not intelligent, but it means you should keep concepts straightforward and concise.

So many marketers are stuck on wordy descriptors, but try to view your website as more utilitarian — the shorter, the better.

To get a sense of where your site ranks on the readability scale, check out www.read-able.com. This is a free readability test tool. Simply type in your website's URL to get a readability score and explanation.

Keep in mind that most often, your viewers are going to scan for keywords that are applicable to what they are looking for on your website, so make sure *your* main points and keywords are front and center. Consider putting them in your headings and breaking up each page by using strategically placed bullet points. This focuses your readers' attention so they know exactly what they should be looking at.

Figure 7-6 illustrates using bullets to break up text and draw the eye. This example is from the Marketo website and explains the company's lead nurturing functionality. Note how "key features" jumps out. The page uses bullets and bold type to draw attention to the key benefits of their lead nurturing software. These benefits also serve as keywords for what your visitors could be looking for.

In fact, according to an eye tracking study by ClickTale, users concentrate more on and are drawn to copy with bullets and bold text. Their study is illustrated in Figure 7-7, which shows how long participants focused on bulleted and bold copy.

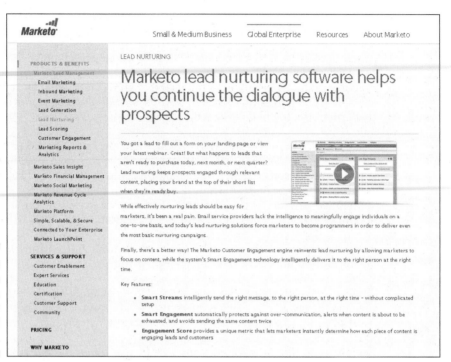

Figure 7-6:
Use bullets
and bolding
to make key
points stand
out.

Figure 7-7:
A ClickTale
eye tracking
study.

Creating Calls-to-Action (CTAs) That Convert

The bread and butter of a great lead generation website are your calls-to-action (CTAs). What is a CTA? According to HubSpot, a CTA is "an image or line of text that prompts your visitors, leads, and customers to take action. It is quite literally, a 'call' to take an 'action'."

But what is that action? It could be anything from contacting your sales team directly, to downloading an ebook, signing up for an event, and so on. A CTA can live anywhere on your website and is typically asking the visitor for his information — resulting in a fresh new lead entering your database.

The trick is making sure that your CTAs are well placed, stand out, provide very clear instructions, and align to a specific lead generation initiative. Figure 7-8 shows an example of a CTA asking the visitor to download an ebook. Notice that there is no question what the website is asking the visitor to do.

Figure 7-8:
A clear CTA.

Working with CTA best practices

Before I dive into specifics around where to place your CTAs for the best conversions, I want to go over some CTA best practices. Although they seem very easy, CTAs can get tricky if you overthink, overcomplicate, and overdesign them.

When developing your optimal website CTAs, here are some best practices to keep in mind:

- ✔ **Your CTA must stand out:** The number one thing to consider when developing the look of your CTA is that it must stand out. This can be done by using a bold color, clever website placement, or by making your CTA appear large on the page. Just be sure that you aren't cluttering your page or taking away from your overall website design.

- ✔ **Clearly define what you want the lead to do:** You need to be very clear and concise when it comes to CTA copy. A lead won't click on a button if she isn't exactly sure what action she will be taking. Start your CTA with a word that's a verb so that it already assumes action will happen. Instead of having a vague button that says *Download*, you can be more exact by having the button text read, *Download ebook*. You want to make sure your lead knows what he is getting and how he is getting it.

- ✔ **Create urgency:** A good best practice is to create urgency with your CTA by offering a time-sensitive special or deal. Let your lead know that by acting now, she can receive an extra discount or a limited offer. For instance, maybe it is the end of the month and you need additional leads, so you are offering a $50 Amazon gift card with a product demo. Make sure that this information is on your CTA to encourage visitors to act immediately.

- ✔ **Position prominently:** Whether it is a CTA on your home page or another page on your site, make sure your chief CTA is positioned in a prominent location. Place your top CTA above the fold (the portion of your website visible without scrolling), have a sidebar that moves as a visitor scrolls, or place it in an obvious spot at the top or side of the page.

Leveraging the home page CTA

Now that I've gone over some key best practices to get you thinking about how to create an effective CTA, I want to talk through some examples. The most important lead-generating CTAs are going to live on your home page. Don't think you have to limit your home page CTA to one. You can have a few: Just make sure you prioritize them through intelligent placement.

As Figure 7-9 indicates, this home page has four CTAs above the fold. The most important ones are showcased as orange buttons — 4 Min Demo, Contact Us, and Free Trial. Additional copy reads *Want to learn more? Get started now*, with an arrow pointing to the CTAs. This draws the eye and entices people to click. Each of these CTAs goes to a form that captures lead information.

Figure 7-9:
Marketo
home page
CTAs.

Also note that the home page has another CTA above the fold: See What We Do. If a person is curious as to what Marketo does, they can click on that CTA and watch an overview video.

Marketo's site also uses secondary CTAs, as illustrated in Figure 7-10, which are slightly below the fold and showcase key content assets. However, the home page CTAs are reserved for pure lead-generation content pieces, so all content that is advertised on the home page links to a form to capture lead information.

Figure 7-10:
Secondary
content
download
CTAs.

The website has more CTAs as you scroll down, but as you get further below the fold, each CTA is a lower priority.

Another great example of a home page CTA that pops is from the software company Zuora. Their primary CTAs are housed on the side of their home page. Take a look at the lower left side of Figure 7-11 as an example. Zoura is strategic about this dynamic placement — their CTAs move with the visitor as he scrolls up and down the site.

Including an obvious contact link

For many companies, a website visitor responding to a Contact Us CTA is lead-generation gold. This means that a visitor is a hand-raiser. You often don't need to nurture her. You don't need sales banging down her door. She is ready to talk to you. It's critical to have an obvious Contact Us button or link.

If a person wants to contact your company and he has to jump through hoops to find your contact information, this is a major lead-generation fail (and a personal pet peeve of mine). There are no excuses for that. If I want to contact someone from your company, I want a form, a number, or *something* to make it easy for me to ask you a question directly or purchase your product or service.

Marketo has a Contact Us button showcased on the home page (as illustrated in Figure 7-9) and on each page on the site. However, one important factor to keep in mind with your Contact Us CTA is that it should go to a very specific landing page. Your Contact Us landing page should have a form where a lead can fill out all of his information, and you might also want to include some additional information on there — your phone number in case a lead wants to call directly, what the lead gains by filling out the form, and some additional content pieces that might answer your lead's questions.

Figure 7-12 shows an example of the Contact Us landing page form. Note that it includes a form and also includes some additional information that a lead might find helpful.

If you have a marketing automation tool, you can often implement progressive profiling. *Progressive profiling* allows you to collect information and build qualification over time. Each time a person fills out a form on your site, the progressive form asks for new and different information.

In addition to the Contact Us CTA on the home page, Marketo includes a Contact Us form on each product page. You certainly don't want someone distracting themselves from getting excited about a feature on your products page by searching for your contact information. Instead, you want to make sure that they contact you immediately!

Figure 7-12: A Contact Us form.

.ıll **Marketo**

1.877.260.6598 | Live Chat

GOT A QUESTION ABOUT MARKETO?

Have a Marketo sales representative contact me. For product support please go to support.marketo.com

First Name:	* Dayna
Last Name:	* Rothman
Work Email:	* email@marketo.com
Phone Number:	* 555-555-5555
Company:	* Marketo
Job Function:	* Content Marketing Manager ▾
# Employees:	* Select ▾
Who Are You?:	* Select ▾
Comments:	

CONTACT ME

* Required. Your privacy is important to us.

We can answer it!

- Wondering where to start?
- Need more pricing information?
- Interested in seeing a live demo?
- Want to speak to Marketo users like you?

Just tell us a bit about you and let us know how we can help.

"At the end of the day its about growing sales... We've seen sales increased by over 150% in just 9 months."

Billy Boyle, Co-Founder, Owlstone

Not ready to talk to an expert yet?

- Watch a recorded demo and see Marketo in action.
- Sign-up for a live demo including a Q&A session.
- Visit the Resource Library and check out our definitive guides, success kits and webinars.

Offering a chat option

A chat option is another touch point that can be a successful lead generation tool on your website. It is no longer used just by the customer support side of the business. Through chat, you can often engage leads who might not be ready to speak to you on the phone — which can be a substantial number of people in today's digital world. Personally, I would rather communicate via email, social media, or chat than call a sales representative, so a chat option is great to capture leads like me. In fact, according to LivePerson, a company that offers chat services, using a chat feature increases conversion rates by 20 percent.

Chat options are common on retail websites, but are also becoming more common for other services. Marketo uses a chat feature that pops up when a visitor has been on the site for a certain number of seconds. You can easily click out of it, or you can engage with a knowledgeable representative who can answer your questions. Depending on where the visitor is on a website, the conversations can be handled either by sales development reps or by customer support agents.

Figure 7-13 demonstrates an example of a chat option. After a person clicks to chat, they have to enter their first name, last name, and email address. After the lead enters the chat, the representative is armed to answer a multitude of questions.

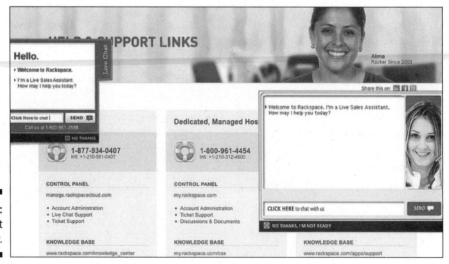

Figure 7-13:
A live chat
window.

Developing Landing Pages That Work

Aside from CTAs, having landing pages that are optimized for conversion is key to a good lead generating website. When a lead clicks on your CTA, you want to make sure that she doesn't bounce — and that certainly *does* happen. By ensuring that your landing page, where a lead lands after she has filled out a form, is clear and speaks directly to the CTA, you have a smaller chance of that lead bouncing.

For instance, if a lead fills out a form to download an ebook and she is sent to a random webpage that has a huge list of ebooks, she might scratch her head, grow impatient, and leave (or bounce). However, if you make sure that she goes to a targeted page that applies specifically to the CTA she clicked, you are in much better shape.

Landing pages can be leveraged on your website for various reasons, including content asset downloads, demo requests, other product-specific information, events, webinars, and so on.

Landing pages are also critical for SEO (search engine optimization) reasons. A relevant ad-optimized landing page has a dramatically higher conversion rate — meaning you get more leads for your money.

Sticking with short forms

Short forms on landing pages always outperform long forms on lead generation tests. In a recent test conducted at Marketo, short forms with 5 fields had a 13.4 percent conversion rate, medium forms with 7 fields had a 12 percent conversion rate, and long forms with 9 fields had a 10 percent conversion rate.

It's common sense, really. People don't like filling out a lot of information about themselves. Not only is it time-consuming for your visitors, but they also don't want to get calls and emails, especially when they're in the early stages of research about your company. So the more information they have to put in, the more time they have to weigh the pros and cons of filling out your form.

As a best practice, only ask for what you really need. And if you have marketing automation, you can employ progressive profiling. That way, your website can intelligently know what information your visitor already filled out. For instance, if he already gave you his name, email address, and title, this information can be retained in your marketing automation system. The next time he fills out a form, you can ask for company, industry, phone number, and so on.

For B2B companies, some marketing products are able to capture the IP address of the website visitor, make assumptions about where she works, and use that information to prefill a form. This assumes that a visitor is researching products or services from work.

When creating a form for a landing page, consider sticking to these five fields:

- First Name
- Last Name
- Work Email
- Job Function
- Industry

For an example of different form lengths and what information you could potentially ask for, take a look at Figure 7-14, which shows the short, medium, and long forms that Marketo tested in their benchmark study.

Short Forms Outperform Long Forms		
First Name: * ▢	First Name: * ▢	First Name: * ▢
Last Name: * ▢	Last Name: * ▢	Last Name: * ▢
Work Email: * ▢	Work Email: * ▢	Work Email: * ▢
Job Function: * Choose One ▾	Company: * ▢	Work Phone: * ▢
Company: * ▢	Job Function: * Select ▾	Company: * ▢
	# Employees: * Select ▾	Job Function: * Select ▾
	Industry: * Advertising & Media ▾	# Employees: * Select ▾
		CRM System: * Select ▾
		Industry: * Advertising & Media ▾
Short (5)	**Medium (7)**	**Long (9)**
Conversion: **13.4%**	Conversion: **12.0%**	Conversion: **10.0%**
Cost per: **$31.24**	Cost per: **$34.94**	Cost per: **$41.90**

Figure 7-14: Varying form lengths.

Designing for success

Well-designed landing pages lead to conversions. This is a fact. A messy, poorly written, and poorly optimized page equals a high bounce rate. Of course, every business is different, with different products and different target audiences, so you need to test to know what works best for you.

However, as a starter, consider these following best practices for landing page design and layout:

- ✔ **Build some templates:** Build some HTML templates to use. If you have a marketing automation tool or email service provider (ESP), this is even easier. But remember, this isn't your home page, so remove all of the navigation. Your templates should be simple — distractions kill conversions!

- ✔ **Always think about graphics:** Your landing page should be simple. Include a logo and a hero shot. A *hero shot* is the primary image that illustrates your CTA. Think of a mock-up of your ebook, a photo of your webinar speaker, and so on. Also think about making your graphics clickable. People tend to click on graphics.

- ✔ **Focus on concise copy:** Make your copy straight and to the point, but give your lead a good reason to give you her information. Here's a simple formula to remember: Set up the problem, talk about your solution (or offer), and deliver the goods (an ebook, video, or webinar registration). Also make sure you have bullet points and a great, eye-catching headline.

- ✔ **Think about reassurance and trust:** Your prospect is risking her privacy by filling out your form. She is probably giving you her email and phone number, so add some reassuring elements to your landing page. Consider mentioning privacy statements, customer testimonials, guarantees, and awards won by your business.

- ✔ **Use confirmation and thank you pages:** It's just plain good manners to say thank you after getting something you want! So have a page that both confirms the form submittal and lets your lead know that you appreciate his time. Do you have something else your lead may be interested in? Make another offer! The confirmation page is a great place to deepen the relationship with additional offers.

- ✔ **Pay attention to your page URL:** This is especially important, and an area that many people ignore. The name of the page, along with the rest of the URL path, is weighed fairly heavily on search engines. You can use up to 1,024 characters, so you don't have to be stingy! Also use dashes between words instead of underscores, for SEO purposes.

- ✔ **Use metadata:** In the early days of Internet search, the importance of metadata was beaten into everyone's heads. *Metadata* are words used within a web page to provide basic information to search engines about that site. For example, if I write a blog post, there could be metadata that states that the author is Dayna Rothman. Although we don't hear about it much anymore, search engines still view it as important. They use it one way or another and typically weigh metadata in results lists. So enter a title and craft good 100-word descriptions as well as keywords.

Figure 7-15 shows an example of a landing page for an ebook from a mobile app development company called Kinvey. Notice the hero shot, the bullet points, the short form, and the privacy information.

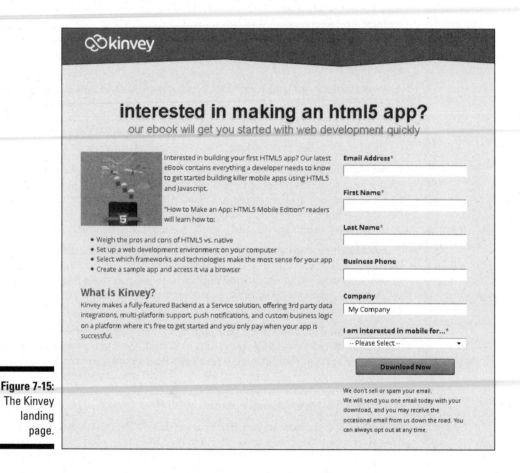

Figure 7-15:
The Kinvey landing page.

Chapter 8

Humanizing Your Brand with a Blog

*W*hen you think of a company blog, "lead generation" might not be the first thing that comes to your mind. In fact, most companies think of a blog as a tool for creating brand awareness and showing the company's personality. This is true; however, a blog can be so much more. A blog done right can be a fantastic tool for lead generation. Why? It helps build trust with your readers, improves credibility within your industry, helps you become positioned as a true thought leader, and enables you to collect lead information through subscriber forms.

Here are some cold hard facts to help convince you that your blog can be one of the top ways to generate quality leads:

✔ Eighty-one percent of consumers trust information and advice from blogs (source: BlogHer).

✔ Ninety-two percent of companies who blog multiple times per day have acquired customers from their blog (source: HubSpot).

✔ B2B marketers who use blogs generate 67 percent more leads than those who do not (source: InsideView).

- ✔ Eighty-one percent of companies consider their blog to be "useful, important, or critical" (source: HubSpot).

- ✔ Businesses that blog more than 20 times per month get 5 times more traffic than those that blog less than 4 times per month (source: HubSpot).

In this chapter, I talk about how you can effectively set up your blog to be an integral part of your lead-generation strategy.

Inspiring Readers with Your Blog Content

Think of your blog as a destination spot and your blog posts as inspirational thought leadership to both leads and customers. As buyers educate themselves through the buying process, why not show off your industry expertise? As I discuss in detail throughout Chapter 6 on content marketing, marketers now must become publishers and work to establish their organizations as thought leaders in their space.

Because a blog lends itself so well to content that is always new and on-trend, it is the perfect venue to really showcase your industry knowledge. Plus, blogs are highly shareable on social channels, so this is a great reason to showcase some of your best content on your blogs.

Hopefully, as a marketer who is in tune with everything that is going on in both your industry and the world of marketing, you subscribe to multiple blogs yourself. When determining how to create blog content that inspires your readers and engages them enough to subscribe to your blog or share it on social channels, think about what content inspires you the most. And don't be afraid to take inspiration from the blogs layout, writing style, or topics.

Going from promotional content to thought leadership

As I describe in Chapter 6, content in general is making a shift from the purely promotional to thought leadership. In order for your blog to be an effective educational resource, you need to embrace this trend. Your blog will never become a destination resource for industry professionals if you're always beating your chest and talking about yourself. Why would a lead who may never have heard of your company care that you won some industry award? He won't. And because he won't care, he will very quickly bounce off your blog onto a competitor's blog that talks about how to solve his biggest challenges.

So what should you be writing about? Best practices, industry trends, how-tos, new theories in your industry, and stories. Make your blog interesting and dynamic. Consider having interviews with influencers in your space or power users from your community, and don't be afraid to be creative and think outside of the box. You might even consider writing poetry in the form of a blog! Take a look at Figure 8-1 for an example of creative blogging in the form of a poem. This post was highly shareable throughout all of Marketo's social channels. Why? Because it was relevant information shared in a fun way.

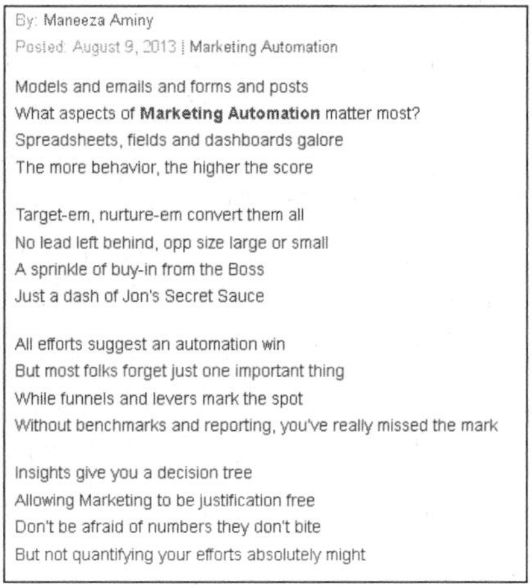

Figure 8-1:
An example
of creative
thought
leadership
in a blog
post.

By: Maneeza Aminy
Posted: August 9, 2013 | Marketing Automation

Models and emails and forms and posts
What aspects of **Marketing Automation** matter most?
Spreadsheets, fields and dashboards galore
The more behavior, the higher the score

Target-em, nurture-em convert them all
No lead left behind, opp size large or small
A sprinkle of buy-in from the Boss
Just a dash of Jon's Secret Sauce

All efforts suggest an automation win
But most folks forget just one important thing
While funnels and levers mark the spot
Without benchmarks and reporting, you've really missed the mark

Insights give you a decision tree
Allowing Marketing to be justification free
Don't be afraid of numbers they don't bite
But not quantifying your efforts absolutely might

And if you *do* want to be promotional, as in talking about a highly successful event that you just sponsored, hosted, or attended, make sure your post discusses more than basic event highlights. Make sure you include some best practices and takeaways that you learned from the event, so that those who couldn't attend can read the highlights and get some actionable takeaways, despite not having been present.

Figure 8-2 shows an example of an event-related post that was crafted to have some clear, usable takeaways.

And even if you have a new product you want to announce on your blog, make sure you position the post as an interesting resource like in Figure 8-3, where a fun video is also provided. People are way more apt to watch and share a video than a stale blog post about your latest announcement.

So let's dig in! Here are my top 4 takeaways from the conference, which represented the best in content marketing trends, challenges, and thought leadership:

1) The New Biggest Threat to Content Marketing: An Over-Reliance on Competent, Professional, On-Strategy Content

A year ago, only the most sophisticated companies had truly embraced content marketing – marketers were just coming to understand that informative, intelligent, and well-made content was integral to a winning strategy. In Doug Kessler's session, "In Your Face Content Marketing," he recalled that last year's attendees were high on early-adopter excitement. In 2012, the biggest threat to content marketing was, as Doug put it, content marketers cranking out crap.

Only one year later, content marketing has gone mainstream. Early adopters have been proven right, but this also means that quality content marketing won't confer the same advantages. To compete, content writers need to do more than cut the crap and up the quality – at this point, we all know that if our content is going to win the trust and love of our future customers, it *absolutely must* be well-written, entertaining, and useful.

The new biggest threat to content marketing is, in the words of Doug, "an over-reliance on competent, professional, well-made, on-strategy content." But why shouldn't we rely on competency and professionalism? What's wrong with well-crafted content that aligns with your company's strategy? For the answer to that, read on.

2) Content Marketing Needs to Tap into Emotions

As Doug explained in his CMW session, content marketing is becoming a "home run game" – most marketing departments generate only a few truly exceptional content pieces each year, and that's fine, because you only need a few. These are the pieces that generate massive engagement – the kind of content used by speakers as examples doing presentations. **These powerhouse pieces are not only competent and intelligent and on-point, they also tap into our emotions.**

Sophisticated marketers have already learned to make smart content – there's really no excuse, at this point, for cranking out crap – but that isn't the end of the line. Home run **content marketing** needs to make people feel something, not just think something.

As many of CMW's presenters demonstrated, one of the best ways to create emotionally resonant content is to 1) do something remarkable, and 2) document yourself doing it. Think of Nike's **Girl Effect** campaign, or Coca-Cola's **Small World Machines** project.

Figure 8-2:
A promotional event post crafted to be thought leadership.

Making sure each post is visual

The next step to having a blog that attracts and excites leads is to make sure that each post is visual and catches the eye. Marketing best practices have shown that visual posts are read and shared more often. People are much more attracted to an online resource that has great imagery than a boring page with no images. Use images strategically on the blog home page itself as well as within each individual post.

When thinking about your overall blog design, consider all the ways you can make your design visual. Consumer blogs traditionally are more visual, but B2B blogs have to also take their cue from some of the top B2C blogs like Mashable, which uses an almost Pinterest-like approach to organizing content, as you can see in Figure 8-4.

Coca-Cola's blog Unbottled, as seen in Figure 8-5, does a great job of using visual imagery to capture the attention of their readers. They have a large area featuring top posts on their blog home page that utilizes a rotator that automatically scrolls through a variety of colorful images.

Meet Dan. Dan walks into the office on Monday morning knowing full well that his budget is due into finance by end of the day. But Dan has struggled all month to get a complete picture of what his marketing team has spent.

Dan thinks about how he is going to figure this all out and he is filled with dread.

To top it all off Dan is stuck in spreadsheet hell. Budget data changes daily and it is distributed across many documents, spreadsheets, and finance systems. How is he supposed to find anything in this mess?

Does this story sound familiar? Too many marketers experience this on a monthly basis. So how do you overcome these challenges?

Introducing **Marketo Financial Management**. A budget and spend tracking software made for marketing teams, so they can run the business of marketing. Now you can get a complete and accurate view to make spending decisions with confidence and to stay in lock-step with finance. Want to learn more? **Sign up today** for one of our upcoming Marketo Financial Management demos.

Watch this video below and learn how Marketo Financial Management can come to your rescue, curing your bad case of the Monday budget blues.

Figure 8-3:
A product launch blog positioned as educational.

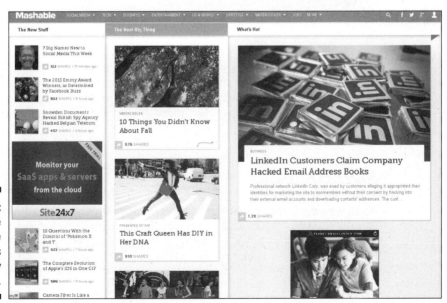

Figure 8-4:
The Mashable blog is highly visual.

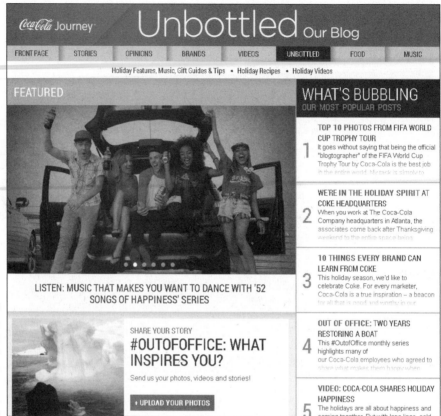

Figure 8-5:
Visual
imagery
on the
Coca-Cola
blog.

The imagery on the home page should then continue into individual posts. Consider including a large featured image and encouraging blog contributors to add images throughout their post to draw more attention and garner more shares. Take a look at Figure 8-6 for an example of how Coca-Cola makes each post visual by having a very large, eye-catching image that draws you into the post.

Newsjacking

Don't underestimate the power of newsjacking. According to author David Meerman Scott, *newsjacking* is "the process by which you inject your ideas or angles into breaking news, in real time, in order to generate media coverage for yourself or your business." This is smart. Very smart. By capitalizing on a popular news item that is being searched often on Google or social channels,

Figure 8-6:
A featured image on the Coca-Cola blog.

your company's blog might get picked up in response. By exposing new people to your brand and providing credible, well-written content, you'll be more memorable as a thought leader. Take for instance a popular movie that's getting a lot of hype. Look for the angle to relate it to your industry. For instance, say that I write a post about five things I learned about marketing from *The Hobbit* when the movie comes out. Now I can use the #Hobbit hashtag when I promote it on Twitter. It becomes searchable to those who are following the hashtag, and I can optimize the post for search engines.

Also, because you are choosing a topic that everyone is talking about, your audience will be excited about the blog and more apt to share.

Figure 8-7 shows an example of a newsjacking blog that took advantage of the news frenzy around Target's release of their Phillip Lim designer capsule collection.

Target Creates a Community: #PhillipLimForTarget

321 SHARES | 235 Like | 64 Tweet | 15 Share | 6 +1 | 1 Share | Like our blog? Share the love!

By: Maggie Jones

Posted: September 19, 2013 | Social Media

Shortly after 12:01am on Sunday, the Phillip Lim for Target Collection went live online. Online shoppers, limited to three items per order, snapped up the fashion designer's skirts, sweatshirts, and tops, priced between $19.99 and $49.99 — quite the steal, considering the three-digit price tags on Lim's usual wares. A few hours later, the Phillip Lim Collection bags — made from high-quality imitation leather, and all priced below $50 — became available, and the true frenzy began.

In Target's major metropolitan locations, shoppers lined up for hours before stores opened on Sunday, where they were allowed to enter in staggered groups. By the end on the day, many of the most desirable items were on eBay, and by Monday, there was

Figure 8-7:
An example
of a news-
jacking.

Newsjacking can quickly go wrong if you are not smart and sensitive about what news you are trying to capitalize on. As an example, designer Kenneth Cole has repeatedly been called out for newsjacking inappropriate topics. For instance, referring to possible military action in Syria, he played off of a quote from the Pentagon stating "there will be no boots on the ground" in Syria. In response, he tweeted "'Boots on the ground' or not, let's not forget about sandals, pumps, and loafers. #Footwear." This angered a lot of people for its insensitivity and was frankly a #fail.

Creating Clear Conversion Goals

Many companies are unsure how to tie lead conversion to their blog because company blogs were originally conceived for brand awareness purposes. However, if you think about your blog through the lens of lead generation, you might be surprised how successful it can be.

People come to your blog and read your posts because they are inspiring, so why not offer them opportunities to view even more content by subscribing to your blog or clicking through to another related resource? Just be sure that your conversion paths are clear and that there is no question what your blog readers should be doing.

Placing your blog subscription forms

The best way to get readers to convert to leads is by prompting them to subscribe to your blog. This means that if a reader fills out a form with her email address, she can get email digests of your blog daily, weekly, or monthly. This is an excellent way to get good leads into your database.

Just be sure that your email subscription opt-in links are well placed and distinctive. Also make sure that your subscribers do not have to put in a lot of information. You should only be asking for their email address and first and last name.

Here are a few examples of different ways to format a blog opt-in:

✓ **Header:** Placing your subscription opt-in form in your header is a great way to catch the attention of your readers. This is often the most logical place that a reader looks. Figure 8-8 shows an example of a blog opt-in on the popular email marketing blog Waldow Social that is utilizing header space for visibility.

Figure 8-8:
A header
blog opt-in.

✓ **Sidebar:** Another very visible place for a blog opt-in, the sidebar is a popular location. It hits a happy medium of being within the field of vision, while not obstructing good blog copy. Consider pinning it to the top of a reader's screen so that as he scrolls down, the opt-in scrolls with him. Figure 8-9 is an example of a sidebar on Copyblogger. Note that their form is very clean and extremely short — they only ask for your email address.

Figure 8-9:
A sidebar
blog opt-in.

✔ **Lightbox pop-up:** There is much debate in the industry about using pop-ups, an opt-in that pops up when someone navigates onto your page. With a lightbox pop-up, the rest of your page blacks out when the opt-in pops onto the screen. Some people find them irritating, but they are worth testing because they're obvious and can't be missed. Marketo's blog uses a lightbox, as shown in Figure 8-10. It pops up immediately when someone unknown comes to the blog and is only presented once every six months, so users aren't bombarded each time they come. Marketo's numbers have skyrocketed since they began using this opt-in, so you should certainly consider using one.

Figure 8-10:
A lightbox
blog opt-in.

Including related resources

Hopefully the topics on your blog relate to other content you have created. For instance, maybe you write a blog about your core competencies in social media marketing. Most likely you have a variety of assets — ebooks, videos, reports, and so on — that are related to social marketing. Make sure you link to all of them in the blog and consider including functionality to enable related resources to pop up on the bottom of your blog when you tag your blog with a keyword or category.

The idea is to keep people on your site and give them more conversion points. They may not have subscribed to your blog, but maybe they want to put in their lead information to download an ebook.

Take a look at Figure 8-11 for an example of related resource tiles after a blog post. Note in this example the blog post is about email marketing, and the related resources are *Comparing Your Email Marketing Results, B2B Email Marketing Success Kit*, and *The Definitive Guide to Engaging Email Marketing*. All of these assets are gated with a form, so if someone decides to click on one of those and leave the blog, hopefully she will first fill out the form to receive the asset.

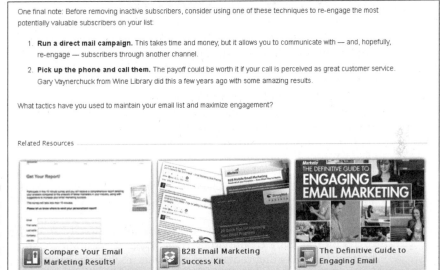

Figure 8-11: A related resource conversion path.

Another example of getting a lead to convert on your blog is simply putting verbiage on the page to prompt him to click to an asset. This could be language like, "If you want to learn more about XYZ, please be sure to download our brand-new ebook."

Figure 8-12 illustrates this strategy. Note how the blog post naturally links to the asset download in the first couple of opening paragraphs.

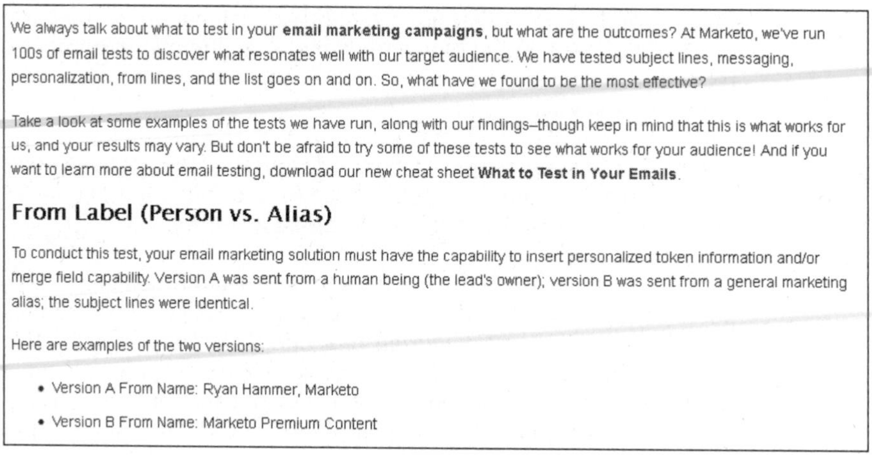

We always talk about what to test in your **email marketing campaigns**, but what are the outcomes? At Marketo, we've run 100s of email tests to discover what resonates well with our target audience. We have tested subject lines, messaging, personalization, from lines, and the list goes on and on. So, what have we found to be the most effective?

Take a look at some examples of the tests we have run, along with our findings—though keep in mind that this is what works for us, and your results may vary. But don't be afraid to try some of these tests to see what works for your audience! And if you want to learn more about email testing, download our new cheat sheet **What to Test in Your Emails**.

From Label (Person vs. Alias)

To conduct this test, your email marketing solution must have the capability to insert personalized token information and/or merge field capability. Version A was sent from a human being (the lead's owner); version B was sent from a general marketing alias; the subject lines were identical.

Here are examples of the two versions:

- Version A From Name: Ryan Hammer, Marketo
- Version B From Name: Marketo Premium Content

Figure 8-12:
A blog link within a blog post.

Leveraging Social Sharing

Enabling readers to share each individual post on social channels expands your reach and increases social validation of your site. But what is social validation and why is it important?

A recent study conducted by *The New York Times* cites that a person is 32 percent more likely to "Like" a post or an article if it has already been "Liked" by others. That is significant. In other words, if your blog post shows it has received multiple social shares, a reader is more likely to share your post on his own social channels. Essentially, the social share validates that this post is good — because it has been Liked and shared by a reader's peers — and therefore, it should also be Liked and shared by the reader. And the more eyes you can get on your content, the more leads you are likely to generate.

So how do you do this? A great way to prompt people to share your post is to ask for the share by providing social sharing capabilities. You can add buttons for many different social networks, including Facebook, Twitter, LinkedIn, Google+ (which I go into detail about in Chapter 9), and so on.

Adding social sharing capabilities also helps give you a benchmark for measurement. As you continue to optimize your blog and your blog posts, how often are your posts being shared? Has the sharing rate gone up or down?

By adding social sharing buttons to your blog posts, you can enable readers to easily share each post with their own social networks. Instead of them having to do the extra work of going to one of their social channels themselves and posting the link, a social sharing button gives them an easy solution. You can populate the post with your own custom messages, and voilà! A reader doesn't have to exert himself too much to share your content.

Adding a Twitter Tweet/Share button

A Twitter sharing button provides your readers an easy way to tweet about your latest blog post to their own social channels. In fact, in a study conducted by BrightEdge, using social share buttons increases mentions on Twitter sevenfold. Including them is a no-brainer. Here is how to implement and install the button:

1. Go to `https://twitter.com/about/resources/buttons#tweet` to choose your button, type the text for the tweet, and provide the URL of your blog post.

2. Consider adding your company Twitter handle (your Twitter identification name), a hashtag (a word preceded by a # sign used to identify or amalgamate a topic) of your choice, and even the Twitter handle of the blogger, if applicable.

3. Copy the HTML code that is generated for your button and place it on your site.

For more information on how to customize your button, feel free to check out Twitter's more detailed instructions at `https://dev.twitter.com/docs/tweet-button`. Figure 8-13 shows you an example of a Twitter Tweet/Share button in action.

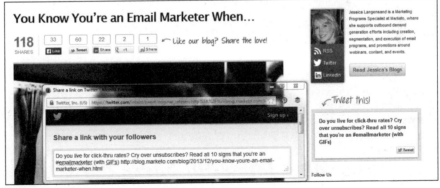

Figure 8-13:
A Twitter Tweet/Share button.

Adding a Facebook Like button

Just like the Twitter Tweet/Share button, the Facebook Like button also enables a reader to easily "Like" your post on Facebook. Clicking a Like button signals to others that, well, someone liked the content that was shared. Content with a lot of Likes gives feedback to others that the nature of the content was relevant, helpful, likable, or amusing — you get the picture. When a reader clicks the Like button in your blog, the post will be shared in her timeline.

1. Go to `https://developers.facebook.com/docs/reference/plugins/like/`.

2. **Using the Layout drop-down list, you can customize the appearance of your Like button.**

3. **Click the Get Code button, copy the code from the pop-up that appears, and place it on your site.**

Figure 8-14 shows an example of the different ways a Facebook Like button can appear on your blog.

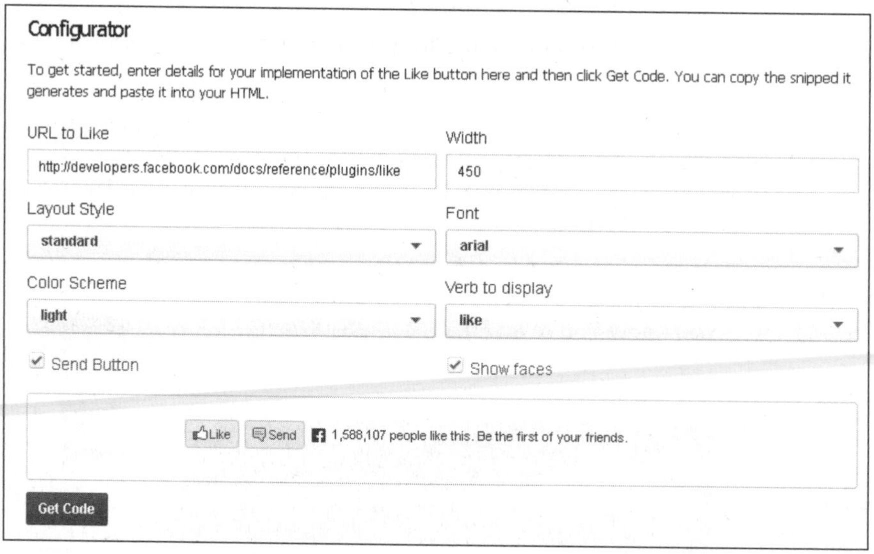

Configurator

To get started, enter details for your implementation of the Like button here and then click Get Code. You can copy the snipped it generates and paste it into your HTML.

URL to Like	Width
http://developers.facebook.com/docs/reference/plugins/like	450

Layout Style	Font
standard	arial

Color Scheme	Verb to display
light	like

☑ Send Button   ☑ Show faces

👍Like   💬Send   📘 1,588,107 people like this. Be the first of your friends.

Get Code

Figure 8-14:
A Facebook
Like button.

Adding a LinkedIn Share button

LinkedIn is a great place for your readers to share their content with other business-minded professionals. The LinkedIn Share button can help you extend your reach. Just like the previous social media buttons I mentioned, the LinkedIn Share button allows readers to share your post with their own networks.

1. Go to `http://developer.linkedin.com/plugins/share-plugin-generator` **to install the Share button plug-in.**

2. **Choose your button style in the Choose a Count Mode area.**

   This area allows you to control how (or whether) a count of how many times the blog post has been shared is displayed.

3. **Craft your message and choose the URL to which you want to send traffic.**

4. **Click the Get Code button, copy the code that is generated, and add it to your site.**

Figure 8-15 shows the LinkedIn Share button generator. As with Facebook, you can customize the look of a LinkedIn Share button.

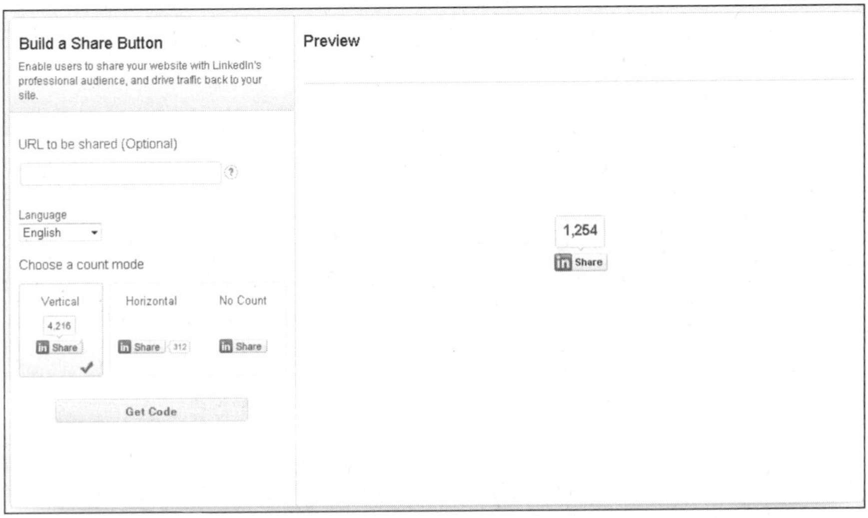

Figure 8-15:
A LinkedIn
Share
button.

Adding a Google +1 button

The Google +1 button prompts readers to +1 your content — basically recommending it to Google and sharing it with others on Google's social media site, Google+ (pronounced "Google Plus"). It is similar to a Facebook "Like." Clicking the +1 button not only recommends your post in search results, but also shares it with your reader's other Google+ connections. This is great to extend your social reach and it improves your search results: Google ranks this content high due to the +1s.

1. Go to `http://www.google.com/webmasters/+1/button/`.

2. **Choose your +1 button style by adjusting the Size, Annotation, and Width buttons.**

   See a preview of your changes to the right.

3. **Add the URL that you want readers to share by clicking on the Advanced Options drop-down list.**

4. **Copy the embedded code and add it to your site.**

Figure 8-16 shows an example of the Google +1 button. You can customize the look and feel for your blog.

Figure 8-16:
The Google
+1 button.

Adding a Pinterest Pin It button

The Pin It button enables readers to share your post on Pinterest. This is particularly great if you have very visual posts. You can even add a Pin It button to all of the images in your post. Make sure you add it for all of your infographics.

1. **Go to** `http://business.pinterest.com/widget-builder/#do_pin_it_button` **and customize your Pin It button with the drop-down lists in the Appearance section.**

2. **The Show Pin Count drop-down list gives you the option of displaying the pin count and controlling its placement.**

3. **Add the page URL in the URL field, the image URL in the Image field, and a description of the pin.**

4. **Click Build It to copy the embedded code and use it on your site.**

Figure 8-17 shows an example of the Pin It button used on blog post imagery.

Figure 8-17:
A Pin It
button.

Handling Commenting on Your Blog

A great way to increase engagement and activity on your blog is to promote and encourage blog commenting. If you can successfully spark a conversation among your readers, they're actively as opposed to passively engaged. Plus, having a conversation with readers through blog commenting is a fantastic way to get your internal thought leaders and sales executives involved in answering the questions of potential leads.

Imagine you work for a company that sells business consulting services, and you write a blog post about best practices in structuring your sales teams to support a service offering you have. You notice that a few people start commenting and asking questions. You even notice that one reader says that he is having a lot of problems with the structure of his sales teams. Right away, you get one of your sales executives to reply to his comment and help him out. Soon enough, a relationship is formed and the lead asks your sales executive to talk offline. An instant (and valuable) bond is formed.

The first step is determining what blog commenting application you want to use — Disqus, Livefyre, WordPress, and IntenseDebate are just a few of the existing providers. You can of course use the native functionality in your WordPress instance for commenting, but a plug-in or additional platform gives you more control over spam and comment management. Depending on your organization and needs, you might need a simple plug-in, or a more robust platform that provides engagement analytics and varying levels of control.

Blog commenting platforms generally have many features, so think about your wish list for functionality before you decide.

You might want to think about and seek out a commenting platform that has the following functionality:

- **Many login options:** Most commenting platforms allow readers to use social sign-on, which makes it easier for your readers to comment if they are already logged in to a social networking site (like Facebook, Twitter, LinkedIn, and so on). They can use their sign-on for those sites without having to create a separate login for your site.

- **Mobile site compatibility:** Many of today's blog readers like to view posts on a mobile device, so make sure your commenting platform supports this.

- **Nested replies:** By having nested replies, your readers can see to which comment a reader is replying.

- **Comment moderation:** You want someone moderating and approving the comments, so make sure your platform has good administrative functionality, and that you have set expectations that someone on the marketing team will need to have this responsibility. You might want to reject comments that seem like spam and include promotional links for other sites. You might also want to keep an eye out for obscene content or commenters bashing your business.

- **Comment voting:** Many new commenting platforms offer users the ability to vote a comment up or down.

- **Comment tagging:** If your commenting application offers tagging options, a reader's friend can easily be brought into the conversation by tagging a username that already exists on the commenting platform or a social media username, further sharing your blog post.

Always make sure you are asking for comments in the blog post itself. If you don't ask for the reaction of your readers, you may not get any. If you are writing a blog post about iPhone versus Android, ask your audience what they think about the debate. You certainly will get a lot of opinions and hopefully some great conversations, which can turn into sales. If you are hesitating to turn on comments because you think you will receive a lot of negative discussions about your product or service, you should rethink having a blog at all. Dialogues between a company and its customers or prospects intentionally create authentic discussions to increase the empathy and bond with constituents.

Make sure you evaluate each commenting platform's ability to prevent irrelevant spam comments from making it onto your blog. Nothing kills a virtual conversation between a blogger and her engaged readers faster than spammers trying to use your blog to sell their unrelated stuff.

Identifying a Guest Blogging Network

Guest bloggers are a great way to increase the reach of your content, and they often provide a different perspective or approach on the topics you usually write about. If you do not have guest bloggers knocking down your door, go out and find them! Put the message out there on social channels, or send out an email blast to your leads and customers asking them to blog.

Don't forget to go after industry influencers and ask them to blog for you. Every industry has a list of thought leaders. Make your wish list and start pursuing them. Reach out through social media, send them an email, or pick up the phone and call. These are the people that can help you ultimately build your following and credibility.

Many people get excited about the possibility of their voice being heard, and you will probably be surprised at how many people might respond to your inquiry. I use guest bloggers all of the time. Each person adds a unique voice to a blog, and he shares the post to his networks as well, which means even more visibility.

But remember, you don't want to just let anyone guest blog on your site. Make sure you have very strict content guidelines. Bad guest bloggers can cheapen the quality of your posts with value-less content, which makes you look bad. Make sure every blogger is well vetted (ask for writing samples, and have them suggest possible topics to get a sense of whether they truly know the space or not), and work with them each time they blog until they understand your voice and how you want your brand to be portrayed.

Creating your blog guidelines

Set clear rules for blogging and write them out in a document that you can send to your guest bloggers. And be specific. If you don't want people writing five-page blog posts, say so. The more specific you can be, the closer your guest posters can get to meeting your criteria.

Here are some things you may want to include in your guideline document:

- ✔ An abstract about your blog that tells your guest bloggers what your blog is about, what sort of content you post there, and your general blog goals
- ✔ What you are looking for in a blogger
- ✔ The kind of post topics you typically accept
- ✔ A brand and tone style guide
- ✔ Suggested page or word count length
- ✔ What should be included in a submission
- ✔ Typical waiting times for a post to go live
- ✔ Number of necessary revisions a post might go through before approval
- ✔ A disclaimer stating that you have the right to edit and amend all submitted posts and that no post is guaranteed to be published

Deciding your guest blog cadence

After you have a fair number of guest bloggers vying to be posted on your site, it makes sense to sit down and think about how often you want to post guest blogs. If you have a new guest blogger for each day of the week, your voice and tone may get muddled, so choose a regular cadence (or pattern) of guest blog posts.

Determining some dates and times also enables you to give each blogger more specific criteria on when his blog will post. On my company's blog, I only allow one guest post per week. The other four days of the work week must host content from internal thought leaders.

Creating an Internal Blogging Program

When I speak with other industry professionals about their blog, I'm often asked how the marketing team can get more blog contributions from internal thought leaders. If the only people who are blogging at your company are the marketing team, the key movers and shakers in your organization aren't getting heard. And *of course* your marketing team is made up of rock stars, but showcasing expert talent from within your company helps you move the sales needle. Some examples of expert voices are your engineering teams if you work for a software company, your practice directors if you are at a services company, or your product management team if you work for a product company. The employees that are closest to the front lines and who can best empathize with your prospect's pains are the ones who can lend thought leadership to your blog.

But when the marketing team goes out to the company and asks others to blog, they hear the same excuses: "We don't have time," "We aren't comfortable with writing," or "We don't know what to write about." As a marketer, you have to make it easy and comfortable for others to contribute. The key to successful inbound marketing and lead generation through content is building that trust as the industry expert with your leads.

So what do you need to do? Create an official internal blogging program and bring out all of the bells and whistles. Create guidelines, pick a theme, train your writers, get a budget approved, and give them incentives to participate. Even consider getting posters, stickers, and T-shirts printed to really get everyone excited.

Developing internal guidelines

The first step to creating an internal blogging program is developing some internal guidelines for blogging. You need to set some parameters to guide your bloggers in the right direction. Similar to your guest blogging guidelines, you want to create a document that is accessible to your team. And be sure to have this document in multiple places, such as an internal landing page, your customer relationship management (CRM) content, or an internal Human Resources (HR) wiki.

Your guidelines should be thorough. Leave no stone unturned. You want internal contributors to see the beauty of how easy blogging can be. In your internal guidelines, consider including

- A program introduction that explains what your blogging program is and how individuals can get involved
- An explanation of what blogging is and why you do it
- Information on your company blog, which can include the type of content you post there and your blogging goals
- Program incentives (if applicable)
- An explanation of the importance of building the company brand and building a blogger's personal brand, which is an important incentive for employees to blog
- An explanation of how your company generates leads through your blog, which can also excite team members to contribute

- ✔ A description of internal roles — who is who in the blogging world at your company

- ✔ Your submission and approval process

- ✔ Resources your department provides (such as copyediting, blog consultations, or training)

- ✔ Post topic ideas

- ✔ Blog guidelines and parameters (include a social media policy if you have one)

- ✔ Blogging 101 (how to begin a first post, how to craft a title, how to write a conclusion, and so on)

Evangelizing your program

It is critical to evangelize your program internally and provide blog training to interested participants. People generally have every excuse in the book for why they can't blog, so sometimes you have to hit them over the head with a frying pan to make them understand exactly what the benefits are.

Start by making a wish list of internal bloggers — either individuals or entire teams. Make sure to spend time meeting with the executives for each department and get their complete buy-in. Craft a presentation and explain to them how a blog can be used for lead generation — feel free to use the many examples from within this book! And explain how if your internal teams start blogging, they can build personal brands for themselves and ultimately for the company. If you win over the execs, you can win over their teams.

Make sure to schedule meetings and training times with each team so that you can have a discussion about your blog and importance of contributing, and so you can train them on how to blog and participate. Not everyone knows how to start writing a blog post or what format a blog should be in, so you want to make sure that all of their questions are answered.

Also, if you have the resources available, offer personal blogging consultations. I have found that people uncomfortable or not used to blogging won't ask questions in front of a group — they would prefer to meet privately to go over their ideas or fears related to writing. If you have the resources, try to provide private personalized time. This goes a long way to encouraging participation.

Note that this can become time-consuming. Consider bringing on an intern who is a great writer to help copyedit posts and train interested contributors.

Crafting incentives for participation

If you have a culture that generally doesn't contribute content, consider offering incentives. Whether you have a small budget or a large one, offering some type of reward really goes a long way. When I launched the internal blogging program at my company, I created prize incentives that participants could win based on the number of posts they submitted. They won a prize in each category after they hit the corresponding post milestone. Figure 8-18 shows the incentive program that I put in place to get people excited to blog.

Figure 8-18: A sample blog incentive program.

When people have an appealing goal to hit, they have an incentive to take time to contribute. Many of my bloggers write their blogs outside of work time, and we have had great success with many people reaching our incentive milestones.

Although you might find that you have an early rush of posts and then some drop-off, you'll find a select group of people who turn out to be strong bloggers. They find that they enjoy participating, they love seeing their name in lights on the website, and you can generally count on these team members to be bloggers for life!

Chapter 9

Creating Lasting Relationships Through Social Media

● ●

In This Chapter

▶ Sharing on social media

▶ Getting the most out of Facebook

▶ Leveraging Twitter

▶ Engaging through LinkedIn

▶ Getting visual with Pinterest

▶ Attracting attention with SlideShare

● ●

*T*he fact that all businesses need to be on social media is not a groundbreaking revelation. Everybody knows that. And hopefully most of you are working on building your social media presence on Facebook, Twitter, LinkedIn, and the other major social channels. (If you aren't, get going on that ASAP!)

However, there has been a significant shift in how businesses are using social media. In the past, it was difficult to tie social media to lead generation, but today's social strategy includes specific tactics for generating leads through social channels. Of course, social media is still extremely important for generating brand awareness and buzz, but the impact that social media has on lead generation is continuing to gain traction.

Here are some cold, hard facts about social media:

✔ One-third of global B2B buyers use social media to engage with their vendors, and 75 percent expect to use social media in future purchasing processes.

✔ Sixty-four percent of marketers rate social media as the most important factor in organic search success, behind only effective web pages, which are cited as most important by 82 percent.

✔ Sixty percent of B2B companies have acquired customers through LinkedIn, followed by 60 percent through the company blog, 43 percent through Facebook, and 40 percent through Twitter.

✔ By spending as little as six hours per week on social media, 64 percent of marketers see lead-generation benefits from it.

It has become increasingly important for businesses to make themselves available to their leads in a personal and accessible way, and social media fits the bill for this type of communication. And because today's buyer likes to self-educate, social media is the perfect outlet to showcase educational content.

Additionally, the casual nature of social interactions is perfect for nurturing leads. Rather than having one-way conversations with your potential buyers, social media marketing allows you to build a relationship with prospects in an informal, personable, and low-pressure way. At the same time, by coming up in the social feeds of high-value leads, you can remain top-of-mind until your lead is finally ready to buy.

Sharing on Social Media

Social media gives businesses the perfect platform to share their expertise in a personal, human way. And because the nature of social media lends itself well to content sharing, you can get access to the networks of your followers through an emphasis on peer-to-peer influence marketing.

A recent study from Nielsen showed that only 33 percent of buyers believe what a brand has to say about itself because people view brand-to-buyer communication as advertising. However, if a buyer gets valuable insight from a peer, he is much more likely to pay attention. By sharing valuable content on social channels, you can tap into the power of peer-to-peer communication and word of mouth.

Sharing on social media and leveraging the power of your followers' sharing network has significant benefits, such as

✔ Increased brand authenticity

✔ Generating a lead at a low cost

✔ Increased trust

✔ Increased network reach

✔ Access to new opportunities

Marketo uses an iceberg analogy to describe social media reach and sharing. On the surface, you see the tip of the iceberg, which represents your social network, including all your Facebook fans, Twitter followers, LinkedIn connections, and so on. But when you look beyond the surface and underneath the water, you see the whole iceberg. You see not only your own direct network but also the friends of those in your network — the iceberg.

Time spent sharing on social media can yield impressive lead-generation results. Marketo takes lead generation on social media sites very seriously. They have developed five golden rules of social media marketing that you should keep in mind when you start developing your campaigns:

- ✔ **Don't take yourself too seriously.** Social media is about being social, and that means you need to have a good personality in order to make your brand likable so that people will want to follow you.

- ✔ **Have great content and good offers.** Without well-produced, engaging content, any tactics you employ will most likely fail.

- ✔ **You need a strong call-to-action.** A strong CTA is just as important in your social media strategy as everywhere else. Be clear about what you want your audience to do after consuming your content or engaging with your brand.

- ✔ **Always add value.** At the end of the day, if you are not providing your prospects and customers some sort of value, you are not doing your job, and social media ultimately won't drive leads.

- ✔ **Social media is a two-way street.** No one likes being talked at. Yes, you can broadcast your message, but remember to keep the lines of communication open in both directions. When contacted, always respond quickly and sincerely. Be sure to mix up your messaging and use a combination of content and offers.

Utilizing the 4-1-1 rule

So what should you share on social channels? You need to have a good mix of educational and promotional content. I like to refer to the 4-1-1 rule to designate what should be shared on social channels. The *4-1-1 rule* was popularized by Tippingpoint Labs and Content Marketing Institute founder Joe Pulizzi and was initially created to use on Twitter.

The rule states that, "For every self-serving tweet, you should retweet one relevant tweet and most importantly, share four pieces of relevant content written by others." Now, you don't have to follow this exactly. The relevant four pieces of content can be written by your company. It is fine to share your own content as long as these pieces are educational. Plus, you want people to fill out forms for your content pieces, so this is critical. Remember, early-stage leads won't fill out forms to get a datasheet if they have never heard about your company, so offering them valuable content prompts them to share their information.

The 4-1-1 formula can easily be applied to each of the social networks. As an example, say I work for a vitamin company and am creating my social media editorial calendar for the day. My posts might look like the following:

Post 1: *Promotional.* Information on our weekend 30-percent-off women's vitamins sale.

Post 2: *Relevant content from others.* Retweet or share an article from *The New York Times* on the importance of taking a multivitamin every day.

Post 3: *Educational content from a well-respected industry thought leader.* Ebook on the right mix of vitamins during pregnancy.

Post 4: *Educational content from company.* Infographic on the increase of vitamin intake since 2007.

Post 5: *Educational content from company.* Blog post on the best new vitamins for 2014.

Post 6: *Educational content from company.* Ebook on what ingredients to look for in your vitamins.

Creating contagious content

In order for your content to be Liked and shared on social channels, it has to be contagious — fun, interesting, and shareable. You won't get very far creating a true social following if all you post is self-promotional items. Why would someone want to tell everyone in her network that your company won some random award? Despite what you might think, she probably wouldn't. But what would she share? Maybe a fun meme that you created to promote your new ebook or an announcement of a contest that you are hosting.

The key to effective lead generation on social channels is a solid social following. People won't be tempted to fill out your forms on social channels if you aren't posting anything interesting.

But what *does* work on social channels? Content that is visual, interactive, and often amusing prompts people to look at, share, and interact with your content. The more people who interact and share your content, the more leads you can get.

As an example, consider a meme that Marketo posted on Facebook to promote a new content asset: a shot of Justin Timberlake with "I'm bringing email back" superimposed on it. The idea was to take an asset theme, which was email marketing, and present it to a social audience on Facebook in a relevant way. It resulted in more than 15,000 likes at the time of this writing, an organic reach of 64,576 people, and 7,100 clicks to the asset. It had a Facebook engagement rate of 17,300 people. Marketo took a pop icon, played off of the lyrics to one of his hits, and included an asset download call-to-action in a way that really engaged a Facebook audience.

A great social post for lead generation has the following characteristics:

- ✔ Compelling messaging
- ✔ Eye-catching visuals
- ✔ Mass-audience appeal and shareability
- ✔ A clear CTA
- ✔ A tone that conveys personality

Getting the Most out of Facebook

Many marketers dismiss Facebook due to its perceived reputation as a personal social network. And although it may be true that Facebook is used to connect with family and friends, businesses can also tap into the huge value that Facebook offers. More than 800 million people use Facebook every day, so if you can show value for your followers, your lead-generation efforts can have a true network effect.

In order to become active on Facebook as a business, you need to create a Facebook Page for your company, if you haven't done so already. Your Facebook Page should include an About section where you can write about your company. Be sure to include an interesting cover image and a profile photo.

Facebook enables businesses to "have a face" and interact with leads and customers on a more personal basis. But because Facebook is such a widely used personal social network, businesses need to strike a real balance between offering content that is valuable for brand positioning and offering content that is fun and shareable.

Ask yourself two questions before posting content on Facebook:

- ✔ Does this piece of content help our brand's likability?
- ✔ Is this piece of content interesting, engaging, and useful?

Because of Facebook's News Feed algorithm, posting for the sake of posting because you aren't sure what message you want to convey can actually *hurt* your chances of being seen and followed. Facebook is constantly updating their platform and they continually try to improve the usability of News Feed. A couple of years ago, EdgeRank was all anyone talked about, but now it seems that EdgeRank is defunct.

Facebook has dropped the name *EdgeRank* and has created an even more complex algorithm. According to a recent *Marketing Land* article and interview with Facebook's engineering manager for News Feed ranking, "Facebook hasn't used the word (EdgeRank) internally for about two and a half years. That's when the company began employing a more complex ranking algorithm based on machine learning. The current algorithm doesn't have a catchy name, but it's clear that EdgeRank is a thing of the past."

But what does this algorithm do? It helps Facebook determine what gets displayed on a user's News Feed. In simple terms, if users or their friends are interacting with your company on a frequent basis, you show up more frequently on their News Feeds. If not, you get dropped and will not appear. Thus, you want to ensure that you are part of the virtuous cycle of showing up on News Feeds with interesting topics to share.

Because engagement is critical to the News Feed, if your content is not shareable and being interacted with, it simply won't show up. And if your content doesn't show up in the News Feed, well, you won't be getting many leads.

What do you have to keep in mind to stay relevant in Facebook's News Feed? Here are some important things to think about:

- **Affinity:** How close is the relationship between the user and content?
- **Weight:** What type of action was taken on the content? A comment might have more weight than a Like, and so on.
- **Decay:** How current is the content?
- **Post types:** What type of posts does a user typically interact with?
- **Hide post/spam:** What type of posts does a user hide or mark as spam?
- **Clicking on ads:** Does a user interact with ads?
- **Device considerations:** Can the device a user is on handle certain types of content?
- **Story bumping:** Is it worthwhile to give old posts new visibility if people are still interacting with them?

Understanding engagement

When it comes to Facebook marketing, you can pay attention to two metrics in order to determine how effective your content is: the engagement rate and the People Talking About This rating.

Your engagement rate is used to measure what share of your audience is engaged with your content. It can easily be determined by the following two metrics:

- ✔ **Engagement rate for posts:** People who Liked, commented, shared or clicked on your post divided by people who saw your post
- ✔ **Engagement rate for pages:** Total engagements (which is the sum of all Likes, comments, and Shares) divided by total fans

By using these engagement metrics, you can determine whether the content you are posting is working, and you can compare the quality of different posts.

The other metric you can look at is the People Talking About This rating. Basically a buzz metric, this rating measures who is talking about you and your posts. This metric can be found right below your page name, as shown in Figure 9-1.

Figure 9-1:
The People
Talking
About This
metric.

Marketo
82,231 likes · 11,953 talking about this

To boost these metrics, businesses need to make sure they are posting on a consistent basis and engaging in a dialogue with their followers.

Telling a visual story

Visual content is critical to engagement on social channels. Because Facebook's News Feed is highly visual, businesses need to develop enticing images that their fans can Like and engage with. Images also bring your lead-generation CTAs to life and encourage more clicks. In fact, a recent HubSpot study found that photos on Facebook received 53 percent more Likes than the average post and 104 percent more comments. And to make it even more compelling for lead-generation enthusiasts, posts with an image received 84 percent more clicks than text-only posts.

So what sort of imagery can you use? Consider promoting a webinar with a custom image, like in Figure 9-2.

Figure 9-2:
A webinar custom image for Facebook.

However, you must make sure that you follow Facebook's imagery rules if you want to promote these posts, which is a must for lead generation. According to Facebook's Help Center, "Images in your ads and sponsored stories may not include more than 20 percent text in the image." Facebook believes that images with less text are more engaging for its audience.

You can see whether your image meets the guidelines by using Facebook's Grid tool. To use the Grid tool,

1. **Go to** `https://www.facebook.com/ads/tools/text_overlay`.

2. **Click Browse to upload an image you want to use in your ad.**

3. **After you upload your image, it appears within the 5 x 5 grid.**

4. **Click the boxes that contain text.**

   If text is present in six or more boxes, the image has more than 20 percent text and is not eligible to be used in an ad in News Feed.

5. **If your image has more than 20 percent text, adjust your image.**

Figure 9-3 illustrates this rule so you can see how this works for ads without text, ads with the right amount of text, and ads with too much text.

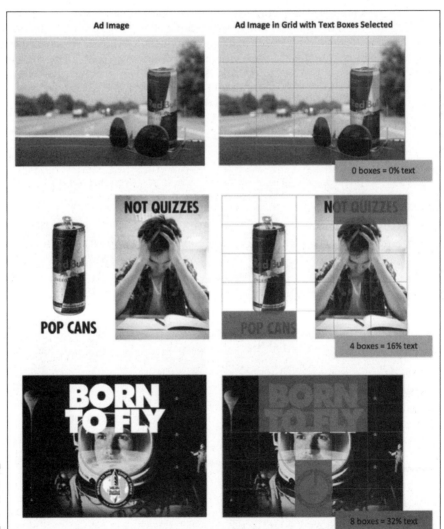

Figure 9-3:
Facebook
image rules.

Developing Promoted Posts

Through Facebook's Promoted Posts, businesses can now further engage their followers and their followers' networks by putting paid efforts behind their top posts. Promoted posts are fantastic for lead generation because they not only show up in the News Feeds of all of your fans, but they're also visible to their networks as well. Remember the iceberg analogy from earlier? This is a great example of tapping into the value of your followers' networks.

Promoted Posts work well for businesses because they enable them to put that extra *oomph* behind posts they believe will generate the most impact and leads. Businesses can promote posts from their News Feeds, including status updates, photos, videos, and offers. Any post they promote appears higher in the News Feed and more people see it. Figure 9-4 shows an example of a Promoted Post appearing in my personal Facebook News Feed. It shows up in-line with my other updates.

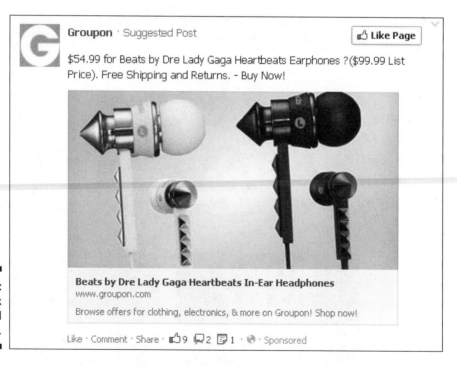

Figure 9-4:
A Facebook
Promoted
Post.

Make sure that if you are using a Facebook Promoted Post, you have a good CTA — downloading a content asset, engaging in a contest or survey, signing up for a webinar, purchasing a product, and so on. And make sure your Promoted Posts have eye-catching imagery. This is critical to engagement.

But how much should you budget for a Facebook Promoted Post and what posts should you promote? Of course, this is all depends on your personal goals and objectives for lead generation through social channels, but according to Jay Baer, social media author and blogger, "If you're at all serious about social marketing, and don't have a line item budget for promoting Facebook posts, you need to add it today." Facebook costs for Promoted Posts are based on your fan count and budget. They can range from $10 to $1,000 or more per post.

Jay also describes a method called STIR that he uses for his own blog, Convince and Convert, to determine what posts to promote:

- ✔ **Shelf Life:** Will the post be relevant four days from publication?

- ✔ **Time:** Has it been at least six hours since publication?

- ✔ **Impact:** Does the post include a link or other CTA that creates desirable customer behaviors (beyond a simple Like)?

- ✔ **Results:** Has the post exceeded a one-percent engagement rate since it has been posted?

Marketo, for example, promotes all posts that have a strong CTA and all content-related posts for brand exposure. They promote their blog posts every day, each new content asset, and anything else that has a strong CTA. Our formula for Promoted Posts is

A fun visual + clever messaging + strong CTA = Eye-Catching Promoted Post

Marketo has seen a huge uptick in visibility from promoting posts. For instance, they recently posted a new ebook about content marketing and spent $1,000 promoting it. The initial post reached only 1,712 people through organic results, but as a Promoted Post, it reached 27,744 people — a huge difference.

Creating sponsored stories

Facebook allows users to create two kinds of sponsored stories — stories that appear in the News Feed and stories that appear on the right side of the home page. Facebook defines sponsored stories as "messaging coming from friends about them engaging with a Page, app, or event that a business, organization, or individual has paid to highlight so there is a better chance people see them." Figure 9-5 shows an example of a sponsored story in the News Feed. Note that this story highlights that a connection of mine likes this page.

Figure 9-5:
A Facebook-sponsored story in the News Feed.

Sponsored stories are a perfect example of leveraging the fact that people are more likely to engage with a company their friends are engaging with. It's called *social validation.*

Sponsored stories can also appear on the right side of the home page where the ads are located. Figure 9-6 shows an example.

Figure 9-6:
A sponsored story on the right side of the home page.

Promoting through Facebook ads

Facebook ads provide highly targeted opportunities to reach your audience. On Facebook, your ads show up on the right side of the News Feed, making them highly visible. Facebook ads are similar to traditional pay-per-click (PPC) ads — you can place a bid for how much you are willing to pay per click, or you can pay per thousand people who will potentially see your ad. But as with Google, your cost depends on how popular your keywords are. Your ads can link to pages on your website or your Facebook page to ramp up the likes.

Facebook targets ads based on keywords within a user's profile and her activity history on Facebook — what she has Liked and engaged with.

Here is a step-by-step guide on creating Facebook ads:

1. **Go to the Facebook Ad tool at** `https://www.facebook.com/ads/create/`**.**

2. **Choose what you want to advertise — this could be anything from your own Facebook page to a blog post or a new product.**

   For the purposes of this exercise, I am going to promote the Marketo Facebook page, as shown in Figure 9-7.

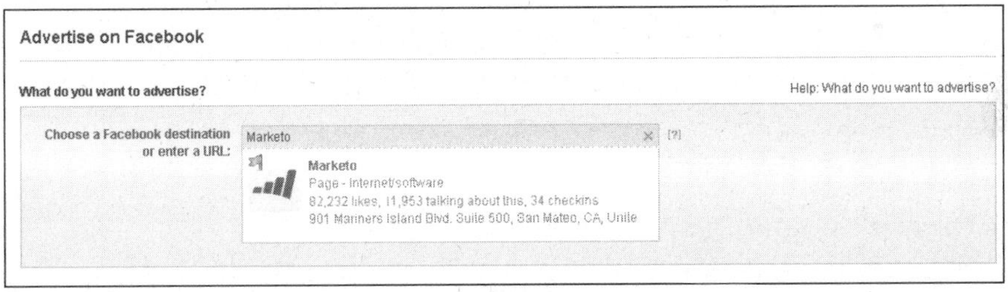

Figure 9-7: Promoting Marketo's Facebook page.

3. **Next, choose what you want to do with your ad: Get More Page Likes or Promote Page Posts.**

   I am going to choose the Get More Page Likes radio button.

4. **Select an image for your ad by clicking Upload Image.**

   Figure 9-8 shows Steps 3 and 4.

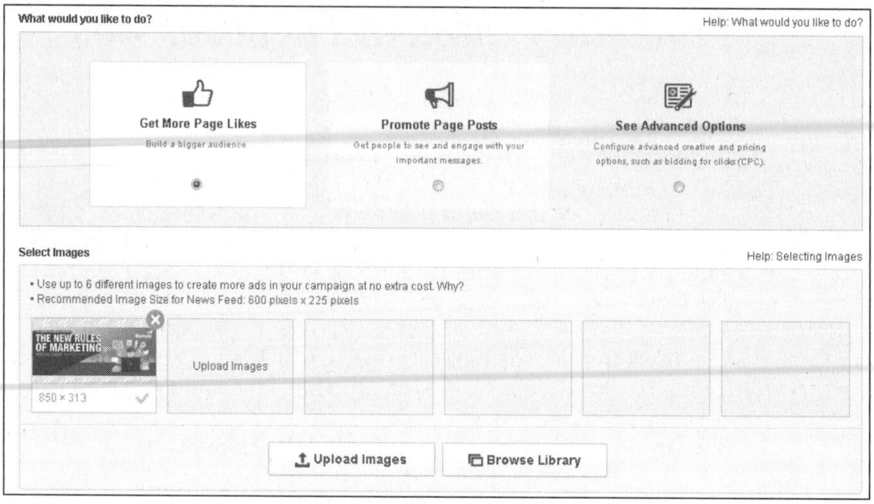

Figure 9-8:
Choosing
what you
would like
to do with
your ad and
selecting
images.

5. **Create your ad headline, text, and landing view.**

   The landing view is where people land on your page when they click your ad. I want them to land on the Timeline. This step also shows a preview of your ad on the right side, as shown in Figure 9-9.

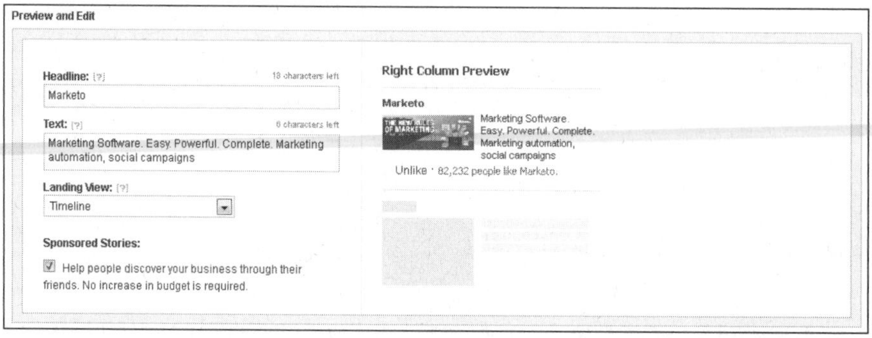

Figure 9-9:
Editing and
previewing
your ad.

6. **Create an audience.**

   I am choosing interests and a location. For my ad, I want people to be interested in the categories *Marketo, software, application software, social medium automation*, and *desktop computer*. I also want to narrow down my audience to include business and technology people. Take a look at Figure 9-10 as an example. I have 11 million in my defined audience so far.

7. **Create a budget.**

   For this ad, as shown in Figure 9-11, I want to pay $20 per day and run my campaign continuously, starting today. You can also include an end date if you want the campaign to end at a particular point in time.

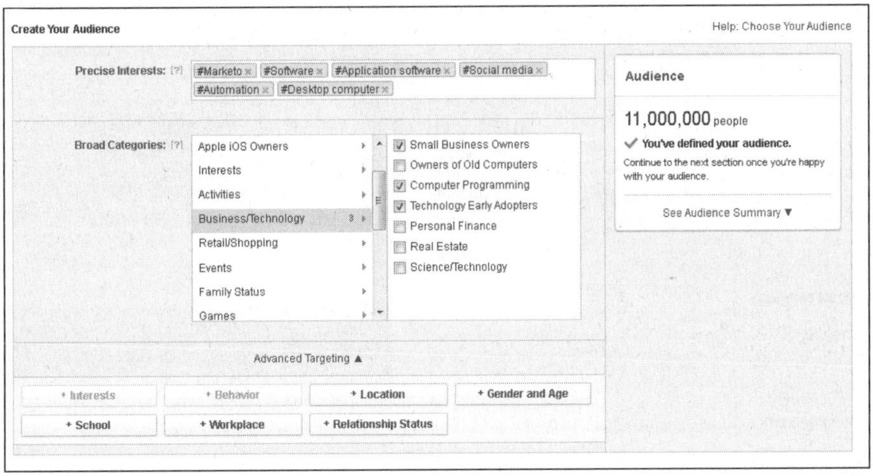

Figure 9-10:
Creating my
audience.

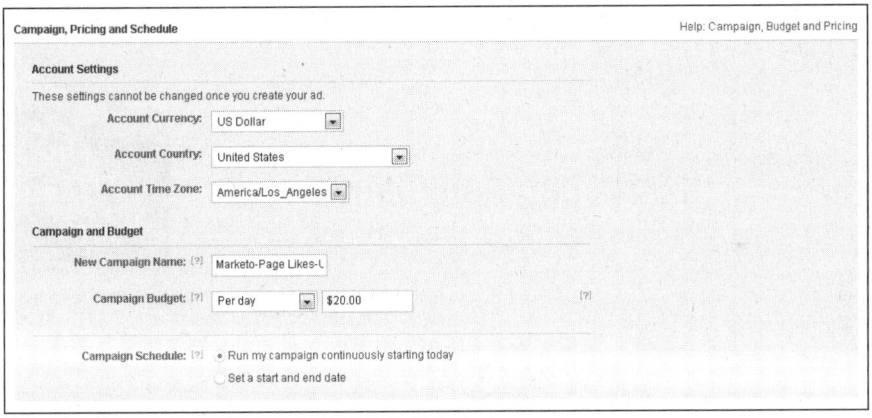

Figure 9-11:
Choosing a
campaign
pricing and
schedule.

Developing Facebook tabs

Facebook tabs are prime real estate because they live at the top of your page, are highly visible, and provide you with the opportunity to embed a landing page, or any other CTA you would like, directly into Facebook. Check out Figure 9-12 for an example of where Facebook tabs are located on your page.

After you click a tab, you can include any information you want. Because you can embed a landing page into these tabs, you can have a form appear within Facebook, which is perfect for your lead-generation efforts. Figure 9-13 shows an example of a tab created in Facebook for a content asset download. Notice that it has a visual banner, concise copy with bullet points, a short form, and a strong CTA. And because the landing page was created within the Marketo software application, leads that came directly from Facebook can be tracked.

Figure 9-12:
Facebook
tabs.

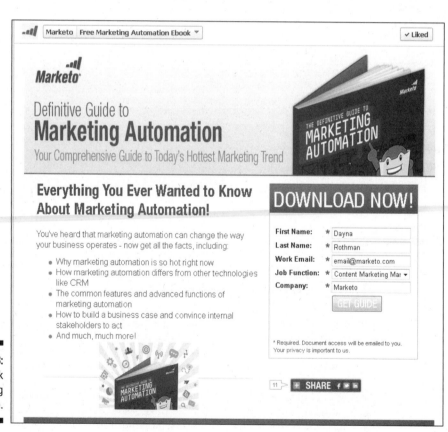

Figure 9-13:
A Facebook
tab landing
page.

Tracking your results

Facebook provides great analytics through their Page Insights. There you can track engagement and ad performance directly in their dashboard. Your Facebook Page Insights dashboard and Admin panel appear at the top of your Facebook company page. To dial down deeper into your analytics, click the See Insights button that appears on the top of your Admin panel.

The first overview Facebook provides is on your reach and engagement metrics. You can see your total Likes, the People Talking About This metric, and your Weekly Total Reach. Make note of whether these numbers are trending up or down — hopefully they're trending up! Figure 9-14 shows an example of this dashboard. The bottom line is Posts, the middle line is People Talking About This, and the top line is Weekly Total Reach.

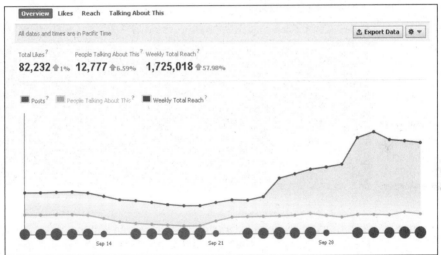

Figure 9-14:
The Overview dashboard.

You can also measure reach by demographics and location, as illustrated in Figure 9-15. You can see what countries, cities, and age groups you are most popular in.

Additionally, you can break down your People Talking About This metric even further by looking at the same demographics, as shown in Figure 9-16.

You can even dive down into the details of each post and look at how many engaged users you have, how many people are talking about each post, the reach, and the virality. This is important so you can compare and contrast how your content is performing on Facebook. Take a look at Figure 9-17, which shows an example of how Facebook breaks these details out.

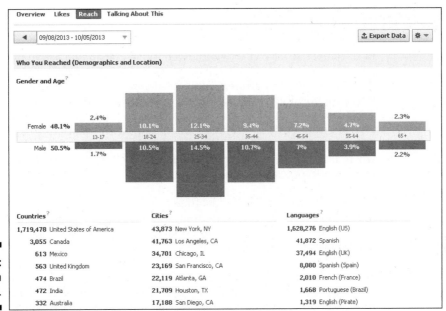

Figure 9-16:
The Reach
dashboard.

Date	Post	Reach	Engaged Users	Talking About This	Virality	
10/4/13	Our friends at Content Marketing Institut...	41,296	1,692	1,316	3.19%	
10/4/13	Attending #Dreamforce this November? J...	10,244	165	120	1.17%	
10/4/13	Happy Friday! It's time for a Friday Photo...	11,888	729	482	4.05%	
10/3/13	Revolutionize your #contentmarketing wit...	26,184	681	359	1.37%	
10/3/13	In this environment, old-fashioned "batch ...	38,832	431	254	0.65%	
10/3/13	Are your #emails optimized for all devices?	8,212	154	92	1.12%	
10/2/13	Trouble backing up your #ABtests? Treat ...	33,424	622	386	1.15%	
10/2/13	It's easy to lose sight of your #marketing ...	16,536	270	166	1%	
10/2/13	What time is it? Hump Day Joke Time! #hu...	14,096	780	365	2.59%	
10/1/13	Afraid of getting trampled by the #mobile...	33,040	589	379	1.15%	
10/1/13	Relationships are hard. Commit to commu...	28,032	582	353	1.26%	

Figure 9-17:
A page post
detail.

Leveraging Twitter

In December 2013, Twitter announced it had 200 million active users, with an expected growth of 400 million users by the end of 2013. Companies that don't have a Twitter strategy and a lead-generation plan are missing out on a huge opportunity. In fact, a recent study published by Mediabistro's All Twitter found that 82 percent of leads generated through social media are referred from Twitter. They also found that Twitter outperforms LinkedIn and Facebook nine to one for lead generation. Twitter is a vibrant community where businesses can interact with leads and industry thought leaders to discuss hot topics and trends.

The beauty of Twitter is its real-time engagement, and because of the wide reach and the nature of the Twitter news feed, it gives businesses a great forum to get the word out to potential customers so they can discover and learn more about your company.

You can also have real-time conversations with your followers, which is a great opportunity for relationship-building. B2C companies do a great job at this, and B2B companies are quickly catching on. As an example, say there's a heat wave going on. Coca-Cola might tweet about the heat, a follower could tweet back that he is beating the heat with a nice cold bottle of Coca-Cola, and then Coca-Cola tweets back with a coupon code and a thank-you.

It is critical to follow the 4-1-1 rule when it comes to Twitter. There is so much going on that that you need to post often; however, you can't be constantly posting your own stuff. (No one likes a narcissist, even in the online world.) Make sure you diversify your presence.

Like Facebook, Twitter also offers many opportunities for lead generation by both using their paid options and by simply adding links to your tweets.

Messaging through Twitter

I am not going to bore you with Twitter 101 here. I hope that you know that a tweet can't be more than 140 characters and you have to craft a compelling message to engage your audience. You should use hashtags when applicable, you should include links to your download forms or assets, you should engage in retweets, and always respond to your audience.

That being said, how do you message for lead generation? There is a simple formula:

Compelling statement + clear CTA + hashtag + link = great lead-generating tweet

Take a look at a simple example from the Microsoft Twitter handle in Figure 9-18. They are asking for a pre-order of the new Surface tablet. It lets their followers know there is a pre-order available, it uses the hashtag #surface to help the tweet find a wider audience, it has a clear call-to-action asking followers to order theirs today, and it provides a link.

Microsoft @Microsoft
24 Sep
Pre-Order now available for #Surface 2 and Surface Pro 2. Order yours today: msft.it/6011wNVV
Collapse
Reply
Retweet
Favorite
Buffer
More

Figure 9-18: A standard lead-generation tweet from Microsoft.

Building promoted posts in search and timeline

Twitter allows you to place promoted tweets in timelines targeted to followers and users who are similar to your followers. These are very similar to Promoted Posts on Facebook. You can take one of your standard tweets and promote it to add that extra boost. These tweets appear in both the timelines of your targeted audience and in search results.

Twitter enables you to target tweets based on the following:

- Interests
- Keywords in timeline
- Gender
- Geography
- Device
- Similarity to existing followers

Take a look at a promoted tweet that landed in my timeline from Salesforce in Figure 9-19 to promote their upcoming conference, Dreamforce. Notice that it has a similar formula to the previous Microsoft tweet. Also note that it says "Promoted by Salesforce.com," so I know that it's a paid tweet. It also shows me who among my followers follows Salesforce. Again, it's some of that ol' social validation in action.

Figure 9-19:
A
Salesforce
promoted
tweet in my
timeline.

Make sure your promoted tweets discuss timely and engaging content such as your new ebook, an event, or a new contest.

One tactic that I have seen work incredibly well is running promoted tweets during an event. Marketo always sees large spikes of activity on their Twitter page if they are attending an event or hosting it. By using promoted tweets, particularly in search results, during one of these high-traffic events, you can be part of these real-time conversations and take advantage of immediate opportunities.

Promoted tweets use a cost-per-click pricing similar to how Facebook ads and Google AdWords operates. Twitter recommends $0.50 to a maximum of $1.50 CPC.

As with any social media lead-generation tactic, make sure you have a dedicated landing page for your offer after a person clicks through.

Promoted accounts and trends

Twitter offers two other promoted ad options — promoted account and trends. A promoted account is just what it sounds like — you get to promote your account in order to gain more followers. The promoted account is featured in the Twitter search results in the Who to Follow area. The promoted accounts are chosen based on who users typically follow.

When someone searches for a keyword and Twitter sees that a user follows similar accounts to the advertisers, your promoted account can appear in their search results.

Take a look at Figure 9-20 to see what comes up in my Who to Follow section. I have Fidelity Investments because I track stock information, and Instagram and Tumblr because I like to track social media sites.

Who to follow · Refresh · View all
Fidelity Investments @Fidelity
Followed by Top Earnings Offer a...
Follow
Promoted
Instagram @instagram
Follow
Tumblr @tumblr
Follow
Popular accounts · Find friends

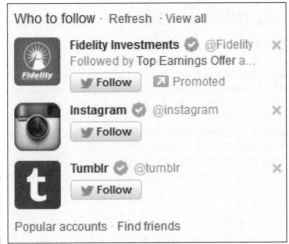

Figure 9-20: Promoted accounts.

The other option is promoted trends, although a promoted trend has a hefty price tag of $200,000 attached to it, according to Mashable. What is a promoted trend? If you are a Twitter user, you probably know that on the left side of your home page, Twitter lists hashtags that are trending throughout the day. If you pay for a promoted trend, your hashtag can appear at the top of the list indicated by a promoted image.

Figure 9-21 shows an example of my Twitter trends. As you can see, most of the trends are related to current events and hot topics. At the top is a promoted trend for an upcoming football game between the Cleveland Browns and the Buffalo Bills. The idea is that a Twitter user sees this is trending and clicks the hashtag or engages with it in some way.

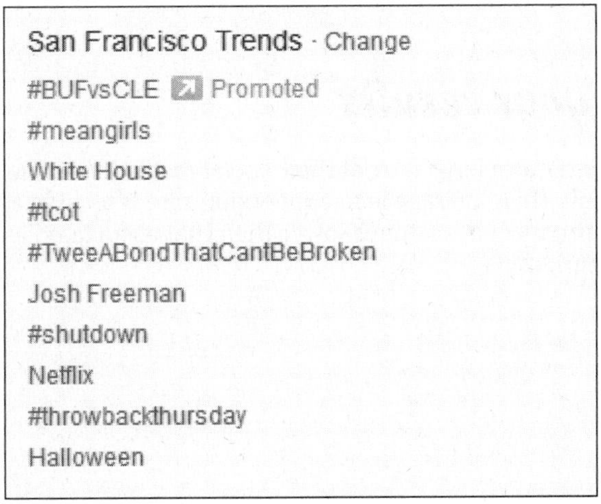

San Francisco Trends · Change
#BUFvsCLE Promoted
#meangirls
White House
#tcot
#TweeABondThatCantBeBroken
Josh Freeman
#shutdown
Netflix
#throwbackthursday
Halloween

Figure 9-21: A promoted trend.

Configuring your Twitter Lead Generation Cards

Twitter Lead Generation Cards enable marketers to collect lead information *directly* from Twitter. A user can fill out his information quickly and securely and never leave Twitter — which is a huge plus for many users.

How do these handy Lead Generation Cards work? When someone expands your tweet, they can see the description of your offer and a strong CTA. The easy part is that the Twitter handle, name, and email address fields are already prepopulated with their information, so they don't have to do very much.

Twitter Lead Generation Cards also have the ability to sync with a marketing automation tool, so that you can keep your lead information all in one place.

 However, note that the Lead Generation Cards only have a single full name field, and most marketing automation platforms collect names in separate first and last name fields. Twitter Lead Generation Cards also do not capture company data. Because of this difference, you cannot at this time push leads from your marketing automation tool to your CRM tool for sales follow-up. However, you can add them manually or upload a list.

Figure 9-22 shows an example Twitter Lead Generation Card. As you can see, there is a compelling image, a clear message, and a CTA. Note how Twitter prepopulates the user's information.

But don't stop after someone fills out your card. Make sure to send a follow-up email to ensure that the lead has taken the correct action — that is, downloaded your ebook, for example. And as extra insurance, add the offer link in your email, just in case they didn't.

Tracking your results

Marketo uses Twitter as a large part of their social media lead-generation strategy. As a result, their average lead conversion rate is as high as 14 percent, and the cost-per-prospect is six times lower than that associated with some other marketing programs.

① Bryan expands @BaristaBar's Tweet to show a signup opportunity
Bryan's info is already filled in. He only has to click the button to sign up.

The Barista Bar @baristabar
Love coffee culture? Love saving $? Join our Coffee Club -
we'll send you deals on our best drinks and treats!
cards.twitter.com/xyz/123...

Promoted by The Barista Bar

Join the coffee club for daily deals
Accept this offer by sharing your email address with Barista Bar:

Bryan Sise
@bryansise
bs ⁄⁄⁄@gm⁄⁄⁄l.com

Join the club!   View advertiser privacy
                                        policy

Customizable call to action

② Bryan's info is securely sent to The Barista Bar
He completed the entire signup in his Twitter timeline.
Now he'll receive great coffee deals by email.

Figure 9-22:
A Twitter
Lead
Generation
Card.

The key is making sure that your results are trackable. If you have a marketing automation tool, you can build landing pages and specialized links, so if a lead comes in from a social campaign, you can look at the campaign performance. You want to know what opportunities came in as a result of a social interaction, and whether social engagement affected an opportunity before it became a closed/won deal. You also might want to track the following elements of your campaigns:

✔ Follower growth

✔ Follower quality and engagement

✔ Reach (how many users favorite and retweet your tweets)

✔ Traffic to your website from Twitter

✔ Conversion (how many Twitter followers fill out your forms and buy your product or service)

You can track activity on your timeline using Twitter's Tweet Activity dashboard to see all of your activity on Twitter, as in Figure 9-23. To get there, go to Settings, click the Ads Info link, and then go to the Analytics tab. Be sure to look for trends and optimize where you see opportunities. Twitter can also show you detailed demographic data so you can see who is clicking your posts and when.

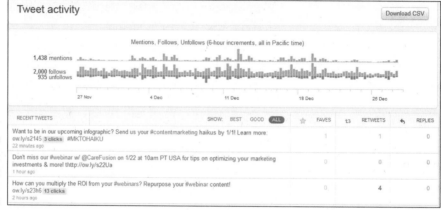

Figure 9-23:
Tweet
activity.

For your ads, Twitter uses the standard metrics such as impressions, retweets, clicks, replies, and follows. You can view these in real time.

Engaging Through LinkedIn

LinkedIn remains the largest professional network with more than 161 million members in more than 200 countries. This is a great network of potential leads — particularly if you are in the B2B space. LinkedIn is perfect for networking and influencer-building opportunities, and they also offer sponsored updates and LinkedIn ads for your lead-generation efforts. And what's more, most LinkedIn users visit the site for pure business purposes — to connect with like-minded professionals, to read industry news, and to connect with their favorite companies. So unlike personal social sites such as Facebook, LinkedIn lends itself well to making business connections. As a result, LinkedIn is the perfect place to showcase your thought leadership and become known as an industry expert.

Building out and optimizing your company page

The first step to optimizing your presence for lead generation is to make sure that your company page is built-out and optimized. The company page tells a user who you are, what you do, and why they should follow you. Keep in mind the following best practices when working to develop your LinkedIn page with lead generation in mind:

- Make sure your company page is well optimized for keywords. People will be searching by using those terms, and you want to make sure that you show up.

- Work towards a daily posting sequence to establish brand positioning on LinkedIn.

- Your company page will have the opportunity to add to and optimize your tabs such as Products and Careers. To do so, simply click the blue Edit button to edit your page and add any copy, images, or videos you want.

- Add videos to your Products tab to further engage followers. Keep the content professional (of course!) and know what specific takeaway you want the viewer to get from watching the video.

I particularly like how Apple presents itself on LinkedIn, as shown in Figure 9-24. They have a crisp, clean image up-top with a compelling message that resonates with me — I can recall how many times my dog has gotten tangled in my computer cords! They also have a section that includes keywords and a variety of updates.

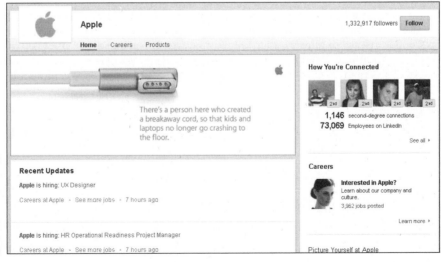

Figure 9-24:
The
LinkedIn
home page
for Apple.

Joining and starting LinkedIn Groups

Engaging in conversations with professionals is what LinkedIn is all about, and LinkedIn Groups do a nice job of facilitating conversations. This is where you and your sales team (who should all be active on LinkedIn) can answer questions, pose questions, and post links to your thought leadership.

It is simple to do a keyword search to find the top industry groups. The results are ranked by group activity, so be sure to join the most active ones. Also, feel free to start your own. If you spend time and give valuable information in your groups, your company will soon be known as a great source of information and will ultimately attract connections. Remember that posting in these groups is important, but engaging is vital. Make sure to add value in your responses to each conversation.

To create a Group, simply go to Interests on the top navigation and click on Groups. Then you can create a Group by clicking the yellow Create a Group button. After you create your Group, you can add information like your logo, Group name, description, and member settings — such as whether you want to approve people before they can join or whether people can automatically join. After you have created your Group, moderate it and answer comments daily.

Also, be sure you are participating in Q&A by doing a search in LinkedIn Answers for relevant topics and then subscribing to the answer feed to further establish your credibility.

Leveraging LinkedIn Sponsored Updates

Just like Facebook and Twitter, LinkedIn has upped the ante for lead generation by offering LinkedIn Sponsored Updates. Through LinkedIn Sponsored Updates, you can promote your message on your followers' feeds and to those outside of your follower network. You can also target who sees your update, making Sponsored Updates even more effective. As with any lead-generation update, you need a compelling image, an engaging message, and a strong CTA.

LinkedIn allows you to target your updates based on

- Location
- Company name
- Job title
- Skills

✔ School name

✔ Group (if they are part of a particular group)

✔ Gender

✔ Age

Sponsored Updates also allow you to exclude options. For example, if you are targeting CMOs and want to make sure marketing managers aren't seeing your message, you can exclude the title *marketing manager*.

Figure 9-25 shows an example on my personal LinkedIn news feed from New Relic. It gives me the opportunity to follow New Relic on LinkedIn, Like the post, comment on it, or share it. Their CTA is to a recent blog post.

New Relic, Inc. · Sponsored

The 'Developer is King' roundtable discussion continues! Hear insights on how these coding CEOs are trailblazing the self-service model and building a community of app developers here: ow.ly/o90Q8

CEO Roundtable Videos: App Developers –Agents of Change and Influence

blog.newrelic.com · Part two of our roundtable series with coding CEOs and founders continues as they discuss the self-service model and building a community of app developers.

➕ Follow New Relic, Inc. · Like (57) · Comment (2) · Share · 19s ago

👍 Neil Smith, Huan Hoang and 55 others

Figure 9-25: A New Relic Sponsored Update.

Like other ad forms, you can choose your budget and decide whether you want to pay cost-per-click (CPC) or cost per 1,000 impressions (CPM).

To post a Sponsored update, go through the following steps:

1. **Click Business Services in the top navigation of your LinkedIn home page and then click Advertise.**

2. **In the Campaign Manager, click Get Started, which brings you to the LinkedIn ad creation interface. Then click Sponsored Update.**

3. **From there, you can name your campaign, choose the update you want to sponsor, and target your update.**

4. **After you have determined your update specifics, you can determine your cost model, daily budget, and start and stop date for your update.**

Setting up LinkedIn ads

LinkedIn ads are a powerful way for companies to target very specific profiles not found in other advertising and social platforms. Because of LinkedIn's focus on professional networking, the data available maps nicely to the lead data you are probably looking for, such as geography, industry, job title, company, LinkedIn group membership, and other demographic targeting.

As with the other social channels, you can set your own budget through pay-per-click or impressions. You can also stop your ads anytime if they aren't working for you, so that gives you the flexibility to test.

LinkedIn also gives you many options to control the look and feel of your ad, including text only, image, and video ads. According to LinkedIn, an image can help your ad get up to 20 percent more clicks, so keep that in mind.

To set up a LinkedIn ad, take the following steps:

1. **Go to** `https://www.linkedin.com/ads/` **and click Get Started.**

2. **Under what type of campaign you would like to create, click the box labeled Create an Ad.**

3. **Next, as shown in Figure 9-26, name your campaign, decide on ad variation, add an image or a video as indicated in the Media Type drop-down list, and create your copy where it says Click to Enter a Headline and Click to Enter Description of up to 75 Characters.**

   You can also see a preview of your ad on the right side of your screen.

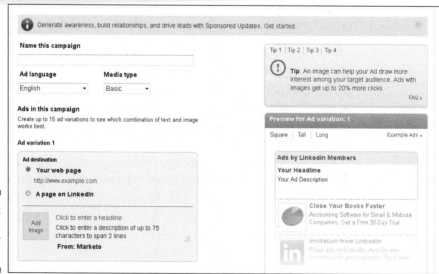

Figure 9-26:
Creating
your
LinkedIn ad.

4. **After you have completed everything, click Next and choose your target audience by location, company, job title, school, skills, group, gender, and age, as shown in Figure 9-27.**

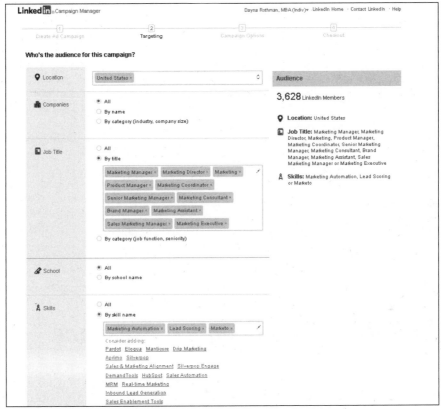

Figure 9-27:
Targeting
your
LinkedIn ad.

5. **The last step is choosing your budget — either CPC or per 1,000 impressions.**

   Here you can also choose how long LinkedIn will run your ad and whether you want lead collection (enabling functionality for a lead to request contact from a company representative). When you are finished, click Save Changes and Checkout. Figure 9-28 shows these final steps.

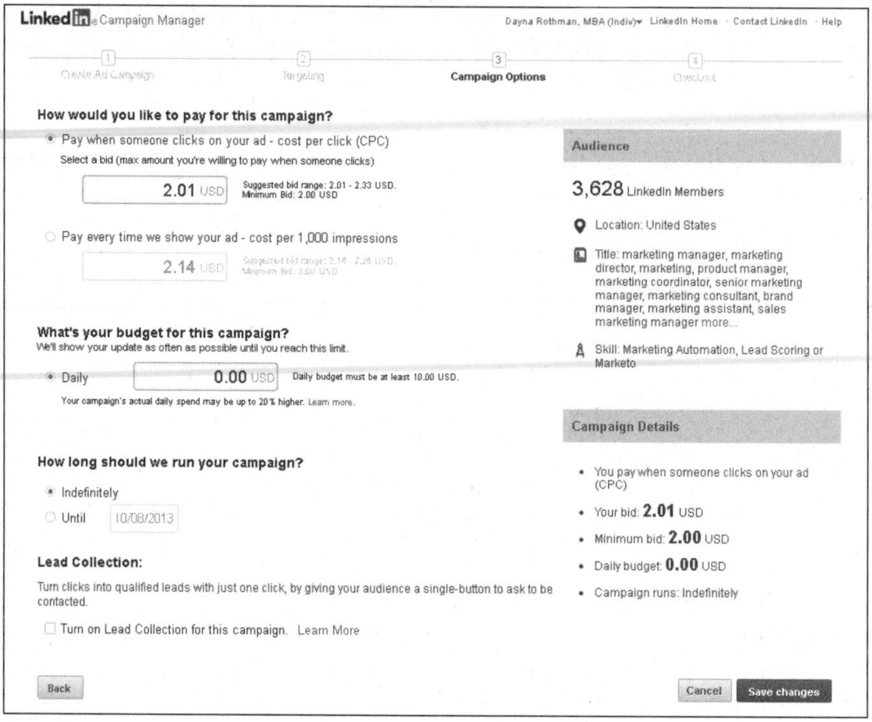

Figure 9-28:
Budgeting
your
LinkedIn ad.

Building Your Google+ Presence

Although there is much debate over Google+'s actual active user data, which they cite at close to 400 million users, we know one thing for sure: Google+ has an impact on search results. Because Google+ is the social network of the biggest search giant, it's natural that search and Goggle+ go hand-in-hand. Because of Google+'s +1s and author rank, Google+ is a must-have for any lead-generation marketer looking to be high in organic search rankings.

Google+ also offers interesting and unique avenues for engagement with leads and followers — including Google+ Hangouts, where you can set up a live telecast between multiple people.

Acknowledging the relationship between Google+ and search engine optimization (SEO)

The critical element about Google+ for lead generation is the clear benefits the social channel has on search results. The first step to start reaping the benefits of Google+'s impact on SEO is enabling Google Authorship for your content via AuthorRank. What is AuthorRank? It takes into account social signals and content authority so that search engines can give smarter, more relevant results. Long gone are the days of keyword stuffing, which flooded the Internet with mediocre, often worthless, content. Useless content reflects poorly on Google's ability to immediately deliver relevant content to a search. Google is now looking at deeper signals that your site is an educational authority. You must link all of your content to your business Google+ page and have influential individuals from your company claim ownership of this content. The kicker is that you must have a Google+ account to enable Google Authorship.

Take a look at Figure 9-29, which shows an example of what Google Authorship looks like when it comes up in Google's organic search results. I did a search for *lead generation*. Marketo comes up on the first page of search results, with an image of Jon Miller, Marketo's cofounder. Jon has claimed Google Authorship of this content.

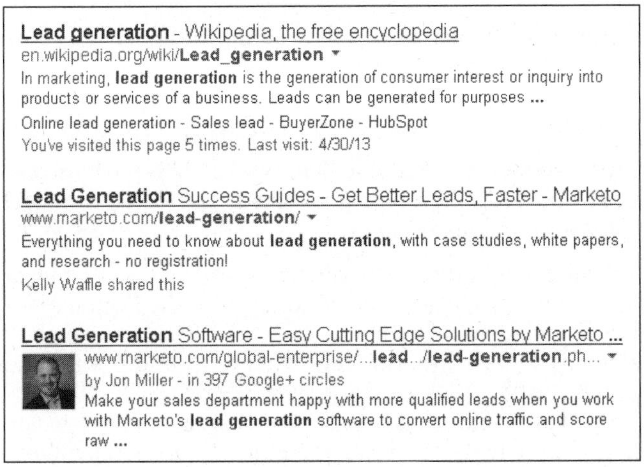

Lead generation - Wikipedia, the free encyclopedia
en.wikipedia.org/wiki/**Lead_generation** ▾
In marketing, **lead generation** is the generation of consumer interest or inquiry into
products or services of a business. Leads can be generated for purposes ...
Online lead generation - Sales lead - BuyerZone - HubSpot
You've visited this page 5 times. Last visit: 4/30/13

Lead Generation Success Guides - Get Better Leads, Faster - Marketo
www.marketo.com/**lead-generation**/ ▾
Everything you need to know about **lead generation**, with case studies, white papers,
and research - no registration!
Kelly Waffle shared this

Lead Generation Software - Easy Cutting Edge Solutions by Marketo ...
www.marketo.com/global-enterprise/...**lead**.../**lead-generation**.ph... ▾
by Jon Miller - in 397 Google+ circles
Make your sales department happy with more qualified leads when you work
with Marketo's **lead generation** software to convert online traffic and score
raw ...

Figure 9-29:
Google
Authorship
in organic
search
results.

To set up Google Authorship, take the following actions:

1. **Go to your Google+ business page and your personal profile (you need to have a Google+ personal profile).**

2. **Let Google know you are a content author by signing into your Google+ profile, going to the About tab, and adding links to the Contributor To section by clicking the Edit button, as shown at the bottom of Figure 9-30.**

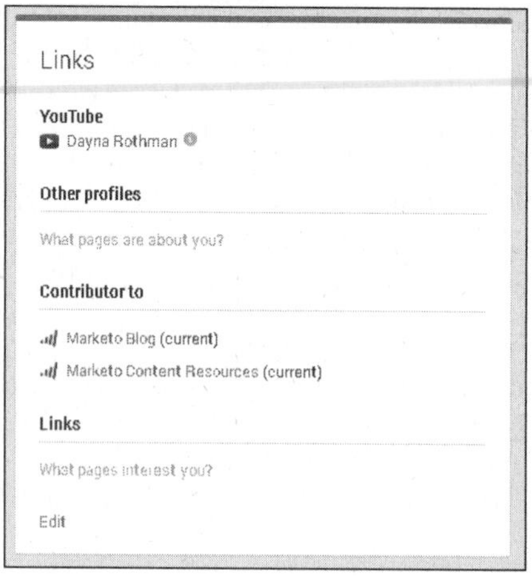

Links

YouTube
▶ Dayna Rothman ⓘ

Other profiles

What pages are about you?

Contributor to

Marketo Blog (current)

Marketo Content Resources (current)

Links

What pages interest you?

Edit

Figure 9-30: Adding contributor links to your Google+ page.

3. **From your content management system (CMS), such as WordPress, Drupal, or SilverStripe, link to your Google+ page by adding `rel="author"` in the link, as shown in a Kissmetrics example in Figure 9-31.**

You can download an SEO plug-in for most CMSs that you can use to add your Google Authorship. You can set up Google Authorship for both your blog and website content.

If you are using WordPress for your blog, for a user to claim authorship, go to the user's profile and select Edit. Under the Contact Info section, you will see an area to enter your Google+ URL. Because you have already linked your profile to your content, your authorship will be set up.

The other important factor that Google takes into account from Google+ is the +1 button. This is fairly simple. Embed the +1 button on your site and blog. (See Chapter 8 if you need a refresher on how to add a +1 button.) When someone +1s your post or page, it shows up in Google search results. In fact, according to a study conducted by HubSpot, websites with a +1 get 3.5 times more visits on their Google+ page, which of course helps with organic search results.

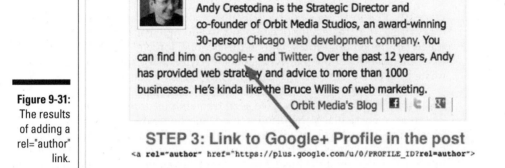

Written by Andy Crestodina

Andy Crestodina is the Strategic Director and co-founder of Orbit Media Studios, an award-winning 30-person Chicago web development company. You can find him on Google+ and Twitter. Over the past 12 years, Andy has provided web strategy and advice to more than 1000 businesses. He's kinda like the Bruce Willis of web marketing.

Orbit Media's Blog

STEP 3: Link to Google+ Profile in the post
`<a rel="author" href="https://plus.google.com/u/0/PROFILE_ID?rel=author">`

Figure 9-31: The results of adding a rel="author" link.

Getting noticed with Google+ Hangouts

The other cool aspect of Google+ is the Hangout functionality. A Google+ Hangout allows you to essentially "hang out" with anyone anywhere and broadcast it live over your Google+ profile. Think of the Google+ Hangout as a casual live event, but online. You can invite your followers to attend and promote your event, just as you would any other webinar. Google+ Hangouts show value in the following ways:

- ✔ **Content:** You can use the Google+ Hangout recording for additional content on your website and for your lead-generation campaigns.

- ✔ **SEO:** The more people who engage with and share your content on Google+, the more likely it is to show up high in organic search results. You can also get additional +1s and engagement if your Hangout is fresh and relevant.

- ✔ **Thought leadership:** One of the best ways to leverage a Google+ Hangout is to do a panel interview or interview with an influencer in your space, a thought leader in your company, or even partners and customers.

Getting Visual with Pinterest

Depending on your business, Pinterest can work wonders as a lead-generation machine. Because the platform is inherently visual, if you sell a product of some sort, Pinterest can be a gold mine. Even B2B companies shouldn't discount it because (hopefully) their content strategy overall is becoming more visual. Pinterest lends itself perfectly to blogs, infographics, slide decks, and more.

Currently, Pinterest does not have paid promotions (although at the time of this writing, they have announced plans to add native advertising). Closely watch how much time you spend on this channel for lead-generation purposes, as it still has not yet been proven, particularly for B2B. You don't want to waste time on a channel that might not have much value for you.

For instance, B2C businesses have seen tremendous growth from Pinterest — particularly the fashion, food, and home décor business. If you are selling clothing, you might have multiple Pinterest boards showing off hot new clothing lines. For B2B, it gets trickier. However, you *should* have a presence on Pinterest because it raises brand awareness and visibility, which is a must for lead generation.

Pinning your top assets

Hopefully you have a good amount of visual content in your arsenal by now. (If you don't, I hope you're starting to think about it now that I've been beating the idea of visual content into your head for the past 100 pages!)

You should be posting the following asset types on Pinterest:

- Infographics
- Visual slide decks
- Ebooks
- Memes and funny images
- Useful collateral pieces
- Blog posts
- Humor
- Product images and photos
- How-tos

Figure 9-32 shows an example of a Pinterest board.

Figure 9-32:
A Pinterest
board.

You can link your image to a chosen website page you want people to go to.
For example, if you pin an image of your latest ebook, you can link it right to
your ebook landing page.

Promoting your events through images

Another great way to leverage Pinterest is by showcasing images at an event
you are attending. Whether it's a fashion show or a tradeshow, you can capture
images of key attendees, vendors, and other exciting happenings at an event. You
can even have a board showcasing everything related to an event, such as invites,
contests, and more. Figure 9-33 illustrates a Pinterest board from Salesforce that
showcases their visual guide to Dreamforce, a large tradeshow. They highlight
things to do in San Francisco, nearby hotels, a survival kit, and so on.

Figure 9-33:
The
Salesforce
Dreamforce
Pinterest
board.

For a B2C example, take a look at Martha Stewart Living's Pinterest board for Gardening Tips & Ideas in Figure 9-34. As you can see, Martha Stewart does a wonderful job compiling gardening ideas and innovations. She also successfully captures her brand by providing easy do-it-yourself activities for her followers.

Figure 9-34:
The Martha Stewart Living's Gardening Tips & Ideas Pinterest board.

Showcasing your company culture

Because Pinterest works so well with candid images to show the human side of a brand, use Pinterest to tell your leads who you are as a company. Never discount the power of showing your humanity to a lead. Today's buyer is looking to create a relationship with his vendor. He needs to buy into your *company* as much as he needs to buy into your product or service. So use Pinterest as a way to show off your company culture, flair, and humor.

Take a look at Salesforce's Pinterest boards in Figure 9-35. They take a very cool approach to the platform and have boards that show off the San Francisco lifestyle, Salesforce office styles, why their employees love working at Salesforce, candid shots around the office, and more. In fact, the majority of their Pinterest boards are about company culture instead of showing off their product suite. Clearly, Salesforce sees Pinterest as a great opportunity to showcase who they are as company — and leads appreciate the transparency.

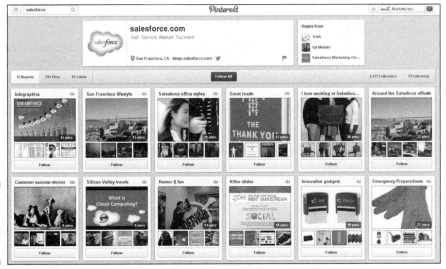

Figure 9-35:
Salesforce's
Pinterest
page.

Attracting Attention with SlideShare

SlideShare (`www.slideshare.net/`) was acquired by LinkedIn in May 2013 and is a community for sharing presentations like PowerPoint, videos, and webinars. The site has 60 million monthly visitors and 130 million page views. SlideShare also offers built-in lead-generation capabilities through embedded forms that can sync to your marketing automation platform.

You can upload slide decks, infographics, ebooks, webinars, and more onto the SlideShare platform. Because it's built as a social network for information sharing, you should treat it as an educational community. SlideShare also features popular assets on their home page for additional exposure.

You should strive to have a slide deck created for SlideShare about once per quarter. Not only because the quality of leads from SlideShare are so strong, but also because you can take an asset and, by repurposing the content in a visual way, give it additional lift.

For instance, Marketo created an ebook a couple of years ago called *Amplify Your Impact: How to Multiply the Effects of Your Inbound Marketing Programs.* The ebook did pretty well, with more than 13,000 views. Marketo then created a visual slide deck from the same content, which got 339,000 views on SlideShare — a pretty significant amount. The result was 4,482 new leads from this asset and 8,519 total downloads of the ebook. Marketo spent $4,620 developing the visual content, which amounted to a cost of about $1 per new lead.

Optimizing SlideShare for SEO

SlideShare offers prime real estate to brand your channel and optimize it for SEO. You can add a featured presentation, upload a custom template, offer social sharing capabilities, and tag each presentation with keywords. And in some cases, creating presentations that rank for certain keywords can be easier than ranking a blog post.

Be sure to include keyword-rich titles, descriptions, and tags to each presentation so that your deck ranks both inside SlideShare and on Google itself. Figure 9-36 shows what happens when you search for the term *visual content marketing* in Google. Marketo also created another visual SlideShare deck on visual content marketing. They optimized it for search results, so you can see it appear on the first page of Google search results. The first organic search result is on Marketo's website and the second one is from SlideShare.

Another benefit is that SlideShare allows users to embed presentations into other people's sites, which is great because that equals an inbound link.

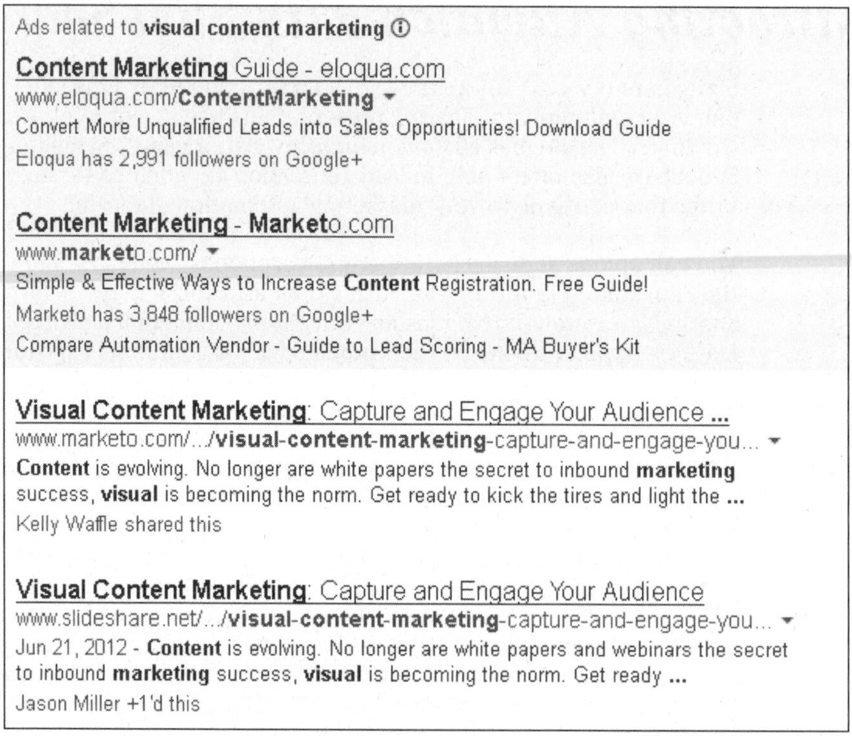

Ads related to **visual content marketing** ⓘ

Content Marketing Guide - eloqua.com
www.eloqua.com/**ContentMarketing** ▾
Convert More Unqualified Leads into Sales Opportunities! Download Guide
Eloqua has 2,991 followers on Google+

Content Marketing - **Market**o.com
www.**market**o.com/ ▾
Simple & Effective Ways to Increase **Content** Registration. Free Guide!
Marketo has 3,848 followers on Google+
Compare Automation Vendor - Guide to Lead Scoring - MA Buyer's Kit

Visual Content Marketing: Capture and Engage Your Audience ...
www.marketo.com/.../**visual**-**content**-**marketing**-capture-and-engage-you... ▾
Content is evolving. No longer are white papers the secret to inbound **marketing**
success, **visual** is becoming the norm. Get ready to kick the tires and light the ...
Kelly Waffle shared this

Visual Content Marketing: Capture and Engage Your Audience
www.slideshare.net/.../**visual**-**content**-**marketing**-capture-and-engage-you... ▾
Jun 21, 2012 - **Content** is evolving. No longer are white papers and webinars the secret
to inbound **marketing** success, **visual** is becoming the norm. Get ready ...
Jason Miller +1'd this

Figure 9-36:
Optimizing SlideShare decks for SEO.

Collecting leads through forms

SlideShare's lead-generation capabilities really stand out when it comes to collecting lead data. SlideShare has the ability to embed a lead-generation form directly into your presentation at the end. If you enable that feature, the form pops up after your presentation, and viewers can enter their information if they want to download the presentation for later viewing or learn more about your company.

Figure 9-37 shows an example of this form. As you can see, the form asks the viewer for first name, last name, work email, phone, and company.

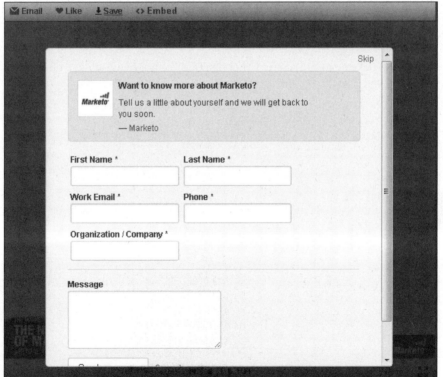

Figure 9-37:
A SlideShare lead capture form.

You can either export these leads and add them to your CRM, or if you have a marketing automation platform, sync directly with SlideShare, if your software has that capability. This way, your leads get directly into your database and you can trigger alerts based on keywords that indicate buyer behavior.

Chapter 10

Getting Found Through Search Engine Optimization

....

In This Chapter

▶ Understanding the major search engines

▶ Learning about Google's algorithm and what it means for SEO

▶ Working with keywords to improve your chances of getting found

▶ Optimizing your site with on-page SEO and link-building techniques

....

*A*ccording to Mashable, more than 1.1 billion people use Google search each month, making 114 billion searches. Pretty incredible, right? It's pretty much guaranteed that your potential leads are conducting millions of searches each month using keywords that describe what you are selling exactly, or the problem you help solve. And if you aren't optimizing your website for search, you are not getting found.

Picture this: You are the sales director of a business looking for customer relationship management (CRM) software. So you search Google for *B2B CRM software*. The sites that are most optimized for search appear in the first couple of pages of results. Most likely, you are going to click the results that appear on the first page. In fact, a recent study done by the company Chitika reports that the top listing in Google's organic search results receives 33 percent of the traffic, compared to 18 percent for the second position. And that's just talking about the first and second results! Imagine if you appear on the second or even third *page*? The farther down in the search results you appear, the less likely it is that leads are going to find your company.

In order to appear on the first page of Google so that leads can find your company immediately, your website needs strong search engine optimization (SEO). Not all companies garner immediate name recognition, and even those that do still use SEO methods to introduce themselves to new audiences. In order to get that brand awareness, you need to get in front of people. Search Engine Land, a news source for everything SEO, defines SEO as "the process of getting traffic from the 'free' or 'natural' listings on search engines. These listings are ranked based on what the search engine considers most relevant to the users. Payment isn't involved, as it is with paid search ads."

Just optimizing your website for search will not guarantee you a page one listing on a search engine. If only life were that easy! Remember that your competition is also vying for this position, and chances are they also know about SEO. Search engines factor in multiple criteria to return websites that they feel are the most useful to their users. Excellent SEO is just one piece of the puzzle. Make sure you also offer a quality product and a good browsing experience for your website visitors.

Maximizing Different Traffic Sources

SEO is an important part of lead generation because it makes your site more visible to potential leads. Without good SEO, you risk never being found. You can conduct as many inbound and outbound programs as you want, but if you don't have SEO, you are missing out on leads who are searching for target keyword phrases that describe your business and could lead them to your website. And it is safe to say that if a lead is searching for target keywords that describe what you are offering, she is probably farther along in the buying cycle than someone who happened upon an ebook through Twitter.

To understand how the search engines function, it is critical to understand the types of search options available to businesses.

Discovering site visitors with organic search

Organic search is the bread and butter of SEO and is really what you will be focusing on optimizing. Organic search results refer to the lists of websites that Google spits out after you type a keyword into its search bar.

Every website is *crawled* (or analyzed) by Google so that Google can determine what a site does and how relevant it is to a given keyword. It makes assertions about what a site does based on patterns of words and phrases within the site. (That is why keywords are so key!) Google's main crawler is called *Googlebot,* and it crawls the entire web *indexing* (also known as organizing) new sites based on guidance from a sophisticated algorithm (also known as a top-secret formula) that identifies which sites to crawl, how often to do it, and how many pages to index from each site.

Google and other search engines use many factors to determine where a site ranks for each keyword, and I'll go into more detail on specific strategy throughout this chapter. For now, the important distinction to make is that the organic search results that are influenced by good SEO are those that come up on the first page of results and are not marked with an Ad Related To label. See Figure 10-1 for an example.

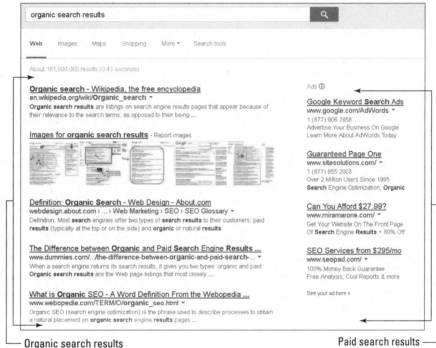

Organic search results   Paid search results

Attracting site visitors with paid search

I will go into much more detail about paid search later in Chapter 11; however, it's important to introduce the concept here because I want you to know the distinction between paid and organic results. Paid results are ads appearing on the very top and the right side of a search results page. Paid ads are purchased through the search engine on a cost-per-click (CPC) model. That means the buyer pays only for the number of times the link for that ad is clicked. For paid ads, you determine keywords, copy, and CTAs (calls to action) to use. In contrast to paid search results, money can't buy you good organic results — instead, you need to understand how to optimize your site properly.

Knowing Your Search Engines

There are three major search engines to consider: Google, Bing, and Yahoo!. Although Google clearly has the lion's share of search usage — 66.7 percent according to comScore — you do want to keep the other search engines in mind too. People have their favorites, and you certainly don't want to alienate those using Bing or Yahoo!.

For the most part, many of the techniques you apply to being optimized for Google apply to the other search engines as well, but there are a few things to keep in mind about each.

Grasping Google

Google is *the* search giant. With 66.7 percent of search traffic, it's safe to say that Google is the one you should be optimizing for. And Google is very tough to optimize for because all your competitors also know that Google is the 900-pound gorilla and are also vying for prominent listings on Google's search results. Google uses a top-secret and complex formula to determine what your website is and where it should rank, and this formula (or algorithm) changes constantly. You need to be up on the trends for how each algorithm change can affect your optimization.

Google also has a variety of tools to help you further optimize and analyze your site including Google Insights, Google Trends, Google Zeitgeist, and Google AdWords.

In addition to web search, Google has image search, news search, shopping, maps, news, videos, blogs, discussions, and more so users can customize and filter their search results.

Figure 10-2 shows an example of the first page of Google results when I search for the term *lead generation,* so you get an idea of Google's layout.

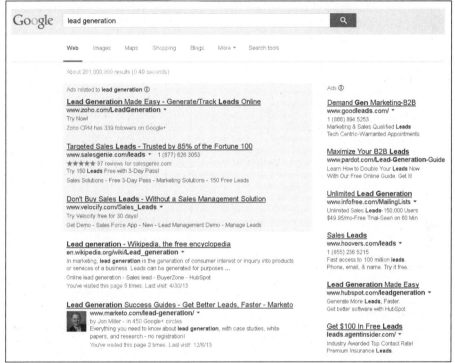

Figure 10-2:
Google
search
results.

Embracing Bing

Bing is Microsoft's search engine. Bing is a fairly new search engine and gets approximately 18 percent of search traffic. It's by no means catching up to Google's 66.7 percent, but it's still notable and worth spending some effort on. Bing also has its own algorithm for determining a page's rank compared to similar pages found elsewhere on the web. Because Bing is a much younger search engine, it's still trying to work out some of the kinks.

Bing does not have some of the rich indexing capabilities that Google has today. According to Search Discovery. an interactive marketing agency, Bing hasn't yet achieved the same sort of eye towards content, authenticity, and social signals as Google currently has.

Figure 10-3 shows an example of Bing's first page of results for *lead generation*. Notice the differences between the top page result here versus that in Figure 10-2. Also notice the addition of Related Searches and Social Results on the right side.

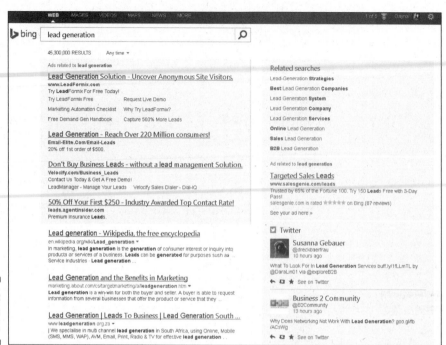

In 2009, Bing and Yahoo! signed a ten-year partnership for Bing's search engine technology to be leased to Yahoo! to provide search results from Yahoo!'s websites. Microsoft had incentive to do so to broaden its coverage against its main competitor, Google, but the jury is still out on the results.

Looking at Yahoo!

Yahoo!'s percentage of search share has dropped to 11.4 percent and continues to drop, presumably due to brand inconsistencies and an older search model. However, as with Bing, you don't want to lose out on those 11.4 percent of leads who are die-hard Yahoo! fans. They search for things while using any of Yahoo!'s sites that provide loyal customers with free email, stock information, fantasy sports leagues, instant messaging, and even weather information.

Like Bing, Yahoo!'s search engine simply isn't as sophisticated as Google's, and instead focuses on traditional SEO ranking factors that fail to recognize the importance of a multichannel world where social media and various devices reign supreme.

In 2009, Yahoo! agreed to lease Bing's search technology under the hood to power search results for their sites. One of the reasons, at the time, was to allow Yahoo! to focus on providing improved visitor experiences on its various website properties. Only time will tell how the effort and recent alliance with Microsoft will affect rankings.

Figure 10-4 shows the results page of the same search term *lead generation* on Yahoo!. Again, notice the differences in layout and the results. Ads appear to the top left and to the right.

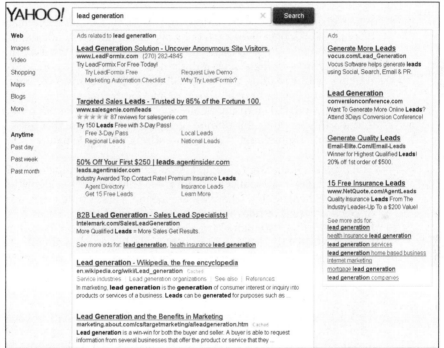

Figure 10-4:
Yahoo!
search
results.

Making the Most out of Google Algorithm Updates

Although Bing and Yahoo! should not be ignored, I'm going to focus mostly on Google for the rest of this chapter, especially because most of your search traffic leads will be coming from Google.

An important thing to note is that in order to be optimized for Google, you need to really keep up with the trends. That means knowing about Google's most recent algorithm updates and what that means for your SEO strategy. Google updates frequently, and sometimes an update can really change how you think about your search engine optimization. Some great resources to find the latest news about SEO are `http://searchengineland.com/` and `http://moz.com/`.

Understanding Hummingbird

When I first started on the outline for this book, Google had released Penguin 2.0. (Google gives each of its algorithm releases code names.) However, because Google changes their algorithm so frequently, they are now onto Hummingbird — which is an entirely new algorithm and a major overhaul. By the time you're reading this, they will most likely be onto yet another code name. According to Google search chief Amit Sighal, the last time the algorithm was updated so dramatically was in 2001. So Hummingbird is a big deal and worth spending a bit of time on, even if by the time this book comes out they're onto Hummingbird 2.0 or an entirely new code name.

The biggest change that Google announced with Hummingbird is its ability to decipher conversational search phrases. That means the algorithm can focus on the *meaning* behind what you are asking, versus only focusing on a string of keywords to give relevant results to the search engine user. Search Engine Land states that "Hummingbird is paying more attention to each word in a query, ensuring the whole query — the whole sentence or conversation or meaning — is taken into account, rather than just particular keywords. The goal is that pages matching meaning and intent do better than pages matching only a few words."

This is a very critical advance in search engine technology because Google is interpreting relevance and actual meaning. The upside for searchers like you and me is that Google will be returning results that make more sense in the context of their search.

But how do you optimize for relevance in Google's algorithms? Read on for more info.

Avoiding over-optimization

In the past, SEO was easy (well, kind of). You chose a few keywords and created pages and pages of copy with keywords stuffed in. This resulted in a website page that sounded unnatural and often contained crappy content.

However, the more keywords you were able to stuff in to a website or page, the greater probability that you'd appear higher up in the search results. Figure 10-5 shows an example of what I mean by *keyword stuffing*. Notice the unnatural placement of the keyword.

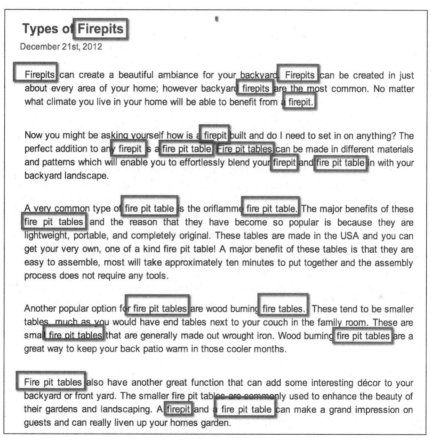

Figure 10-5:
Keyword
stuffing.

Over the years, Google figured out that keyword stuffing and over-optimization did not necessarily mean the best results for their audience of searchers. In fact, many times, a user clicked the first search result, only to be brought to a page filled with keywords without any real relevance to their initial query.

As the web has become more and more complex, search engines have followed suit, and Google now realizes that keywords alone mean nothing to relevant search results. Instead, quality content is what should be awarded higher placement in results. So yes, keywords are important and I'll talk about them at length, but keyword stuffing is a big no-no and can in fact downgrade you in search results.

Getting quality link-backs

Another key to a relevant and helpful website is quality link-backs from other well-regarded sites that also rank high on Google search results. Google believes that if other good websites are linking back to you, your site must also have something worth talking about, and thus, one that people would be interested in discovering.

Quality link-backs are typically given to destination pages such as a blog or other high-quality content because external websites want to focus on linking to interesting content, not keyword-stuffed pages.

Leveraging authentic content

Google and other search engines are heavily weighing content as a determining factor in where the website should rank. If a site is offering educational content to its visitors, it most likely has information that a searcher would find helpful. If a site has nonsensical information due to keyword stuffing or content that is way too basic for any searcher with common sense, the visitor leaves that website, and the search engine that provided this irrelevant site loses some credibility in this person's eyes. This could lead to searches being conducted on a different website, which means fewer eyeballs on the original search engine site, which means that website eventually has to lower the price it charges for people to advertise on their site. (Those costs-per-click will go down.)

Google is looking at authentic content on all of your pages including your home page, product pages, your blog, content resource center, and any other place on your site that has copy.

Google is telling users that it will penalize the use of sneaky, keyword-stuffed tactics like hidden text, so be careful of using some of these old SEO tactics. You won't necessarily get a warning email from Google if you're guilty of these things. You'll get the message loud and clear, however, when your search engine ranking drops like a brick.

Connecting social media

Another indicator of a high-quality website is social signals — how often are people engaging with you on social channels such as Twitter, Facebook, and Google+? Google's algorithm looks at the following when determining rankings based on social signals:

- Engagement on social channels such as your content being shared
- Mentions on social channels

> ✔ Linked content such as the `rel="author"` tag for Google+ (see Chapter 9 for more information on this and how to set it up)
>
> ✔ Backlinks from content-sharing sites like Pinterest

Choosing Your Keywords

The first step to creating your SEO strategy (after learning the search engine optimization basics and looking up Google's latest and greatest update), is to choose your keywords. Ask yourself what you want to rank for. This can be answered after asking yourself and your team a series of simple questions:

> ✔ What does my company do?
>
> ✔ What is the key search term(s) people use when they want to learn more about my business?
>
> ✔ What are my different product/service lines?
>
> ✔ What needs do my product/service fill?
>
> ✔ What are the features of my product/service lines?
>
> ✔ What keywords do my competitors rank for?
>
> ✔ Where am I ranking now for these keywords?
>
> ✔ What is the traffic opportunity for each keyword? (Read the Tip in the following section to discover how you can easily find out.)

Building a better keyword list

After you have the answers to the preceding questions, you can start thinking about what keywords make sense and then create a strategy to optimize for your chosen terms. Note that you won't have a fully baked and executed strategy overnight, so plan on instituting a step-by-step approach to optimization. Start with your top keywords, and then go from there.

If you are having trouble coming up with keywords, leverage Google Keyword Planner. You must have an AdWords account to access the tool (which you should have anyway), and you can search for keyword ideas and get estimates for search volume. It's a terrific place to start. Simply go to the Tools and Analysis navigation in your Google AdWords account and click on Keyword Planner in the drop-down menu.

Initially, a great way to keep track of your keywords and priorities is to create a spreadsheet that lists each keyword, keyword phrase, its priority, and the page URL you want your keyword to link to, which should be the page that you want to rank for. To determine keyword priority, think about the keywords that map closest to your core competencies as a business. For instance, if you own a hair salon, your top priority keywords might be *salon, hair, hair salon, beauty, hair styling,* and so on. And then, you might choose keywords like *waxing, coloring, makeup application,* and so on, for the next level of priority.

Optimizing for keywords

There are many ways to optimize for keywords throughout your site. After you choose and rank your top keywords and determine which page you want to rank for each term, you need to make sure each page is optimized — meaning you are making it easy for a search engine to know exactly what your page is talking about.

Of course, the first step to keyword optimization is through on-page SEO and good content, which I talk about more in depth in the next section. However, there are a couple of additional techniques you can use to make sure each page is optimized correctly for each keyword:

- ✔ **Headline:** Your headline on a web page should always match your keyword page titles. If a visitor clicks your page title in the search engine results, she expects a certain outcome. It is critical for user experience and keyword consistency to make sure your headline (H1, in HTML-speak) delivers the right message. Note that your H1 doesn't have to match your title exactly, but it should be similar enough that your visitor isn't confused. For instance, if I search for *marketing automation* on Google, I expect to go to a page that has a headline about marketing automation, such as "Marketing Automation Success Center." If I go to a page that says "lead nurturing software," I might be a tad confused.

- ✔ **Images:** Using images on your page can help your SEO rankings. Also note that your image can come up on Google image search, so you want to make sure all of your images are optimized. Moz, a popular SEO blog and consultancy, suggests that your image have a title, a filename that contains keywords (as opposed to unrecognizable abbreviations), and `alt` attributes (alternative text that is rendered when an image can't be seen, for instance, if someone views your page on a phone. The alt text tells a viewer what he should be looking at) as a good SEO practice. Each of these elements can be added via your website content management system (CMS).

Creating power content

Instead of keyword-stuffed content, create what's called *power content* for optimization. Power content is educational, informative, credible, and uses natural keyword placement for emphasis. To rank for certain words on certain pages, create power content to optimize your web site pages to be premiere educational resources on each subject. You want people to come to your site not only to view your content resources, but you also want to create a main page that people view as the definitive page on your keyword.

For example, Marketo wanted to rank for the keyword phrase *marketing automation* and chose their resource page, where all their content was housed, as the primary page URL they wanted to drive traffic to. They added power content to the page to help it rank.

Figure 10-6 shows an example of power content. Note that it reads naturally and answers many questions a visitor might have on the subject of marketing automation.

Marketing Automation Success Center

Marketing automation is a category of technology that allows companies to streamline, automate, and measure marketing tasks and workflows, so they can increase operational efficiency and grow revenue faster.

WHAT IS MARKETING AUTOMATION?

IDC predicts that the overall market for automating marketing will grow from $3.2 billion in 2010 to $4.8 billion in 2015.

Three key trends have been driving companies to adopt the technology.

- Changing buyer behaviors forced companies to change how they market and sell.
- The 2008 recession permanently altered how companies approach revenue generation and measurement.
- The software-as-as-service (SaaS) delivery model made the technology available to many more companies than ever before.

Marketing automation software is used in many modern marketing processes, including lead generation, segmentation, lead nurturing and lead scoring, relationship marketing, cross-sell and up-sell, customer retention, and marketing ROI measurement.

Some of these practices are possible at small volumes without software, but technology becomes essential with any scale. In particular, these processes all require:

- A central marketing database. A place for all your marketing data, including detailed prospect and customer interactions and behaviors, so you can segment and target the right message to each customer. Think of this as "system of record" for all your marketing information.
- A relationship marketing engine. An environment for the creation, management and automation of marketing processes and conversations across online and offline channels. Think of this as the "orchestra conductor" for your customer interactions.
- An analytics engine. A way to test, measure, and optimize marketing ROI and impact on revenue. Think of this as the place you go to understand what worked, what didn't, and where you can improve.

BASIC MARKETING AUTOMATION WORKFLOW

Nate Dame from SEOperks believes your power copy should include the following elements:

- ✔ Describe your keyword — what is it?
- ✔ Why is it important? How will this page help you?
- ✔ Three to five types, options, or topics related to your keyword
- ✔ Data and statistics (if available)
- ✔ One or two experts on a topic and a quote
- ✔ Why your company should be selected
- ✔ Conclusion
- ✔ A strong CTA
- ✔ External resources and further reading

Perfecting On-Page SEO

On-page SEO applies to the techniques you can use to make a certain page rank for a keyword. Remember that you want to assign one page to one keyword, so on-page SEO is very important — Google needs to know what should rank for what keyword.

The most important factor of on-page SEO is ultimately the content. At the risk of sounding repetitive here, great content drives relevancy, which aids greatly in boosting your website to the top of the search results. According to Moz, your content must have the following attributes:

- ✔ **It must supply a demand:** Great SEO on-page content fills a need. The highest ranking goes to the page that answers that need most specifically. Good content can be web copy, video, images, or sound.

- ✔ **It must be linkable:** People need to link to your content. If people don't link to your content, the search engines won't rank it high.

To set the stage, Figure 10-7 shows a skeleton layout of a perfectly optimized page for the keyword term *chocolate donuts*.

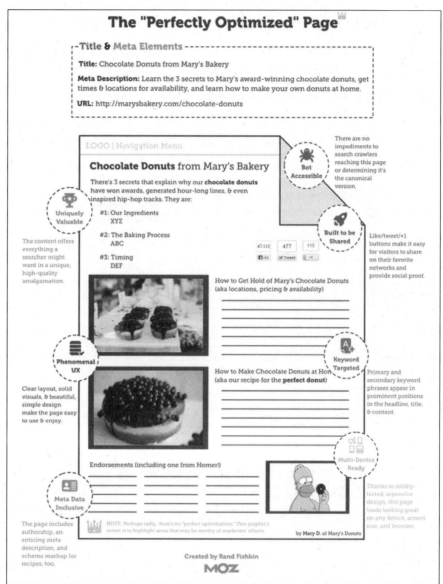

The "Perfectly Optimized" Page

Title & Meta Elements

Title: Chocolate Donuts from Mary's Bakery

Meta Description: Learn the 3 secrets to Mary's award-winning chocolate donuts, get times & locations for availability, and learn how to make your own donuts at home.

URL: http://marysbakery.com/chocolate-donuts

LOGO | Navigation Menu

Chocolate Donuts from Mary's Bakery

There's 3 secrets that explain why our **chocolate donuts** have won awards, generated hour-long lines, & even inspired hip-hop tracks. They are:

#1: Our Ingredients
XYZ

#2: The Baking Process
ABC

#3: Timing
DEF

How to Get Hold of Mary's Chocolate Donuts
(aka locations, pricing & availability)

How to Make Chocolate Donuts at Home
(aka our recipe for the **perfect donut**)

Endorsements (including one from Homer!)

NOTE: Perhaps sadly, there's no "perfect optimization." This graphic's intent is to highlight areas that may be worthy of marketers' efforts.

by Mary D. of Mary's Donuts

Bot Accessible — There are no impediments to search crawlers reaching this page or determining it's the canonical version.

Uniquely Valuable — The content offers everything a searcher might want in a unique, high-quality amalgamation.

Built to be Shared — Like/tweet/+1 buttons make it easy for visitors to share on their favorite networks and provide social proof.

Phenomenal UX — Clear layout, solid visuals, & beautiful, simple design make the page easy to use & enjoy.

Keyword Targeted — Primary and secondary keyword phrases appear in prominent positions in the headline, title, & content.

Multi-Device Ready — Thanks to solidly-tested, reponsive design, this page loads looking great on any device, screen size, and browser.

Meta Data Inclusive — The page includes authorship, an enticing meta description, and schema markup for recipes, too.

Created by Rand Fishkin
MOZ

Figure 10-7:
An optimized page.

Assigning title tags

After you have created content that is both linkable and in demand, you need to think about your title tags. A *title tag* describes a document or page. It appears in browsers, search engine result pages, and external websites. Your title tags should always align with a keyword term you have deemed important.

Figure 10-8 and Figure 10-9 show examples of title tags in each key location.

Figure 10-8: A title tag in a browser.

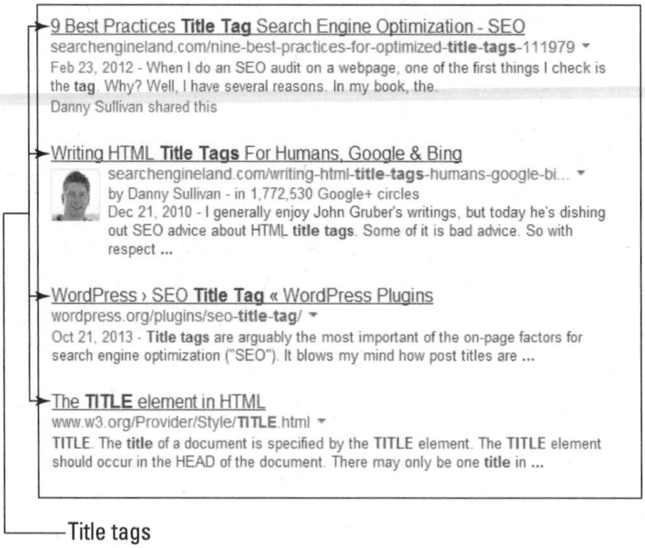

Figure 10-9: A title tag in a search engine result page.

The key to success with title tags is to accurately describe the content on each page. If your title tag is not relevant, viewers will bounce and the user experience will be hindered.

Here are some best practices from Moz to ensure your title tag is relevant to your visitors:

- ✔ Watch your length. Try to have titles fewer than 70 characters. If they're longer, search engines will cut off your headline.

- ✔ Place important keywords close to the beginning of your title tag.

- ✔ Assess how well-known your brand is — if it is well-known, include it in your title tag because it may induce more clicks.

- ✔ Create a compelling and interesting title tag.

Structuring your URLs

Your URL is what appears in the browser bar at the top of your page when visitors navigate to your site. Your URL should be concise and include keywords. You also want to structure your URLs to mimic your site's page structure in order to show a clear hierarchy. Search engines use this to determine how items relate to one another on your page and in the overall context of your keywords.

Figure 10-10 shows an example URL.

Figure 10-10:
A URL with a clear hierarchy.

Press Releases | Marketo News

www.marketo.com/about/news/press-releases

Note the hierarchy here. We know that Press Releases are in the News section, which is in the About primary navigation. It is logical, obvious, and I know exactly what the page is from looking at the URL.

Wording your meta description

Meta keywords may be a thing of the past, but you do need to focus on creating a good meta description for your page. A *meta description* is what the search engine pulls as the description to your page for search engine results, as seen in Figure 10-11.

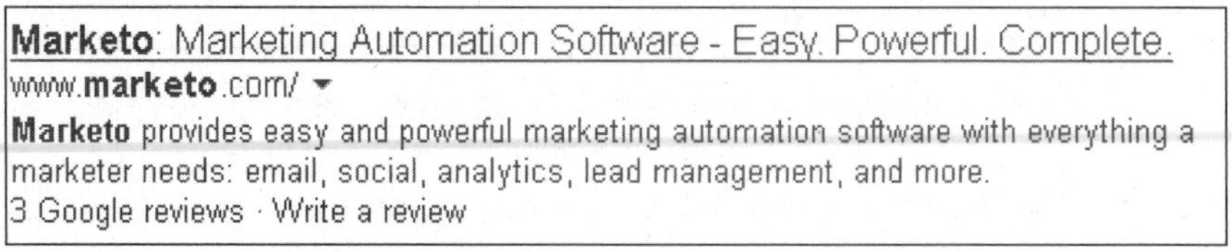

Figure 10-11:
A meta
description
in search
results.

> **Marketo**: Marketing Automation Software - Easy. Powerful. Complete.
> www.**marketo**.com/ ▾
> **Marketo** provides easy and powerful marketing automation software with everything a marketer needs: email, social, analytics, lead management, and more.
> 3 Google reviews · Write a review

This is your chance to up the ante and entice more leads to click. Think of your meta description as an online ad or even a tweet. Note that meta descriptions are only 160 characters, so you need to keep them short, sweet, and interesting. For optimal lead generation, think about including a strong CTA so you can ask for the click.

Utilizing Links in a Natural Way

Establishing authority on one (or all) of the major search engines requires a strong mix of on-page SEO and link-building efforts. Your content is only good if people actually link to it — this is what the search engines are paying attention to. Google determines authority through great content and a strong link-building profile.

Link building is the practice of adding links to your site *and* getting sites that rank high on Google to link to your content. When measuring link value, Google tends to look at the following factors:

- Overall popularity of the site — both globally and locally
- Having the right keywords in the anchor text
- Having a trusted domain
- Analysis of other links on the linking site
- Social signals from the linking site

You don't just need links — you need *good* links from reputable sources. Basically, those spammy links or links from cheap websites that you paid a pittance to keyword-stuff just aren't going to fly. In the end, you can't fake credibility.

Starting with on-page links

On-page links send a signal to Google that you have chosen a primary page to rank for each keyword. In order to do this, you need to build links throughout your site by linking the intended keyword to the intended page.

Figure 10-12 shows an example for the term *email marketing*. Marketo wants their email marketing resource page to rank for that term, so all of the link building they do externally reflects this.

A Smart Database with Smart Lists

That's why **modern, engaging email marketing** needs to be powered with a behavior-smart database at the core. This database serves as the system of record for all prospect and customer interactions within marketing, sales, and transactional systems. The result: a single place from which marketers can build highly targeted campaigns tied to trackable information about each individual contact.

With a smart database, marketers can easily target their subscribers using demographic AND behavioral filters and triggers, such as:

- **Demographic:** name, location, age, registration source, household, preferences, score, custom fields, etc.
- **Email history:** sent, opened, clicked, bounced, unsubscribed, etc.
- **Social:** shared content, referral, poll answer, etc.
- **Website:** visit, clicked link, completed form, referral source, search query, etc.
- **Campaign history:** campaign membership, campaign response, campaign success, etc.
- **Custom:** purchase history, deposit, withdrawal, cart abandonment, data usage, etc.

"Smart lists" can combine filters to create specific target segments: subscribers aged 18-25 who shared content via social, or customers with balances above a certain amount who visited the loans page twice in the last month. Plus, you can track campaign and response history for a solid record of how segments have performed.

This type of **email marketing system makes marketing self-reliant**, so that marketers can easily create and manage sophisticated behavioral-targeted campaigns on their own, without having to enlist the help of technical support. That means they spend less time modifying spreadsheets and waiting for IT, and more time building engaging, relevant campaigns.

Figure 10-12: Natural on-page link building.

Any post about email marketing on their blog is linked to this page. Note that you want to make sure your language is natural. Remember the "no keyword stuffing" rule? The same is true when you are dealing with link building. Use natural language. No stuffing.

Leveraging influencer relationships

In addition to on-page links that you create yourself, you also need other sites linking to your page. This can be done naturally by producing good-quality linkable content, but you also want to do some influencer outreach to get other sites with high domain authority to link to your page. Influencers in your space can be people and sites with high trust and authority, press and media outlets, sites with lots of social followers, or other influential people that you want to or currently do business with.

If you include influencer quotes and links on your own pages, they often link back to you. Reach out to influential people for each topic, ask for a quote, provide a link for them, and ask for a link back. Most influencers will be more than willing to help you, especially if you provide a link back to their site as well. Take a look at an example in Figure 10-13 of influencer quoting in event marketing power copy.

Figure 10-13:
An influencer quote in power copy.

essential to any company's bottom line.

THE IMPACT OF EVENT MARKETING

Events must be memorable to make an impact. Of course the desired impact depends on your goals, but most companies want events to be more than just a staged advertisement for their brand. When done well, events have the power to create a lasting and powerful impression of all that your company can deliver. By allowing people to experience and interact with your company, product or service while participating in an event, you are connecting with potential buyers.

"Not all events are created equal. Companies must consider live events an extension of their brand and content marketing and build events that really engage. For me that means thinking about the customer experience you REALLY want to portray. A 6x6 static stand is unlikely to meet that need!"

– Craig Hanna, EVP North America, **Econsultancy**, **@Cragster**

If you maintain these relationships, you can reach out to them from time to time to ask for favors or links. Influencer marketing is hard and probably should be a *For Dummies* book all its own, but it's an important concept when it comes to SEO for lead generation. If the influential people in your space trust and value your content, Google will rank it highly, and you can also build trust with your leads because your site is being linked to from influential sources that they trust.

Defining Your SEO Measurements and Analytics

To determine how successful your SEO strategy is at attracting leads and increasing your position in Google's rankings, you need a solid set of metrics. But first, you need to make sure you are benchmarking by measuring where you rank when you begin your SEO efforts so you know how far you have come:

- ✔ **Search engine ranking:** For each keyword, determine where you are ranking now, and make sure you keep track of rank as you increase the level of your SEO strategy over time. Note when you dip, and note when you climb. You should keep tabs on activity for all of the three major search engines.

- ✔ **Referring visits:** This is a log of all the traffic sources to your site. You want to look at direct navigation (when someone types in your URL directly), referral traffic (traffic coming from links on another website), and search traffic (traffic coming from any of the three major search engines).

- ✔ **Keyword phrase traffic:** Which keywords are sending traffic to your site? Are your efforts surrounding your top keywords bringing in more traffic? Or do you need to do something different? Also see what keywords you might not be targeting that bring in heavy traffic.

- ✔ **Conversion rates:** In the spirit of lead generation, you want to figure out who is converting from which keywords. You might need an SEO-specific tool to figure out this data, but ultimately you need to determine which keywords are converting and which aren't out of all of the traffic coming to your site from a search engine. That data can help you to determine where you should be spending your time.

- ✔ **Specific page traffic:** Which of your pages is getting the most traffic from search engines? And are these pages the right pages? You can also look at indexing by seeing whether Google is indexing your pages properly by doing a simple search to see where and how your page shows up. And if Google isn't, you need to work on determining why.

Part III

Linking Outbound Marketing with Lead Generation

Visit www.dummies.com/extras/leadgeneration to discover the best practices for sales enablement.

In this part . . .

- ✔ Get started with pay-per-click (PPC) ads and other paid channels
- ✔ Learn to target the right audience with direct mail
- ✔ Connect and create relationships with both online and offline events
- ✔ Discover how to hire and develop a sales team that closes

Chapter 11

Helping Buyers Find You with Pay-Per-Click Ads

. . . .

In This Chapter

▶ Understanding and leveraging Google AdWords

▶ Writing ad copy that compels and converts leads

▶ Creating your first ad with Google AdWords

▶ Measuring your ad performance over time

. . . .

*P*ay-per-click (PPC) advertising is a highly effective form of lead genera-tion that leverages online ads on a variety of websites, including search engines. For a PPC ad, an advertiser pays only if a visitor clicks on the ad. PPC ads are typically highly targeted using demographic and search criteria. Some PPC ads can also be behavioral, appearing on various websites that a lead visits after he leaves your page.

In today's noisy, multichannel world, PPC ads help your brand be seen across multiple channels including search and other websites. Wherever your lead goes, you go! Plus, if you aren't yet appearing on the first page of Google, PPC ads can help you be seen by your target audience, as paid advertising appears on the first page of results.

Getting Started

In this section, I focus primarily on search engine PPC ads because they are often the highest converting. The first step to getting started with PPC ads is to determine your goals. What are you trying to get leads to do? A good thing to note here is that you are now paying for ads and are starting to delve in outbound marketing techniques, so think clearly about your CTAs and your offers.

Every good PPC campaign should have a custom landing page. I highly urge you to stay away from using your home page as the landing page. More on PPC landing pages later in this section.

Starting a Google AdWords account

One of the first things you need to do is to create a Google AdWords account so you can create your ads and research your keywords. Go to `www.google.com/adwords/` and create your account.

To create a campaign, you have to make decisions about the following settings:

- **General:** Name your campaign so you have a clear idea what your ad is relating to. Come up with a standard naming convention that works for your company so that you can quickly scan for a campaign among a list (you will be building several over time).

- **Type:** Google allows their users to set their ad type based on goals such as Search and Display. That way, you can tailor your setup process to the type of ad you are placing.

- **Location and Languages:** You can select options for your ad to display only for people searching in certain locations. You can also specify a language. This option lets you fine-tune your target audience.

- **Networks and Devices:** Google allows you to control where your ads appear — directly in search results on its own websites or on partner networks (where other websites may lease Google's search bar and results, instead of spending energy building their own). You can also target certain devices, such as smartphones and tablets.

- **Bidding and Budget:** Set your bids and budgets. Your default bid is the most you're willing to pay per click for ads in your ad group. Your budget is the average amount you want to spend each day, total, on your campaigns.

- **Ad Extensions:** You can also include additional information on your ads such as links, your location, phone number, or Google+ page address.

After you get the hang of Google AdWords, you can then go in and set a campaign start and end date, schedule your ads for certain days of the week, or schedule your ads when they are most likely to get more clicks.

Take a look at the Google AdWords dashboard in Figure 11-1 to see what your PPC campaigns look like in the tool.

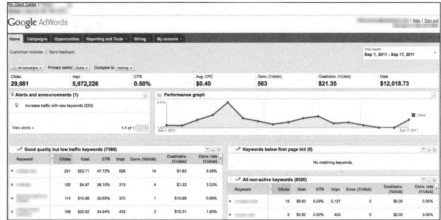

Figure 11-1:
The Google
AdWords
dashboard.

Creating your offer mix

When starting to create your PPC strategy, you want to first think about your objectives. What are your goals for your PPC ads? Driving opportunities or conversions? Or are you focusing on brand awareness? Because each company is different, your offer mix will be unique based on your business priorities.

As you do with many lead-generation strategies, think about how your PPC ads map to the sales funnel. You want to catch leads in each stage of the sales funnel; therefore, you have to create ads and offers that map to lead buying stage and search queries.

For instance, if someone searches for *what is marketing automation*, she's most likely in the beginning of researching marketing automation, so that person should be provided with a top-of-funnel-targeted ad and asset. If your lead is searching for the definition of your product, she certainly isn't ready to buy.

In contrast, if someone searches for *comparing marketing automation vendors*, that person is farther along in the buying process and therefore should get a mid- to late-stage ad and asset discussing the differences between various vendors.

Here are some desirable outcomes for PPC that you might want to keep in mind as you determine your offer mix:

✔ Attracting site visitors that are actively looking for your product or service

✔ Keeping tight control of messaging throughout your buying funnel

✔ Increasing keyword ranking and traffic to your website

✔ Gaining insight into people's search queries and behaviors

✔ Tracking ROI details through paid advertising metrics

✔ Increasing your database size

Defining your audience

As with any successful lead-generation campaign, with PPC, you need to define your audience. Defining your audience also helps you conduct more thorough keyword research, determine who and how you can target leads, and have more proactive brainstorming sessions.

Based on the goals you determine, ask yourself the following questions:

✔ Who is my key target audience for this campaign?

✔ Am I going to be targeting based on physical location?

✔ Am I going to be targeting based on device (mobile, tablet, computer)?

✔ What pain points or questions will my ad address?

✔ What point in the buying cycle do I want to focus on with my ads?

✔ Do I want to be targeting people searching for competitors' keywords?

By answering this short series of questions, you can frame your list and have a better understanding of your ad copy, landing page copy, and the right CTA for your audience.

Choosing your keywords

After you have your goals outlined, know where your PPC ads fit in your funnel, and have started a Google AdWords account, it's time to choose your keywords. The best place to start is with a brainstorming session between you and your team. For each top keyword, think of all the iterations or phrases that might pertain to your goals.

Many keywords are similar to your SEO keywords that were discussed in Chapter 10; however, your PPC goals might differ from your SEO goals, so think outside of the box and map your PPC keywords to your sales funnel.

Keep track of your brainstorming keywords in a spreadsheet. Here is an example of what a brainstorm might look like for the phrase *lead generation:*

Lead generation

Generating leads

Lead-generation marketing

Lead-generation management

Managing lead generation

Lead-generation tools

Tools for lead generation

What is lead generation?

How can I do lead generation?

Lead-generation solutions

Sales lead generation

Lead-generation programs

Programs for lead generation

B2B lead generation

Automated lead generation

You can also reference a keyword tool. Google AdWord provides a Keyword Planner. Simply go to the Tools and Analysis navigation on your home page and click Keyword Planner. Alternatively, you can also do a Google search for *keyword tool* or *keyword generator* and find tools that way.

Take a look at Figure 11-2 for a look inside Google Keyword Planner and its feedback for the keywords *hotels cabo*. Their tool shows you relevant keywords, average monthly searches, competition, and average cost-per-click (CPC).

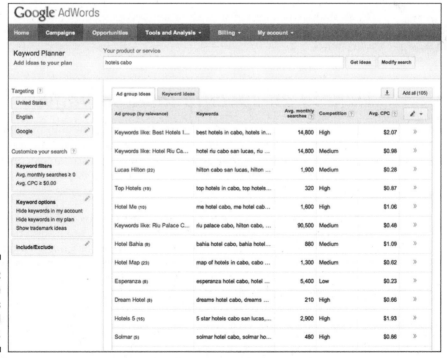

Figure 11-2: Google AdWords Keyword Planner.

From the information you gather with a keyword planner, you can then determine which keywords are your best bet for generating leads.

Then combine like keywords together to form ad groups. According to *Web Marketing Today*, an online magazine that includes marketing tips and advice, a best practice is 10–15 keywords per group. Sometimes, however, it makes sense to do more or fewer. Groups and segmentations can be determined by like words or meanings. Using my *lead generation* keyword example, I can have a group for lead-generation software and include all of the iterations of lead-generation software.

Think about running a negative campaign using *negative keywords* — choosing keywords that will *not* trigger your ad. For instance, if you are a consignment store selling used designer shoes, you can set up a campaign that doesn't trigger your ad when someone searches for *new designer shoes*. Negative keyword usage can help you parse out good leads from bad.

After you have your keywords selected, ask yourself

- ✔ How relevant is this keyword to my website, my products and services, and my content?
- ✔ If someone searches for this keyword, will she find my offerings useful?
- ✔ Do I have content to offer for this keyword or will I have to create this content?

You should also make a clear distinction between early- and late-stage keywords. The ad copy and offers that you create should map tightly to your funnel.

Making ad-specific landing pages

All PPC ads should go to a landing page that speaks to your exact offer. It is a bad practice for a PPC ad to go to a page on your website. You want leads to engage with your offer and ultimately fill out a form so you can get that valuable conversion. If your landing page doesn't speak to your ad or their search query, they will bounce.

In the next section, I cover what you want the user experience to be when it comes to PPC ads and landing pages. I have entered the search query *how can I track marketing analytics* in Google. On the results page, I see three ad options. I'll click the Marketing Analytics Guide — Equate Marketing with Revenue ad. Sounds perfect and aligns to my initial query.

Take a look at my search query and the related ads in Figure 11-3.

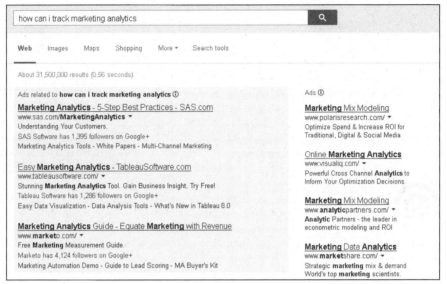

Figure 11-3:
A Google
search
query.

After I click the ad, I'm brought to a specific landing page that is unique to my ad, as shown in Figure 11-4. Notice that the main heading (H1) of the landing page closely matches the ad.

The landing page also follows these standard lead-generation best practices by having

✔ Engaging graphics

✔ Bold copy

✔ Bullet points that clearly outline what is in the asset download

✔ A clear CTA button

✔ A short form

The main point to take away here is that once I click on the ad, I am brought right away to a page that speaks to my search. As a result, I am way more apt to fill in my information. If I had been brought to a generic website page, I probably would have left to go search for something else more applicable.

Marketo

THE DEFINITIVE GUIDE TO MARKETING
METRICS & ANALYTICS

REVENUE
ROI
PROJECTIONS   LEADS

Finally, a book dedicated to driving and calculating Marketing success.

This all-encompassing guide to **Marketing Metrics and Marketing Analytics** shows marketing professionals how to talk the talk of C-level executives in terms of forecasting and reporting, and walk the walk to the revenue table by leveraging the metrics that matter. With compelling **graphics and real-life examples** of Marketo's own metrics and tactics, this guide offers best practices and techniques for harnessing data to not only prove, but improve ROI.

This 70 page guide will show you:

- The right metrics for understanding and interpreting marketing results
- Why measuring marketing programs is difficult, and how to do it correctly and efficiently
- Revenue metrics that gets the executives' attention and prove marketing ROI
- The critical elements of a marketing dashboard
- And much, much more!

The bottom line of any business is the top line: **Revenue** and **Growth**. Let the Definitive Guide to Marketing Metrics and Marketing Analytics help you gain the insights you need to grow your company's revenue and demonstrate the true value of your marketing.

DOWNLOAD DEFINITIVE GUIDE

Work Email: * drothman@marketo.com
Company: * Marketo

DOWNLOAD GUIDE

* Required. Your privacy is important to us.

Tweet +1 Share
Like Be the first of your friends to like this.

Figure 11-4:
A model
PPC landing
page.

Creating Your Ad Copy

The next step to a great PPC campaign is writing your ad copy. This is tricky because you have limited space to get your message across. Basically, you have one 25-character headline and two 35-character lines to entice your leads to click. Pretty challenging, right?

Creating ad copy is a critical part of your PPC campaign. However, don't worry too much because you can easily test your copy and change your ads instantaneously through AdWords.

Here are five golden rules of PPC ad writing according to Search Engine Watch:

- Use clear, easy-to-understand words
- Use vivid, emotional language

> ✔ Focus on both keywords and more importantly, the intent behind them
>
> ✔ Have a clear compelling offer and CTA
>
> ✔ Don't go overboard with abbreviations and truncated phrasings

Be sure to do some competitive research to see what your competitors are doing. Make sure your copy stacks up to theirs!

Targeting and relevancy

Consider what your leads are searching for when they come across your ad, and write copy that resonates with their need. Be sure to address pain points directly, either by calling them out or by creating copy that addresses the issue. If your ad isn't relevant, your lead will not click.

As an example, I searched for *buying a CRM solution*. Take a look at the results in Figure 11-5. Out of the paid ads at the top of my search, the ad from Business-software.com is the most relevant to my search in both headline and copy. If I click their ad, I'm promised an analysis of the top 40 CRM vendors. This is perfect for my query.

Figure 11-5:
Relevant
headlines
and copy.

Top 40 **CRM** Vendors Rated 1 (650) 288 3452
www.business-software.com/Best**CRM** ▾
2013 Top 40 **CRM** Software Rankings. Download Report from Top IT Analyst
Business-Software.com has 509 followers on Google+
Top 6 Free CRM - Top 15 Cloud CRM - Top 40 CRM

Crafting your title

Your ad headline is what stands out the most, and a winning headline grabs the attention of your lead and compels her to click. Headlines are so important, in fact, that 80 percent of people will only read a PPC ad headline, whereas only 20 percent actually read the rest. You have very limited real estate to create a title that draws your leads to you.

Create headlines that are emotional. If a person is searching, he is looking for information or, better yet, he has a problem that needs to be solved. Emotional writing elicits an emotional response from your lead. Use strong verbiage and don't be afraid to use words or phrases such as *now*, *warning*, *#1*, and so on. As a test, I conducted a search for *PPC ad help*. Figure 11-6 shows the ads that appeared in my search results. All three ads used emotional language to draw me in, such as *best* and *leader*. Each business wants me to believe that they are the best at what they do.

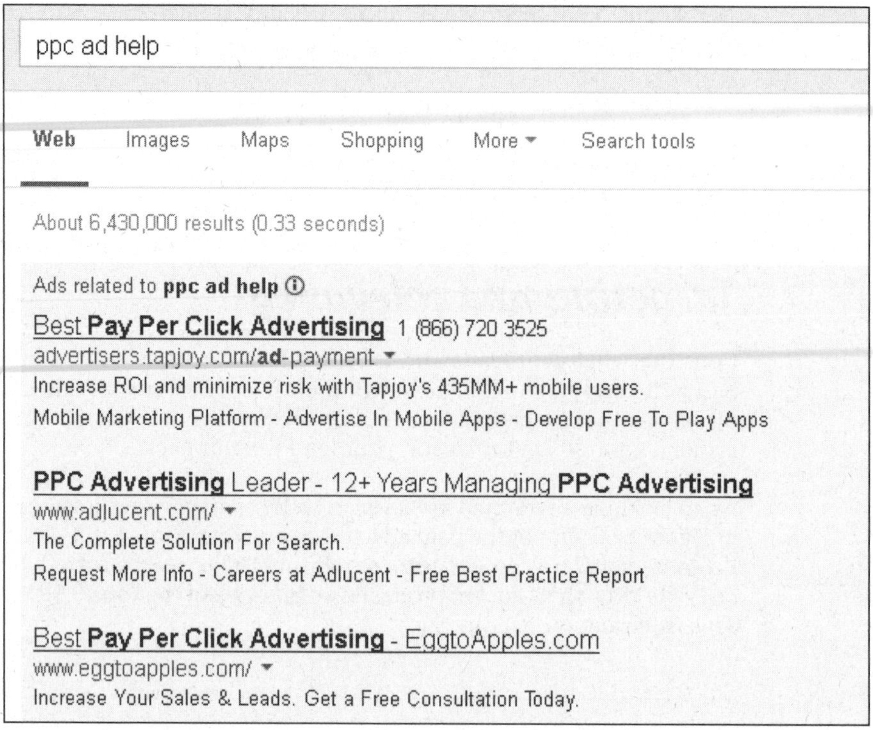

ppc ad help

Web   Images   Maps   Shopping   More ▾   Search tools

About 6,430,000 results (0.33 seconds)

Ads related to **ppc ad help** ⓘ

Best **Pay Per Click Advertising** 1 (866) 720 3525
advertisers.tapjoy.com/**ad**-payment ▾
Increase ROI and minimize risk with Tapjoy's 435MM+ mobile users.
Mobile Marketing Platform - Advertise In Mobile Apps - Develop Free To Play Apps

PPC Advertising Leader - 12+ Years Managing **PPC Advertising**
www.adlucent.com/ ▾
The Complete Solution For Search.
Request More Info - Careers at Adlucent - Free Best Practice Report

Best **Pay Per Click Advertising** - EggtoApples.com
www.eggtoapples.com/ ▾
Increase Your Sales & Leads. Get a Free Consultation Today.

Figure 11-6:
Emotional
PPC
headlines.

These headlines show authority by using language that describes the advertiser as a leader in the space. As a searcher, I want to click the ad for the company that is the *best* at helping with PPC ads.

In my search, I found another great example of a creative PPC headline.
Figure 11-7 shows an ad from a company called BoostCTR. They use a question in their headline to grab my attention.

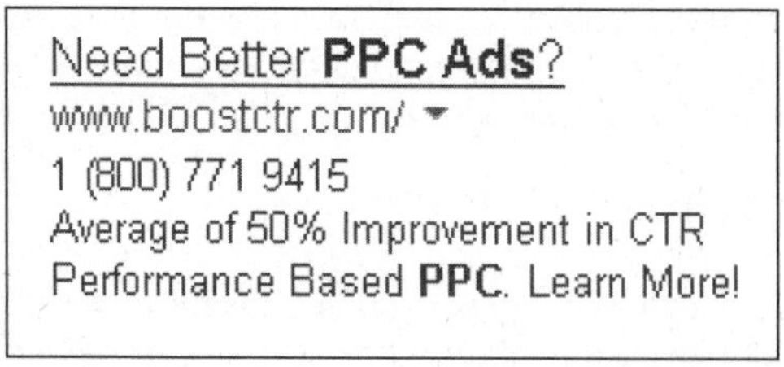

Need Better **PPC Ads**?
www.boostctr.com/ ▾
1 (800) 771 9415
Average of 50% Improvement in CTR
Performance Based **PPC**. Learn More!

Figure 11-7:
Using ques-
tions in PPC
headlines.

Here is another great example from BoostCTR, as seen in Figure 11-8. For my next search, I input *writing PPC ad copy*. Their ad popped up again — not only with a question this time, but also with an affirming statement of 50 percent click-through improvement. They're speaking directly to me through a question, but also showing authority by claiming my CTR will go up 50 percent if I use their service.

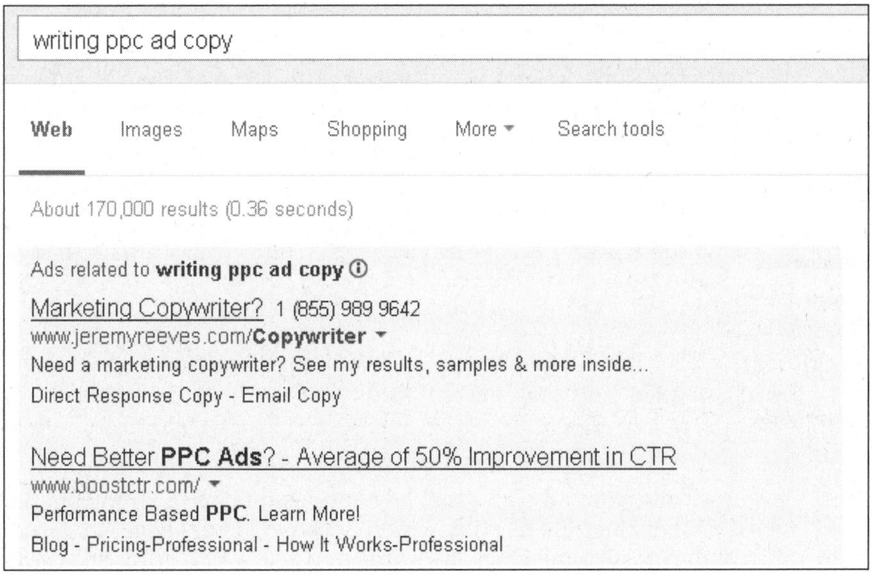

> writing ppc ad copy
>
> **Web**   Images   Maps   Shopping   More ▾   Search tools
>
> About 170,000 results (0.36 seconds)
>
> Ads related to **writing ppc ad copy** ⓘ
>
> Marketing Copywriter? 1 (855) 989 9642
> www.jeremyreeves.com/**Copywriter** ▾
> Need a marketing copywriter? See my results, samples & more inside...
> Direct Response Copy - Email Copy
>
> Need Better **PPC Ads**? - Average of 50% Improvement in CTR
> www.boostctr.com/ ▾
> Performance Based **PPC**. Learn More!
> Blog - Pricing-Professional - How It Works-Professional

Figure 11-8: Showing authority and ROI in PPC headlines.

Writing your ad copy and CTAs

Your ad copy is also critical to lead conversions, and you have to cram in a lot in a very small space. It needs to show value, credibility, and must stand out. Whereas you might shy away from capital letters and exclamation points in your regular marketing copy, all bets are off for PPC: You have to grab the attention of a lead amidst a sea of search noise.

Each ad should focus on one keyword, show value, and have a strong CTA if applicable. Take a look at the results I get when I search for *sales performance* in Figure 11-9. The first hit I get is from a company called Fantasy Sales Teams. Immediately I'm drawn to the name of their company. But more importantly, their ad copy speaks to their audience and includes a compelling reason for me to click. Who wouldn't want to model a sales contest after fantasy sports? It's a win-win and they clearly understand their audience.

Ads related to **sales performance** ⓘ
FantasySalesTeam® - Fantasy**Sales**Team.com
www.fantasy**sales**team.com/
Run better and more engaging **sales** contests modeled on fantasy sports!
Contact Us - How It Works - About Us - Benefits

Figure 11-9: Compelling PPC ad copy.

When I conducted the search *marketing analytics* shown in Figure 11-10, an ad from Tableau Software came up with a strong CTA to try their software for free. They have very concise copy reading, *Gain business insight. Try Free!*. Their call-to-action is clear.

Marketing Data **Analysis** - Stunning **Marketing Analytics** Tool
www.tableausoftware.com/
Gain Business Insight. Try Free!
Tableau Software has 1,238 followers on Google+
What's New in Tableau 8.0 - Get Your Free Trial - Data Analysis Tools

Figure 11-10: A strong CTA in PPC ad copy.

Basically, your ad copy must be concise and have a strong point-of-view or CTA. LunaMetrics recently released a handy cheat sheet that lists out some of the most compelling CTA words to use in a PPC ad. String these words together and voilà! You have strong ad copy. See a snippet of their cheat sheet in Figure 11-11.

LunaMetrics™ Call-to-Action Cheat Sheet

Be	(2)	Rush	(4)	Attain	(6)	Connect	(7)
Do	(2)	Save	(4)	Attend	(6)	Consult	(7)
Go	(2)	Seal	(4)	Beware	(6)	Contact	(7)
Act	(3)	Send	(4)	Browse	(6)	Deliver	(7)
Add	(3)	Shop	(4)	Create	(6)	Develop	(7)
Aid	(3)	Sign	(4)	Decide	(6)	Elevate	(7)
Buy	(3)	Sort	(4)	Design	(6)	Enhance	(7)
Get	(3)	Stop	(4)	Double	(6)	Imagine	(7)
Let	(3)	Take	(4)	Engage	(6)	Improve	(7)
Nab	(3)	Talk	(4)	Enlist	(6)	Lighten	(7)
Opt	(3)	Test	(4)	Enrich	(6)	Package	(7)
Own	(3)	Tour	(4)	Enroll	(6)	Perform	(7)
Pay	(3)	Turn	(4)	Ensure	(6)	Prevent	(7)
Put	(3)	View	(4)	Escape	(6)	Produce	(7)
Run	(3)	Zing	(4)	Exceed	(6)	Program	(7)
See	(3)	Apply	(5)	Expand	(6)	Qualify	(7)
Tap	(3)	Begin	(5)	Expose	(6)	Realize	(7)

Figure 11-11: The LunaMetrics call-to-action cheat sheet.

Creating a sample PPC ad

Now that you have a good sense of how to write your ad headline and copy, dig in and actually create a sample PPC ad via Google AdWords:

1. **Sign into your Google AdWords account and click Create Your First Campaign.**

2. **Next, fill in the following information:**

   - **Campaign Name:** Name it anything that's easy to remember.

   - **Campaign Type:** You can choose Search Network Only or Leverage Partner Sites. Your choice dictates the networks you are participating in.

   - **Location:** Enter an area to target or exclude. Click one of the radio buttons to select a very large area, such as the United States. Select Let Me Choose and enter your choice in the box below to select a more specific region or city.

   - **Language:** English is selected by default. Click Edit to select another language.

   - **Bid Strategy:** Set your own bids or have AdWords set your bids.

   - **Budget:** Enter the maximum dollar figure you'd like to spend daily.

   - **Ad Extensions:** You can extend your ad with location information, site links, phone number, and your Google+ profile.

3. **The next step is to create the ad itself. Name your ad group, write your headline, write your copy, and select your keywords.**

   Note that Google AdWords has a preview screen on the right side so you can see what your ad looks like.

4. **Click Save and Continue and enter in your billing information.**

Tracking Your Ad Performance

PPC ads have very clear performance indicators and metrics. Because your ads are easy to adjust, it's important to constantly keep track of the results so you can optimize your ads. Writing the right ad copy and getting the click can be a guessing game, and by vigilantly checking metrics, you can be agile and pivot strategies when needed.

Google Quality Score

The Google Quality Score aligns nicely with many of their new algorithm updates because it takes a look at the relevancy and quality of your ads, keywords, and landing pages. Having a high Quality Score means more than just being in the Google club. It also means that you might have a better ad position than someone who has a low score. By having a high Quality Score, you can also be eligible for certain ad extensions, and it affects your CPC, so this metric matters.

According to Google, your Quality Score is based on the following elements:

- **Expected Keyword Click-Through Rate (CTR):** Metric calculated based on past CTR and historical performance of the keyword in your ad
- **Display URL's Historical CTR:** How often your display URL receives clicks
- **Account History:** Overall CTR numbers on all ads and keywords
- **Landing Page Quality:** How relevant your landing page is and how easy it is to view
- **Keyword/Search Relevance:** How relevant your keyword is to what a searcher is looking for
- **Keyword/Ad Relevance:** How relevant your ad is to your keyword
- **Ad Performance:** How an ad performs on Google and partner sites
- **Targeted Devices:** How well your ad performs on multiple devices such as laptops, mobile phones, and tablets
- **Geographic Performance:** How successful you have been in regions you are targeting

Exploring basic PPC metrics

There are many standard metrics for PPC measurement. Many can be found in Google Analytics — they give a very easy read-out of performance — but it's good to know basic definitions and what you should be looking out for.

Here are some standard measurements that you want to keep in mind:

- **Impressions:** The measurement of how many times your ad is displayed when someone types in your search term. Note that this metric does *not* track clicks: It only tracks the number of times your ad actually appears.
- **Click:** The number of times your ad is actually clicked by a searcher.

✔ **Conversion:** The number of times a lead takes an intended action — that is, downloading a piece of content or attending a webinar. You can keep track of conversions in both Google Analytics and your marketing automation program.

✔ **Spend:** The amount of money you spend on a campaign.

And now you can have some real fun! You can combine these measurements to come up with other awesome measurements to analyze campaign performance:

✔ **Click-through rate (CTR):** This is the percent of impressions that yield clicks (clicks divided by impressions).

✔ **Cost per click (CPC):** This refers to the amount you are spending per click when you look at your entire campaign spending (spending divided by clicks).

✔ **Conversion rate:** This is your main metric and probably the most important of all paid search metrics. This is the percentage of clicks that actually convert (conversions divided by clicks).

Creating conversion tracking

It's important for you to know when a conversion ultimately came from one of your kick-butt PPC campaigns, so you can justify the monetary investment that you have invested into lead generation. In order to track that process, you need to set up conversion tracking. What is that, you say? *Conversion tracking* is when you (or your web developer) place a piece of code from Google AdWords in your landing page or thank-you page so you know how often a lead converts from your ad. The beauty here is now you know how well your ads are performing.

If you have a marketing automation tool, you can set up separate tracking codes for each landing page so the data reports back to your marketing automation platform. Then you can change a lead score and include your PPC ad in your reporting.

Some marketing automation tools now report back to Google with lead status information so you can view conversion data from your marketing automation directly in AdWords. Why is this useful? In the past, Google AdWords was only able to measure online conversions, but with these new integrations, you can now track when a click on your ad resulted in a qualified lead, opportunity, or new customer.

Chapter 12

Casting a Wide Net with Content Syndication

*Y*ou have to reach your buyers where they are, and they won't always be on *your* website or *your* channels. So how do you reach them? Content syndication is a great option to spread the reach of your content to leads who may not otherwise have shown interest.

Content syndication is the tactic of placing your high-value content assets on third-party websites, often gated with a form. The process of syndicating your content can be a paid program through a vendor, or it can be non-paid through RSS (Really Simple Syndication) feeds and social channels. It is a good lead-generation practice to consider using both paid and non-paid efforts in your content syndication to get additional reach and fresh, new leads for your database.

The trick with content syndication is determining what sort of content is relevant on what channel.

Accomplishing Your Goals with Content Syndication

Content syndication achieves many lead-generation goals, but keep in mind that your goals for paid and non-paid programs will differ. As with any paid outlet, you want to make sure your money is going to the acquisition of *good* leads. Where non-paid channels are concerned, you might have different goals.

Here are some basic questions to ask yourself when you're creating your content syndication plan. The answers to your questions can help determine which assets to offer and how you will measure your ROI:

- ✔ Is your goal to drive net-new top-of-funnel leads?
- ✔ Is your goal to drive mid-funnel leads that indicate buying intent?
- ✔ Is your goal to improve your SEO through increased content consumption?
- ✔ Is your goal to get more brand exposure?

Without clear and well thought-out goals for content syndication, you could actually hurt your brand awareness *and* SEO. If you put your content on a vendor site that doesn't have a good reputation or if the site outranks you in the Google search results, it could be bad for your brand. Think about it this way: If you put your best content on a site that appears higher in search results, you are risking your leads going to the syndicated site instead of your site. Remember: A key lead-generation goal is driving traffic to your *own* website and your *own* forms.

Generating targeted leads

Content syndication is excellent for generating leads and growing your database, particularly if you are using paid channels because they offer such precise targeting. Syndicating content through publishers increases your chance of adding new leads to your system through expanded reach and the ability to gate your assets with forms.

Paid syndication vendors offer many targeting options, and you can often target leads based on the following criteria:

- ✔ Geographical location
- ✔ Job type and role

✔ Company size

✔ Industry

A good content syndication vendor syncs with your marketing automation tool through an Application Programing Interface (API) so you can get all of your leads routed directly into your system. From within your marketing automation tool, you can score the leads, add them to lead nurture programs, and email them at will. If a content syndication vendor does not sync to your marketing automation platform, you might spend countless hours manually sorting through and uploading spreadsheets into your system.

After you have syndicated content leads in your database, your follow-up plan is critical. Many of these leads download your asset and never think about your company again. By engaging them through lead nurturing, you can introduce them to your company and lead them through your sales funnel.

Lead generation, and content syndication in particular, is a numbers game. No vendor can guarantee that someone who downloads your asset will become a customer — so the more good leads you can gather through the right vendor, the more opportunities you will have to close a deal.

Considering SEO implications

So here is the rub with content syndication — it can be effective for SEO or it can have negative SEO implications, depending on a variety of factors.

Here are the pros of content syndication for SEO:

✔ You can build brand authority on search engine sites by having quality content available on multiple sites.

✔ It's a great link-building strategy to get link-backs to your website.

✔ It can extend your overall reach.

✔ It can contribute to increased traffic, which increases rank.

Clearly those are some really great benefits. However, here are the cons:

✔ Search engines might see your content as duplicate content, if you are already saying the same thing on your website (which is obviously bad).

✔ The site you syndicate on might outrank you on Google; therefore, when someone is searching for one of your keywords, the vendor site could come up first.

Eek! Not good. These drawbacks pose a problem, particularly for smaller companies that do not yet have a huge web presence. But there are some handy tips that can keep content syndication positive instead of negative:

- ✔ **Consider promoting an abstract instead of the entire content asset:** You can write a compelling blurb with key takeaways and post a link to the content. The key here is to make sure your abstract is compelling, or you won't get the click.

- ✔ **Guest posting instead of syndicating:** If you are worried about duplicate content and being outranked, consider guest posting instead, which can be a form of content syndication where you write a unique article for another site. When the article describes who you are, you will have a link back to your site. You can also often include links back to your site within the blog copy itself, depending on the website's guest blogging guidelines.

- ✔ **Make sure you are using legitimate vendors:** Google penalizes you if you are using a syndicator that looks like a content farm (that posts a ton of random content with no regard to audience — basically, content spam). Make sure the site is reputable and appropriate for your industry.

Working with paid content syndication

Working with paid content syndication vendors gives you the biggest return on your efforts. You can get targeted leads, a high volume of readership, and often email program accompaniment, where the vendor sends out an email with your content to contacts in their lead database on your behalf. Paid content vendors typically charge per click or per form fill, depending on their service offering.

There are content sites like Outbrain.com, shown in Figure 12-1, that provide links to related content on websites for media outlets such as *Time,* CNN, and *The Washington Post.* Your content shows up right beside the featured content on those sites, so visitors see your content as having high authority.

Or you can put your content directly on an aggregator content syndication site such as TechTarget, which provides visitors industry-based resources. Figure 12-2 shows an example of a TechTarget property *ComputerWeekly,* which provides IT pros with the latest tech news.

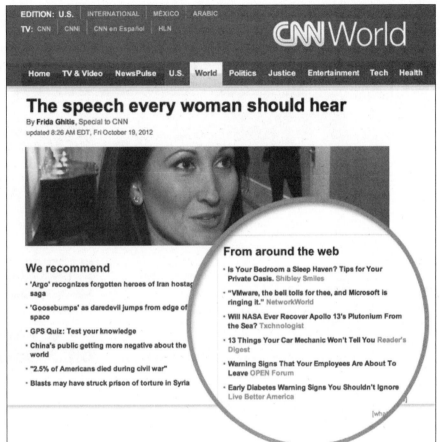

EDITION: **U.S.** | INTERNATIONAL | MÉXICO | ARABIC

TV: CNN | CNNi | CNN en Español | HLN

CNNWorld

Home | TV & Video | NewsPulse | U.S. | **World** | Politics | Justice | Entertainment | Tech | Health

The speech every woman should hear

By **Frida Ghitis**, Special to CNN
updated 8:26 AM EDT, Fri October 19, 2012

We recommend

- 'Argo' recognizes forgotten heroes of Iran hostage saga
- 'Goosebumps' as daredevil jumps from edge of space
- GPS Quiz: Test your knowledge
- China's public getting more negative about the world
- "2.5% of Americans died during civil war"
- Blasts may have struck prison of torture in Syria

From around the web

- Is Your Bedroom a Sleep Haven? Tips for Your Private Oasis. Shibley Smiles
- "VMware, the bell tolls for thee, and Microsoft is ringing it." NetworkWorld
- Will NASA Ever Recover Apollo 13's Plutonium From the Sea? Txchnologist
- 13 Things Your Car Mechanic Won't Tell You Reader's Digest
- Warning Signs That Your Employees Are About To Leave OPEN Forum
- Early Diabetes Warning Signs You Shouldn't Ignore Live Better America

Figure 12-1:
Related content on major news sites.

I recommend using a combination of the two. Some of these sites also offer paid email programs that email your content to the contacts in their database. Take advantage of this option as well.

For a more robust example of paid syndicators, take a look at Table 12-1, which shows a list of potential options, including site name, reach, number of monthly downloads, cost, and frequency of lead reports.

Figure 12-2:
Syndication
aggregate
sites.

Table 12-1		Paid Content Syndicators		
	Reach	*Downloads/ Month*	*Cost*	*Freq. of Lead Reports*
emedia	3.5 million	70,000	$35–80	Weekly or monthly
Find White Papers	>25 million	100,000	$30 minimum	Daily
IDG TechNetwork	125 million	10,000	$45 minimum	Weekly
Incisive Media/ IThound.com	6.5 million	20,000	Won't share	You choose
Insight24	35 million	Only tracks leads	Case by case	Weekly
NetLine	75 million	200,000	$30 minimum	Real time, daily, weekly, or monthly

	Reach	Downloads/ Month	Cost	Freq. of Lead Reports
PaperShare	New network	>40,000 since launch	$5,000-10,000 annually	You choose
QuinStreet	20 million	Won't share	Won't share	Real time, weekly or monthly
RetailWire	50,000	3,000	$3,500-$40,000	Weekly
TechTarget	10 million	200,000	Varies	You choose
Toolbox.com	3.3 million	25,000	Won't share	Daily or weekly
UBM TechWeb	9.73 million	>200,000	$41 average	Weekly
Spear Marketing	Consults its network of media partners and negotiates a package of content postings and other promotions for you. Clients spend a minimum of $10,000 on media alone, plus a management fee.			

Courtesy of Ten Ton Marketing

Choosing the right content

After you decide on a list of vendors that are suitable for your business and content syndication goals, take time to think about what type of content you want to use on these sites.

For example, Marketo typically uses mid-stage content offers when implementing a paid content syndication program. By mid-stage, I mean content that indicates buying intent. For Marketo, these assets are buying guides, ROI calculators, cost calculators, and some other premium (gated) content.

Because we pay per click or lead, we want to make sure the people who are filling out our forms on syndication sites are good leads — true hand-raisers. Figure 12-3 shows an example of what we use on some of our content syndication networks and the registration form that accompanies our content offers.

However, note that the goals for content syndication are very lead-focused — that is, Marketo wants new leads in their database. They aren't quite as concerned about brand awareness and SEO when it comes to syndication efforts.

☑ Yes   **The ROI of Marketing Automation** [paper]
Today's fastest growing companies are using repeatable marketing and sales 2.0 techniques to grow revenue predictably and reliably. Download this paper and learn why companies that implement marketing automation software to support their marketing and sales efforts are better equipped to manage lead flow and process leads more efficiently.

Marketo

☐ Yes   **Deploying Customer Service in the Cloud: The Four Phases from Implementation to Transformation** [paper]
How will you serve consumers in an environment where customer engagement is rapidly shifting? This business guide reveals best practices to implement an agile customer service experience strategy to serve customers on their own terms across all channels

ORACLE

☐ Yes   **Federated Knowledge Supercharges Field Service Operations** [case study]
With a rapidly expanding portfolio of high-tech products, Tokyo Electron's field service team needed a next-generation solution to speed the identification and retrieval of critical engineering and service information from a growing and highly decentralized global knowledge infrastructure.

coveo

☐ Yes   **The Definitive Guide: Marketing Metrics & Analytics** [paper]
This comprehensive guide shows marketers how to talk to CxOs about forecasting and reporting, and drive revenue by leveraging metrics that matter. With compelling graphics and real examples, learn the best practices for harnessing data to prove and improve marketing ROI.

Marketo

3. Complete Registration Form

Email*	First Name*	Last Name*

Not you? Clear form and reload page

Job Title*	Company*	Industry*

Company Size*	Phone*	Country*

Figure 12-3:
Mid-stage content and syndication.

Choosing the right vendor

Vendor selection for content syndication can be tricky and you need to be very vigilant. Make sure you get a full pitch and look over a potential vendor's advertiser material very closely. Some vendors take permission to republish content as permission to repurpose it as well. Be *very* cautious whom you share your content with. You should also know what other websites your syndicator places content on so you can make sure those sites are reputable as well.

Ask potential vendors how often they add new prospects to their database. You want to make sure your content is being seen by fresh, new leads. If you are always showing your content to the same old leads, you will get just that — *the same old leads.*

To ensure that you get the freshest leads possible, give your syndication program a break before renewing with that vendor. If you stop using a vendor for two to three months, this gives you a higher chance of getting fresh leads when you do renew.

Also find out whether your vendor offers paid email programs to their contact databases. This is a terrific way to get in front of fresh people. Because these sites have so much traffic, their lead databases are relatively large.

Testing in paid content syndication

You're paying for leads with content syndication, so testing the results is critical. Be sure to test the following elements in your syndication programs:

- ✔ **Content asset:** Does early- or mid-stage content work better?

- ✔ **Content types:** Which type of content performs best? Ebook? Reports? Videos?

- ✔ **Vendor:** What vendor delivers you the best and most relevant leads?

- ✔ **Form length:** If you can, ask for different forms lengths so you can test what leads to more form-fills.

- ✔ **CTA:** What is your CTA? What works for this audience?

- ✔ **Email copy:** If you do paid email campaigns, what copy resonates most with the audience?

Implementing Non-Paid Content Syndication

There are many non-paid syndicators to leverage as well. Some sites like Business 2 Community allow blog authors to syndicate their work for free if they are set up as featured authors on their site.

You can also reach out to your own network to find out what industry sites might want to syndicate your thought leadership content. You might be surprised to find that a lot of them would be more than happy to receive your ebooks, blogs, videos, and infographics. You can check to see whether these sites want an RSS feed of your content, or you can simply ask to repurpose blog posts and other assets.

Guest blogging on other sites is also a great way to dabble in non-paid content syndication. Take one of your ebooks and repurpose some content, or write an original or amended post.

Also consider cross-posting your content manually on sites like StumbleUpon and Reddit.

Sharing your content through Really Simple Syndication (RSS) feeds

When working with non-paid channels, many sites offer opportunities for you to syndicate your content or blog through a Really Simple Syndication (RSS) feed. An RSS feed enables you as a publisher to syndicate content automatically to sites that you want to syndicate to. That way, you have to do very little on your end and your content just feeds into the site automatically.

As an example of what your content looks like to an end user, take a look at Figure 12-4, which shows the syndication site Business 2 Community. Most of their articles are RSS feeds. For instance, Marketo shares their RSS feed with Business 2 Community. Each time a new blog publishes, it appears on the Business 2 Community site a few days later.

Figure 12-4:
The syndication site Business 2 Community.

An RSS feed is XML-formatted text and is simple to read through automated processes. Figure 12-5 shows an example of what this feed might look like. The data included in a typical RSS feed is a link, the headline, and a description of the content.

```
{
  "rss": {
    "xmlns:taxo":  "http://purl.org/rss/1.0/modules/taxonomy/",
    "xmlns:content": "http://purl.org/rss/1.0/modules/content/",
    "xmlns:rdf": "http://www.w3.org/1999/02/22-rdf-syntax-ns#",
    "channel": {
      "title": "Artima Articles",
      "description": "The most recently published articles at Artima.com.",
      "item": [
        {
          "guid": {
            "content": "http://www.artima.com/articles/defining_done.html",
            "isPermaLink": "false"
          },
          "title": "Defining \"Done\" in User Stories",
          "description": "An increasing number of organizations are taking the plunge to Scrum,
with or without professional coaching. Developers transitioning to Scrum can avoid many pitfalls by
following a handful of hard-learned principles. In this article, I discuss a common mistake with
the popular &quot;user story&quot; requirements format: poorly defined done criteria.",
          "link": "http://www.artima.com/articles/defining_done.html"
        },

        // additional item entries ... ...
      ]
    }
  }
}
```

Figure 12-5:
A sample
RSS feed.

To get your RSS feed, follow these simple steps:

1. **Your feed's URL is probably** `http://yourwebsiteaddress.com/feed`.

   If you're using Feedburner, your feed will be `http://feeds.feedburner.com/yourdomain`.

2. **After you have figured out your feed's URL, you can add an RSS Subscription button to your website, like the one shown in the following figure.**

3. **Through your Subscribe button, visitors and websites can subscribe to your RSS feed.**

You can also do a Google search for RSS directories to submit your feed to. These are syndication aggregators as well. However, be wary when using directories. Make sure they are reputable. You don't want to be associated with a spam site.

Sharing your content through social media

Social media sharing can also be considered a form of content syndication. The best approach here is to work with thought leaders in your industry and ask for the tweet or the post. In exchange, you can offer to share their content.

The key is to create ongoing relationships with these influencers and make yourself a valuable resource for them as well. Just make sure that the content you are asking influencers to share is high-value and shareable. It should demonstrate thought leadership, appeal to emotions, and entertain. No one wants to share your message if you approach them with a totally self-promotional request, and you might risk hurting the relationship you have built.

The upside to creating influencer relationships for the purpose of social content syndication is that you both get the benefits of each other's network and reach.

Another suggestion is to work with customers and leverage them as advocates on social channels. Many companies have advocacy programs that incentivize customers for sharing content and posting reviews. Your customers will tell your peers. Remember what I said about peer-to-peer sharing? It holds much more authority than you sharing your own message through your own megaphone.

Chapter 13

Targeting with a Personal Touch Through Direct Mail

. . . .

In This Chapter

▶ Understanding how to include direct mail as part of the modern marketing mix

▶ Designing your direct mail to drive leads farther down your funnel

▶ Discovering the dos and don'ts of direct mail engagement

▶ Combining your inbound, outbound, and direct mail efforts into an integrated campaign

. . . .

*Y*ou're probably rolling your eyes at me and saying "Dayna, isn't direct mail a thing of the past?" My answer is no, direct mail is actually still very relevant and effective. If you're curious about why I say that, read on.

The key to effective direct mail is approaching it in the right way *and* integrating it with other outbound and inbound lead-generation strategies to make it part of a full campaign.

In fact, direct mail can be highly personal and creative, depending on your mode of attack and how you target your list. If you don't believe me, take a look at some of these convincing stats:

✔ Seventy-three percent of U.S. consumers said they prefer direct mail for brand communication because they can read information at their convenience. *Source: Epsilon's 2012 Channel Preference Study.*

✔ Fifty-six percent of U.S. respondents agreed with the following statement: "I enjoy getting direct mail from brands about new products and services." *Source: Epsilon's 2012 Channel Preference Study.*

✔ Forty-eight percent of the U.K. population surveyed responded to a direct mail piece they received in the past year. *Source: Central Mailing Services 2013 Direct Mail Statistics.*

✔ Eighty percent of marketers forecasted investment in direct mail and 28 percent reported increases in their budget. *Source: Target Marketing Magazine's Media Usage Forecast 2013.*

✔ U.S. advertisers spend $167 per person on direct mail to earn $2,095 worth of goods sold, which is a 1,300-percent return on investment. *Source: Print Drives Commerce 2013.*

Hopefully these stats convince you or at least open your mind to learning more about direct mail for lead generation. The key is to make sure your campaigns are targeted, creative, and integrated with the rest of your lead-generation strategies.

Making Direct Mail Work for You

Direct mail is a great opportunity to target a select group of leads in a creative and unique way. It also can get pretty expensive. I recommend that you not do large mass-mailings. They are impersonal and rarely creative. You don't want your direct mail piece ending up straight in the garbage, so how can you ensure that your mailer is actually engaged with, and (no surprise) demonstrates a return on those marketing dollars? Read on to find out more.

Setting your objectives

As with everything lead-generation related, what are your goals and objectives for your program? Maybe it's moving a selection of hot prospects down your funnel, or maybe it is an exclusive event invitation. Direct mail is expensive, so make sure you know exactly what you want to get out of it. Here are some sample objectives that you might have for direct mail:

✔ Closing key target accounts

✔ Moving key target accounts down your sales funnel

✔ Accelerating lead movement towards the end of the month

✔ Demo requests

✔ Introducing new leads to your company

✔ Sending personalized invites to an event

✔ Cementing relationships with key influencers in a company

Sending general blanket mailers with no clear CTA or goal leads to lackluster reception and conversions. The more specific you can be with your goals, the more you can target and segment your audience and creative approach.

Defining your audience

The most important element of a direct mail campaign is ensuring your mail is highly targeted to the correct audience. Your direct mail piece should be personal and speak directly to your audience. For instance, if you are targeting a handful of important accounts to move them closer to being customers, you should personalize each direct mail piece to your list of decision-makers.

Even if you are sending a more generalized mailer to either a purchased list or your database, you should still be segmenting your list based on demographic or behavioral data.

Take a look at Figure 13-1 for an example of effective targeting. This is a direct mail piece sent out by a company called Hop and Peck in the U.K.. They make handcrafted wooden toys. They created a direct mail campaign to target moms. They used a highly personalized approach, down to the name of the recipient and their child's birthday.

Figure 13-1:
A targeted and personalized direct mail campaign.

What did they do right? So many things. They understood their audience, personalized each response, and created copy that spoke directly to the lead on an emotional level.

They could have sent out a general mailer that just contained information about the company. But that wouldn't have garnered an emotional reaction from their audience in quite the same way.

Choosing your offer

You need a strong CTA in order for direct mail to work for you. What do you want a person to do upon receiving your mailer? Call for a demo? Go to a landing page to download a content asset or sign up for a webinar?

Direct mail CTAs are trickier than web CTAs because you have to entice a lead to stop what he is doing to call a number or go online. Here are some tips to make your CTA stand out with direct mail:

- **Use strong language:** You need to get your lead excited! Use strong, expressive language to incite an immediate response.

- **Use a PURL (Personal URL) CTA:** Include a PURL in your direct mail piece. People are often more incentivized to take an action if they see a personalized URL. Your PURL should then lead to a personalized landing page that speaks directly to your recipient.

- **Don't have too many CTAs:** It is tempting to use as much real estate as possible to overload your mailer with CTAs. Too many CTAs are the kiss of death and a sure invitation to pitch your mailer into the garbage. If you have more than one CTA, create a hierarchy so your lead knows exactly what the most important element is.

- **Speak directly to your lead:** Use a recipient's name in the CTA. If you are speaking to the lead directly, she is way more likely to act.

- **Offer an incentive:** Want the lead to sign up for a demo? Include an offer for a $50 Visa gift card. Your lead is way more likely to take action if there is a WIIFM (What's In It For Me).

- **Consider using a QR (Quick Response) code:** Including a QR code is another quick and easy way for your lead to get to a landing page with an additional offer or CTA. All he does is snap a picture of the code and he can go to a dedicated landing page.

- **Always have a landing page:** No matter what your CTA is, always have a landing page created exclusively for your direct mail piece. The user experience should be seamless and consistent.

Figure 13-2 shows an example of a Pitney Bowes direct mailer that has many of these suggested CTA elements. The copy is personalized, uses strong language, has a PURL CTA that asks the recipient to visit a landing page, and offers an appealing incentive.

Syncing to your marketing automation

Many marketing automation tools have the ability to integrate with direct mail campaigns. This is an effective option to ensure an integrated campaign approach and proper follow-up for your program. For instance, many marketing automation platforms can send a trigger email when someone has signed for a direct mail piece, or when a recipient visits their PURL or scans a QR code. Additionally, a visit to a landing page can also trigger an increase in lead score.

Follow-up is a critical element, so by syncing a marketing automation platform to your campaign, you can ensure a timely follow-up to hundreds or thousands of leads and have insight into your lead's actions.

Another way that you can include direct mail with your marketing automation is to trigger a direct mail piece to be sent out after your lead hits a certain score threshold, or if he has engaged with a particular email campaign.

Joining forces with marketing automation also enables you to track direct mail performance, which helps you track ROI. And for an expensive program like direct mail, knowing how leads interact with your campaign is a critical element.

Focusing on Creative Execution

The key to a successful direct mail campaign is creative execution: in other words, what your direct mailer looks like. I caution you against sending out a typical postcard. Think outside of the box for your direct mail pieces, have an eye-catching design and theme, and don't be afraid to use some mixed media by sending out packages instead of postcards. And because you are hopefully sending out your direct mail pieces to a targeted list, you can get a bit more creative and have a bit of a higher budget to make your mail pieces really pop.

Choosing the right medium

Most marketers think of direct mail in terms of only a 4 x 6 postcard. And yes, this *could* work, but have you thought about all the other forms direct mail can take?

To illustrate my point, check out these truly creative and inventive non-postcard direct mailers. These pieces have a theme and are highly memorable to the leads who receive them.

Figure 13-3 shows an example of a Cox Business campaign sent from a sales rep when a new lead enters their system. This package includes a postcard with a three-dimensional hand that pops out and reads, "Nice to meet you." The outside of the card has the name of the sales rep. Cox also includes a coffee cup that says, "Find out how we can perk up your business," and a Starbucks Via coffee packet. Cox hits the nail on the head with this campaign. It not only has that personal feel but uses a different medium and includes a functional element — the cup and the coffee.

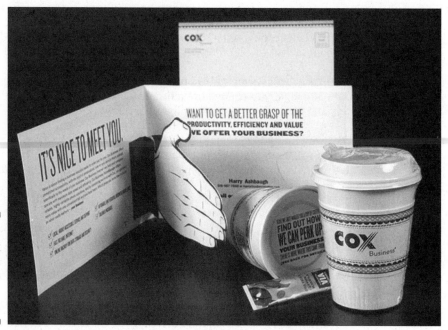

Figure 13-3:
A Cox
Business
"Nice to
Meet You"
campaign.

Another great campaign is Infinity Direct's marketing apothecary bag piece, shown in Figure 13-4. As a marketing agency, they needed something that appealed to marketers, so they took a creative approach by sending a 3D pop-out apothecary bag that included "marketing malady cures" such as "Functional Blog Balm" with directions like "Use for treatment of tight deadline syndrome." They also included a PURL for a personalized landing page.

Figure 13-4:
Infinity Direct's marketing apothecary bag.

The campaign in Figure 13-5 was sent by advertising agency Publicis to clients to let them know that in lieu of a holiday gift, they had donated to a local food bank in their names. They sent each client a customized paper plate that included information about the donation. The interesting angle? The paper plate, of course!

Avoiding the junk mail look

It's important to avoid a junk mail look when working with direct mail. People hate junk mail, and there are a ton of vendors out there sending busy, overloaded junk mail pieces. And what happens to these gems? They end up in the garbage. So make sure that your mail piece doesn't look like junk mail — which is achieved by clever creative, good targeting, and strong, clear CTAs.

Figure 13-5:
Publicis's
Paper Plate
campaign.

What are some don'ts when it comes to direct mail? Here are two important concepts to keep in mind.

- ✔ **Don't use gimmicky language:** Stay away from a ton of copy on your direct mail piece that says "Free," "No Gimmick," "Pre-Approved," and so on. This type of language is a junk mail red flag.

- ✔ **Stay away from a busy design:** Marketers sometimes think the more they can jam on a direct mailer, the better, but in fact, the exact opposite is true. Your mailer should have a clean, streamlined look and be well-designed. A busy design looks like you threw it together in Microsoft Paint and printed it out yourself.

Figure 13-6 shows an example of two direct mail pieces that could easily be construed as junk mail. They break my two golden rules by using busy design and lots of gimmicky language.

Having an Integrated Approach

Your direct mail piece will be that much more effective if you combine with other channels by adding a PURL to a personalized landing page or website, sending out an email follow-up, or sending out a tweet to your lead. Because you can get creative with direct mail, it lends itself very well to a multichanneled approach for more of a campaign feel.

Another important element to an integrated direct mail campaign is appropriate follow-up through email, social channels, or ultimately a sales call, depending on lead's actions. By ensuring you close the loop on your direct mail pieces, you can have a much higher ROI.

Chapter 14

Seizing the Opportunity to Connect Through Events

*W*hether you are participating in or hosting an offline tradeshow or an online webinar, event marketing is a terrific opportunity to attract new leads, move leads through your sales funnel, and close deals. Why? Because events offer an unparalleled chance for personal communication directly with the leads you want to attract and close.

Events enable you as a marketer to truly define your brand, clarify your solutions and products, and establish strong personal connections with event participants. Events also give participants a chance to interact with *your* customers, and as I've mentioned before, peer-to-peer recommendations are truly king when it comes to spreading your message. Imagine how powerful it can be for a lead to have direct interaction with one of your customer advocates.

Compared to most outbound marketing techniques, events provide you with the greatest opportunity to close deals and provide a lively, interactive, and educational forum to position your business as a true thought leader. Like the direct mail approach I discuss in the previous chapter, events can also get very expensive, very quickly. Make sure that when you are about to invest in a lot of cash for an event, that you are set up to tie metrics to it, so you can gauge the effectiveness of your investment.

Figure 14-1 shows a chart from a CMO Council survey on what role trade-shows and events play in a marketer's overall marketing mix. Sixty-four percent say that events help them source new prospects and business opportunities.

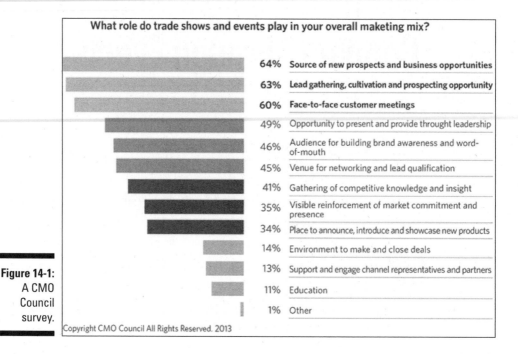

What role do trade shows and events play in your overall maketing mix?

64%	Source of new prospects and business opportunities
63%	Lead gathering, cultivation and prospecting opportunity
60%	Face-to-face customer meetings
49%	Opportunity to present and provide throught leadership
46%	Audience for building brand awareness and word-of-mouth
45%	Venue for networking and lead qualification
41%	Gathering of competitive knowledge and insight
35%	Visible reinforcement of market commitment and presence
34%	Place to announce, introduce and showcase new products
14%	Environment to make and close deals
13%	Support and engage channel representatives and partners
11%	Education
1%	Other

Figure 14-1:
A CMO Council survey.

Events can take many forms. They can be offline in the form of tradeshows, conferences, and field events, or online in the form of webinars and virtual tradeshows. The key to successful lead generation through events is to diversify your event strategy by having a solid mix of tactics.

Leading Through Webinars

Webinars are my favorite type of event. I love them because they give you the biggest bang for your buck and you can execute many of them at once. In fact, Marketo has a full-time employee devoted to nothing but eating, sleeping, and breathing webinars. Webinars are delivered via the web and can happen in real time or on-demand, by viewing a recording. They typically last for about 30–60 minutes, can include one speaker or even a full panel, and enable interaction amongst participants in the form of questions or polls. But don't be afraid to mix it up if you have a creative idea for engaging your audience.

Webinars are a splendid way to generate new leads, as well as nurture leads that are already in your database. You can also tailor webinars to different stages of the sales funnel. For instance, your webinar mix for a given month might looks like this:

- ✔ Week 1: Thought leadership TOFU (top-of-funnel) webinar
- ✔ Week 2: Thought leadership joint TOFU webinar with partner
- ✔ Week 3: Thought leadership MOFU (middle-of-funnel) webinar
- ✔ Week 4: Product-specific BOFU (bottom-of-funnel) demo webinar

Note that in a four-week spread, you can cover all stages of the funnel, speaking not only to all of the leads in your database, but also to any new leads you have acquired.

You can sprinkle in paid webinar programs as part of your mix. Many industry publications and organizations offer sponsored webinars. Take advantage of this program so you can get access to new leads and databases. These organizations often have a lead-sharing program for you to acquire all of the leads that signed up for your webinar.

So what is the ideal number of webinars you should participate in per month? It depends on your business. I would say if you are a small company, shoot for *at least* one webinar per month. If you are a medium-sized company, shoot for three to four webinars per month. Large companies should be participating in multiple webinars per week. My employer sometimes does as many as 20 webinars per month, with a solid mix of paid, thought leadership, and sales (promotional) webinars.

 It's critical to set expectations for registration and attendance when embarking on your webinar program. On average, you can expect that one-third of the people who register will attend your webinar. Keep that in mind when setting registration and attendance goals.

Educating your audience

First I want to focus on a critical part of creating the perfect webinar — education. The majority of your lead-generation webinars should be focused on education and thought leadership. Just like with content marketing and other lead-generation programs, in order to get leads into your funnel, you need to give your audience a *reason* to sign up for your webinar. And by offering industry best-practices or bringing in a well-known speaker, you can generate much more interest.

Where many companies fail is providing high-quality thought leadership webinars that map to early stage leads. Instead, they produce webinars that are very product-centric. By hosting lots of TOFU webinars, you have a vehicle to draw leads in. Later, you can serve them promotional content.

How does this work? Well, for example, Marketo produced a webinar called "The Definitive Guide to Marketing Automation." Obviously marketing automation is Marketo's core competency, so it's easy to create a webinar talking specifically about their capabilities. However, in order to attract leads, they included educational content on general marketing automation. This content could be applied to their platform in addition to any other marketing automation platforms out there. That way, they could get leads interested in what they had to say without trying to make a sale before the audience was ready to buy.

Setting up your webinar program and calendar

Webinars and events in general need to be well coordinated so you can plan them in conjunction with your other programs. You also need to plan events far in advance so you can send out promotions and follow-ups. Plus, you need to think about who is going to run your webinars and what platform you want to use.

When initially creating your webinar program, think conservatively. Tackle one to two webinars per month and then increase from there, depending on how each webinar is received, how much effort you put into production, and how many leads were generated. You also want to pick one day and time per week to run webinars for consistency.

Keep track of your webinar calendar either on a Google Calendar so it can be shared with everyone, an Excel spreadsheet, a whiteboard calendar, or a calendar that is available in your marketing automation tool. Each calendar entry should have the following information:

- Title
- Speakers
- Time
- Dial-in and URL details for participant login

When creating your program, you need to choose a webinar platform. There are many platforms available such as Citrix, GoToMeeting, WebEx, and ReadyTalk. Choose your platform based on your needs, how many attendees you expect at each webinar, cost, and what sort of interactivity you are looking for.

Many platforms offer the functionality to create polls, upload videos, and chat with the audience. Figure 14-2 shows an example of a webinar instance in ReadyTalk. Make sure your platform is easy to use and intuitive.

Figure 14-2: A sample webinar dashboard.

Knowing what to do before an event

Preparing for a webinar is the most time consuming and difficult part, so have all of your ducks in a row. You need to coordinate your speakers, help develop presentations, set up your event in your webinar platform, and more. I go into more promotion and follow-up details at the end of this chapter because those apply to all events, but here are some webinar-specific action items you need to keep in mind:

✔ **Decide on your topic:** You should map your webinar program to your buying stages and business priorities, so the first step when thinking about a particular webinar is deciding what stage of the funnel the webinar maps to and who your audience is. Then you can decide on a topic that makes sense.

✔ **Choose your speakers:** You want to make sure you choose speakers that are subject matter experts (SMEs) on your topic. Speakers can be chosen from within your company or externally. It is also a good practice to consider switching it up — have one internal speaker and one external thought leader.

✔ **Write your abstract:** Next you need to create an abstract. Your abstract is what you add to your landing page, give to your speakers, and use for social promotions. Your abstract should include a short paragraph about the webinar itself, a few bullet points about what the viewer can learn, and speaker bios. Figure 14-3 shows a sample abstract from a Curata webinar.

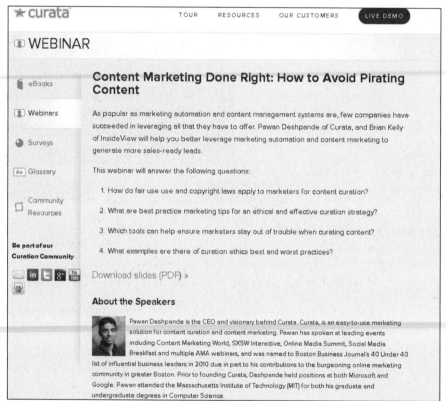

Figure 14-3:
A Curata
webinar
abstract.

✔ **Create your webinar event:** You also want to make sure you create the event itself in your webinar platform. Every platform is different, but you will likely have to schedule it and input the abstract. After you schedule it, you should get a dial-in number for participants, a dial-in number for speakers, and a URL for participants. You can use that information in your promotions.

✔ **Build a webinar landing page:** Every webinar should have its own landing page complete with the abstract and signup form. If you have a marketing automation platform or an Email Service Provider (ESP), you can make the landing page yourself using an easy landing page creator.

✔ **Schedule and conduct content sync calls and platform training:** You should schedule an initial call with the speakers a few weeks before your webinar to discuss content. About a week before your webinar, have another call to do platform training (if needed) and another content sync. In my experience, full dress rehearsals aren't necessary, but it's up to you.

The key is to make sure you are in constant communication with the speakers and that you stay on top of the process to ensure a smooth webinar.

Creating the right presentation

Whether you are the speaker or are just coordinating the webinar, you need to make sure you create the right presentation and that it accomplishes your lead-generation goals.

Here are some best practices to take into consideration when designing your slides with lead generation in mind:

✔ **Keep it entertaining:** On average, only about one-third of the people who register actually attend your webinar. And of that one-third, you have to make sure you *keep* them interested. Boring decks encourage drop-offs. Use memes, cartoons, and engaging slides to bring the energy level of your deck up. Check out Figure 14-4 as an example. Notice how the slide includes memes and compelling imagery.

Figure 14-4: Using fun imagery in slides.

✔ **Include a few links:** Throughout your presentation, include a few links that participants can follow to download more information via a form. Make sure that your link pertains to the content. Figure 14-5 shows an example of using a link in a slide.

Figure 14-5:
Using a link
in a slide.

✔ **Always include your Twitter handle and tweetables:** Help your audience out by including pre-written tweetables throughout your deck. That way, your audience doesn't have to create their own tweets. And of course include your Twitter handle. An example of tweetable takeaways is shown in Figure 14-6.

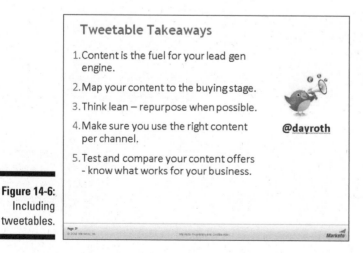

Figure 14-6:
Including
tweetables.

✔ **Consider a poll:** If your webinar platform can accommodate it, consider including a poll in the middle of your presentation. Not only does a poll increase engagement, but you can also gain additional knowledge about your buyers.

✔ **Leave time for Q&A:** This seems obvious, but it can be overlooked. Always include time for Q&A at the end of your presentation — ten minutes is a good goal. Q&A gives you time to speak directly with your audience and answer any questions they might have.

Repurposing your webinar content

After you have your webinar recording (well, you should — your vendor should be able to record webinars), what can you do with it? Here are a few important steps to consider:

1. **Post your webinar recording to your website resource center.**

2. **Create a landing page that hosts your webinar content with a form.**

3. **Email the link to your resource page to those who registered, regardless of whether they attended.**

4. **Have your social team share and tweet out your webinar landing page and ask people to fill out a form for access.**

5. **Post your slide deck on SlideShare (`www.slideshare.net`) for extra exposure.**

Testing out sponsored versus hosted webinars

You can host your own webinars or work with a trusted vendor to sponsor their webinars. There are certainly benefits to both, and I encourage you to try both options to see how they work for your lead-generation strategy.

If you are creating your own hosted webinars, you will be responsible for the entire process — from ideation and choosing speakers to creating content and promotion. If you have a small database of leads, you might have trouble getting high attendance rates. That is where paid (or sponsored) webinars come in handy — you can showcase your expertise while having the advantage of the vendor's database.

Building Your Virtual Event Presence

Think of virtual events as a hybrid between webinars and physical events. A *virtual event* is an online tradeshow that incorporates many elements of a physical tradeshow including booth space, thought leadership presentations, and networking opportunities. Participants can visit a virtual booth, collect some virtual "swag" (promotional) items, meet your team, and ask questions.

In a virtual event, attendees can experience the event from the comforts of their own desk (or even home) without having to incur the typical travel expenses. So instead of having to get gussied up to attend a physical event two hours or two states away, your attendees can experience the same content from their couch — in a Snuggie, sipping on a cup o' joe.

Virtual events are also a cost-effective option. If you are hosting your own virtual event, it's far less costly than hosting your own *physical* summit. And if you are sponsoring a virtual event, the time commitment is slim and the setup easy. The best part? The payoff is similar to that of a physical event — you still get that personal connection and can showcase your product, thought leadership, and move buyers through your funnel.

Creating your presence

When participating in a virtual event, you need to think about your look and feel and how you want to convey your presence overall. You wouldn't go to a tradeshow without thinking about how your booth is going to look, what contests you are going to run, and what you are going to give away. A virtual event requires the same amount of thought.

Here are some simple items to think about when creating your virtual event presence:

- **Controlling the look and feel:** Most virtual event platforms allow you to choose the look, feel, and colors of your booth. Make sure you use your company colors and logo. Note that the default settings in a virtual event platform are not always the best, so make sure you customize it as much as you can. Figure 14-7 shows an example of a customized booth for the company InXpo. Note the prominent placement of their logo and the company colors included throughout.

- **Holding contests:** You can create a contest at your booth to further incentivize visitors to participate. You can host an overall contest and draw a winner from leads, or you can offer prizes throughout the day for completing specific actions such as attending a session, downloading some content, watching a demo, or completing a survey.

Figure 14-7:
An example
of a virtual
booth.

✔ **Adding a video:** Consider adding a video to your booth. It can either be a video about your company, or, even better, a personal hello from an executive. This increases the overall personalization of a virtual event.

✔ **Utilizing the networking lounge:** Have a representative from your company staff and be present at the networking lounge feature in your virtual event platform. Engage attendees and draw traffic back to your booth. The networking lounge also provides the opportunity to answer any questions attendees may have about your product or service.

Including thought leadership

Virtual events give you the chance to showcase some of your core thought leadership in the form of sessions or booth collateral. If you have a session, think of it like a thought leadership webinar. Most of your attendees are likely to be early stage because attending a virtual event is low-commitment, low-cost, and a great way to get introduced to a variety of companies at once.

Many virtual events offer tracks based on the personas of the targeted attendees. For instance, you could have session tracks that appeal to different groups of marketers such as a social media and content track, an email marketing track, a marketing analytics track, and so on. It's important to include your content where it makes sense and can be most relevant.

The second way to showcase your thought leadership in a virtual event is through booth collateral. Most virtual event platforms offer vendors the ability to add assets to their booth, so attendees can add each asset to a *virtual briefcase*. Attendees can then download the assets and even score and rank them based on their relevance and helpfulness.

Think about the asset mix you want to include. If you get spots for four assets, I would include two early-stage assets, one mid-stage asset, and one product-specific late-stage asset. That way you can make sure you are appealing to buyers no matter where in the funnel they fall.

Figure 14-8 shows an example of a virtual event resource center. Attendees can download and rate each asset.

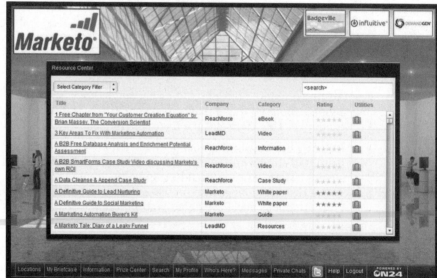

Figure 14-8:
A virtual event resource center.

Hosting your own virtual event

I want to take a minute to talk about hosting your own virtual event, which can be a really effective lead-generation strategy. This means you are funding the event, choosing your own platform, creating the content, and recruiting exhibitors. Last year, Marketo hosted a virtual event and had more than 10,000 registrants to the event, with an attendance of almost 4,000, and 1,800 fresh leads in their database. Those are pretty good numbers.

When you host your own event, consider the following logistics:

- ✔ **Platform selection:** You need to choose a platform to run your event such as ON24.

- ✔ **Theme selection:** Choose a consistent theme to showcase. Your messaging should match your theme.

- ✔ **Session coordination:** You need to choose thought leaders from your own organization and consider using presenters from partner organizations to participate in educational sessions.

- ✔ **Partner and exhibitor sponsorship:** To fund your event, you can ask exhibitors to sponsor. Provide different levels of sponsorship just as you would a physical event.

- ✔ **Assigned staff:** You need a booth manager and other staff to manage your virtual event and interact with attendees.

- ✔ **Coordinated promotion and follow-up:** More on this later, but you will need a steady roll of promotion and follow-up correspondence, particularly if you are hosting your own event.

The beauty of hosting your own event is the difference between renting and owning attention. If you own the attention, you get to present your own content and create an event around your own wants and needs. Plus, the leads you get are yours and yours alone!

Engaging Your Audience Through Physical Events

Now for the big kahuna: physical events! These events require a ton of time and effort and have a *lot* of moving pieces. Physical events can come in many forms such as tradeshows, conferences, field events, and seminars. But the most popular (and best in my opinion) for lead generation is the tradeshow. And that is what I am going to focus on because tradeshows take the largest amount of coordination, are the most expensive, and are often ones that marketing folks spend money on with unimpressive results.

Physical events are fantastic for face-to-face communication with new leads, opportunities soon to become customers, and customers, of course. For new leads, you can introduce them to your company and make them feel special through personalized communication and various incentives. And for those mid-stage leads who are almost ready to buy, that extra personal touch can really seal the deal.

There is a lot to consider when participating in a physical event. Depending on your sponsorship level at a tradeshow, you could have a booth presence, a speaking session, lunch sponsorships, and so on. In other words, it's a lot to think about and plan for. You can't just sign the contract, show up, and expect everything to work for you!

You need to plan your goals and think about your ROI numbers. Tradeshow participation is generally expensive, so your executive team will certainly want to see the return on their spending.

Your tradeshow goals might look like the following:

- ✔ X number of scanned leads
- ✔ X number of new scanned leads
- ✔ X number of opportunities created
- ✔ X number of prospect meetings
- ✔ X number of upsells
- ✔ X number of customer meetings
- ✔ X number of closed deals

In order to determine ROI for your event, you need to come up with some baseline metrics.

Setting the stage and creating a theme

Just as with a virtual event, with a physical event, you need to think about your booth and overall theme. If you are an exhibitor, you will likely get a booth that is commensurate with your sponsorship level. Make sure you check out what the rules are when it comes to what you can and cannot have at your booth.

Your key objective at a tradeshow is to stand out from the crowd. Depending on how large your event is, there could be hundreds or thousands of exhibitors, so you need to really pull out all of the stops to get leads to come to your booth.

Some items to keep in mind when thinking about your theme and décor:

- ✔ New products or services you want to showcase
- ✔ Colors you want to include in your booth
- ✔ Where your logo will be located

✔ Whether you need demo stations or lounge areas

✔ Where your welcome area will be

✔ Where you want to put your booth collateral and swag

✔ What you are planning on including at your booth that is fun and engaging

✔ Whether you plan on featuring any video content on a screen

✔ Whether you want a large overhead sign featuring your logo

Take a look at Figure 14-9, which is a rendering of Marketo's Dreamforce (Salesforce's major user summit) booth. As you can see, the booth features multiple demo stations, signage, an overhead hanging sign, and a car giveaway. Plus, everything is in purple, Marketo's color.

Figure 14-9:
A Dream-
force booth.

Why is this important? Well, you want to really come out with a bang and impress your leads. But don't think that bigger is always better. You can have a really fantastic event presence with a smaller booth. Just be creative with it!

Another important aspect of setting the stage for success at a physical event is your staff. Make sure you have enough staff on hand to scan lead badges and speak with interested leads as they enter your booth. If you are giving demos, make sure you have qualified employees on hand at all times so if a lead asks a question, they can actually answer it.

Attracting an audience with games and interactive booth tools

Aside from your booth appearance, what else is going to attract attention? Fun stuff! Have something fun and interesting in your booth. There is so much noise from competitors at an event that you want something in your booth to make leads stop and say "That's cool! I want to check it out!" This can be in the form of games and interactive booth tools.

This is by no means an exhaustive list of items you can include in your booth to add intrigue and interest, but it's a great start:

- **Spin-to-win:** Include an interactive spin-to-win wheel at your booth. You can give away small items like Starbuck's gift cards or large items like televisions or even cars. Just remember — a badge scan for a spin!

- **Interactive iPad games or videos:** Set up an iPad wall and give attendees a chance to learn more about your company. An iPad enables them to take a self-guided tour through what you do and what you have to offer.

- **Photo booth or meme generator:** Have a photo booth with props and have attendees come in and get their picture taken. Make sure your photo printouts have your company branding or event theme on them. Consider having a meme generator in your booth. Attendees can get their photos taken and match them up with popular and funny phrases, and then retrieve their photos online and post them to Twitter and Facebook. Take a look at the meme booth in Figure 14-10.

- **Food and drinks:** Another way to get people in your booth is by offering up food or drinks. I have seen this work quite successfully at a number of tradeshows. Think popcorn, coffee for the weak and weary, or even Dippin' Dots ice cream. People generally get pretty hungry and thirsty at tradeshows, so offering food is certainly a way to strike up a conversation and get people to stick around.

There is much debate in the industry on whether to hire so-called *booth babes,* models who attract attendees to your booth. In my opinion, whether to hire booth talent depends on your industry. If you are in the automobile space, booth talent is sometimes a must and is commonplace in the industry. However, if you are in the technology, insurance, or a more B2B space, think twice. You can sometimes generate bad quality leads and alienate a demographic of buyer. Also, booth talent often cannot answer detailed questions about your company. So, proceed with caution!

Figure 14-10:
A meme booth at a physical event.

Generating demand with contests and sweepstakes

Contests and sweepstakes are an effective lead-generation tool at tradeshows before, during, and after an event. Contests and sweepstakes get people excited, attract potential leads to your website, give people a reason to click on your pay-per-click (PPC) ad, and are very shareable over social channels.

To ramp up registrations and spread the word about your presence, consider offering a contest leading up to your event. Maybe you want to give away a free event pass and an all-expense paid trip for one winner. Create a landing page, add a form, send out an email blast, and promote it on social media. Holding a contest that relates directly to the event serves multiple purposes — it promotes the event to increase overall attendance, promotes your attendance at an event, increases brand awareness, and gets new leads into your database.

Take a look at an example from Apttus, a company that sells a custom pricing and quoting application, promoting a contest for Salesforce's Dreamforce tradeshow. Figure 14-11 shows the PPC ad that they created to promote the conference. This came up when I searched for the keywords *Dreamforce contests*.

Figure 14-11:
A Dream-
force
contest
PPC ad.

Going to **Dreamforce** 2013? - Win a Free Leadership Pass Upgrade
www.apttus.com/ ▾
Exec Content VIP Perks Enter to Win

When I click the ad, it brings me to a landing page that tells me about the contest — winning a Dreamforce Leadership Pass upgrade, which is shown in Figure 14-12.

During the event, you can run a high-value contest and give away an item such as an iPad or even a car if you have the budget! You can give the item away for a badge scan or even for a tweet. If it is a smaller item, consider doing daily giveaways.

I have also seen photo contests work really well on social channels during an event. Have attendees tweet out photos to a specific hashtag and tag your company. Choose the most creative image or have your followers vote. If you are giving away a large item like a car, consider showcasing the car in the booth to get everyone excited.

After the event, think about how you can further engage those who attended. Ideas that I've seen work well include holding a blog contest for the best wrap-up post, submitting photos from the event, or simply filling out a post-event form on social media or through an email.

The idea is to get leads engaged and excited about your company. The more attention you can bring to yourself in a noisy event, the better.

However, one warning here — don't go overboard and do more than you can. Consider your event goals, the number of team members you have, and your budget. It's a shame to blow the bank on an event with memorable games and prizes that just isn't going to give you the ROI you need to justify your purchases.

Choosing booth content and swag

At your booth, you want to provide attendees both content to promote your company and thought leadership, and you want to have swag items — that is, stuff to give away in your booth. Typically, when people attend an event and are perusing the exhibit hall, they are very open to reading materials about your company and accepting promotional materials.

My advice on content at the booth is to keep the paper to a minimum because it may get tossed in the end. By paper, I mean datasheets, pricing sheets, brochures, and so on. Instead of giving away a huge heap of tree-killing paper, consider offering a portable mini-USB drive to your attendees with all of your product information content on it.

If you must have printed collateral at your booth, make sure it is something valuable. Consider printing and binding a copy of a thought leadership ebook that you have, or if someone in your company wrote a published book, give that away. Another item that could be a cool content giveaway is a printed infographic, as seen in Figure 14-13, that tells your attendees who you are and what you do.

Figure 14-13:
A foldable infographic as a booth giveaway.

The next set of items you want to think about are your swag items because these will also drive people to your booth. Swag items can be great branding opportunities in the form of shirts, hats, bags, and more. But get creative! Tradeshow attendees *love* swag.

Consider guerilla and outdoor marketing at your events

Another way to get the attention of event attendees is to dabble in guerilla marketing tactics and other outdoor activities. Guerilla marketing tactics are using unconventional marketing tactics to send a message locally and often on the street.

Here's an example of a guerilla marketing campaign that I created while working at a cloud technology consulting firm called Bluewolf. We were giving away Salesforce training to unemployed individuals who submitted videos on why they wanted to be trained. The campaign was during the Occupy Wall Street movement, so I named the program the Pinkslip campaign and used traditional propaganda-type design as my creative.

The campaign was scheduled to launch at a Salesforce's New York City user conference, so we decided to do some guerilla marketing outside the event to promote the program. I got a large group of people together, gave them all matching shirts containing the Pinkslip messaging, and handed out various picket signs. We chanted outside the conference center about our Salesforce training program and handed out fliers that contained links to our landing page.

This got a *lot* of attention outside of the conference. Take a look at an image from the campaign in Figure 14-14. We were able to pivot off of a hot topic that people were talking about at the time, which made our guerilla tactic a success. We also used a daring approach to get our message across.

Figure 14-14:
The Pinkslip guerilla marketing campaign.

What else are you doing outside of an event to make your presence known? Consider a mix of the following tactics (depending on your budget):

- Contact local businesses and see if you can rent some space for prospect meetings. Make sure your signage is out front.

- Contact customers to see if you can put signage in their windows if they are near the event hall.

- See if your event offers any additional sponsorship opportunities like sponsored breakfasts or lunches, happy hours, or additional signage.

- Host a party or happy hour after the event closes and invite attendees.

- Make a video at the event and ask attendees, influencers, and analysts to join.

One thing to consider if you decide to embark on guerilla or outdoor marketing outside your event: Ask the city and the event host what you can and can't do. There may be rules and regulations around where you can put signage and so on. For the Pinkslip campaign, I found out the hard way that I was not allowed to stage any sort of marketing outside of Salesforce's event. They shut my mock protest down in about two hours. So make sure you ask your host whether whatever you have planned is okay and within the rules!

Syncing with marketing automation

Many marketing automation platforms offer functionality specific to events — both online and offline. Because there is so much correspondence around events, it's important to make sure you are tracking attendance and engagement. Marketing automation simplifies your event marketing, but it also makes it highly effective. Integrating marketing automation and events can help drive success in the following ways:

- ✔ **Get registration and attendee information:** With marketing automation, you can determine how many people were invited to an event, how many people attended, and who engaged with your team at an event.

- ✔ **Send invites and follow-ups:** You can easily send invitations and follow-ups through your marketing automation tool. If you are holding a webinar, use marketing automation to follow up with attendees quickly.

- ✔ **Align your sales and marketing teams:** Increase lead scoring for event attendees through marketing automation and alert sales when hot leads attend.

- ✔ **Track event ROI:** Prove how valuable your events are — see how attendance tracks to revenue goals and closed deals.

There are many easy functions within marketing automation that help make your event programs a success.

- ✔ **Progression status:** As shown in Figure 14-15, you can easily see who was invited, who registered, who attended, and who didn't show. You can also see who downloaded slides, who visited your booth, and other actions a lead could have taken.

- ✔ **Asset view:** You need multiple emails and landing pages for your event to be successful. A marketing automation tool combines all your event assets in one place, as shown in Figure 14-16.

- ✔ **Cloning:** You can use the cloning functionality in a marketing automation tool to easily re-create your event programs without having to build new programs each time. You can clone landing pages, emails, and event flows. Just make sure you remember to change your assets with the new event information!

⊟ **Results**	
Total Members:	190164
Acquired By:	36
Success: ◉	692
⊟ **Members by Progression Status**	
Invited:	188077
Pending Approval:	0
Wait Listed:	0
Rejected:	0
Registered:	0
No Show:	1395
Engaged: ◉	0
Attended: ◉	683
Attended On-demand: ◉	9

Figure 14-15: Progression status in Marketo.

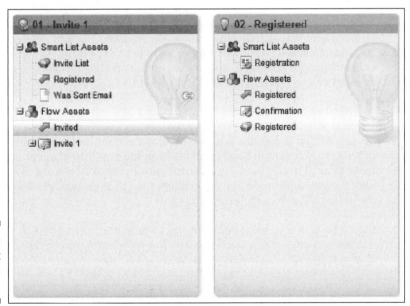

Figure 14-16: An asset view in Marketo.

Having an Event Promotion and Follow-Up Plan

Every successful event needs a successful event promotion and follow-up plan. No one will attend your event if you don't promote it, and you might leave a bad taste in the mouths of your attendees if you don't follow up.

You need to communicate with your audience early and often leading up to an event, engage with them during an event, and keep in touch afterwards — it's definitely a lot to think about. But if you can successfully execute your plan, you can show your leads a lot of love and move them through the sales funnel to become customers.

Thinking about pre-event promotion

You need to get people to your event so you can wow them with your event presence. And how do you do that? You need an event promotion plan to get as many attendees as you can.

Make sure you think about your event promotion in a multi-touch fashion — that is, make sure you include email, social, direct mail, PPC, and more to get the most bang for your buck. But remember to take into consideration what sort of event you are hosting or sponsoring as you create your plan — not all promotional tactics make sense for all events.

A critical element of proper event promotion is segmentation, so you can get the best attendees registered for your event. Take time to think about data quality so that you know you are inviting the right people. For instance, if you are having an event in San Francisco targeted towards VPs and up, it wouldn't make sense for you to invite a coordinator living in New York. By thinking about segmentation before you embark on a promotional plan, you can try to avoid these types of mistakes.

Figure 14-17 shows an example of what segmentation might look like in your marketing automation tool. You can filter out demographic criteria to make sure you are inviting the right leads.

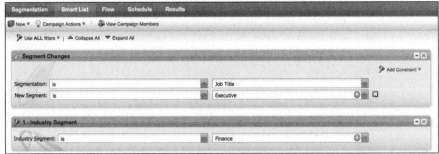

Figure 14-17:
Event seg-
mentation in
Marketo.

After you have your list right and you know who to invite, you can get moving on the promotions. Think about using the following tactics:

- ✔ **Email:** How many emails you send out and when you send them out depends on your event. If you are hosting a webinar, a good best practice might be two emails sent out two or three weeks before your event. If you are planning for a large tradeshow, consider starting your promotion earlier to make a bigger splash. You'll want to send out an event reminder to all registered attendees one week before your event. You also might want to consider sending a day-of reminder as well.

- ✔ **Sales outreach:** Your sales teams can be a vital part of helping to promote your event. Have them do personal outreach to target attendees before the event. Also make sure your sales teams are setting up meetings at the event if you are attending in person. Another way to take advantage of sales outreach is to use an automated voicemail campaign through a service such as Boxpilot to ask for registration or confirm attendees.

- ✔ **Direct mail:** Sending out direct mail is a way to create an impact with your audience. Send out personalized event invitations to target attendees. Include a Personalized URL (PURL) to send each lead to a personalized web page.

- ✔ **Paid promotions:** Utilize paid promotions like banner ads, PPC ads, SEO, and billboards to promote your presence at an event.

- ✔ **Partner promotions:** Got partners attending the same event? Do some co-promotion. Send out co-sponsored emails or do a pre-event webinar together to gain more traction.

- ✔ **Public relations:** Connect with your PR team to create press releases and buzz around your event. Your team should be crafting press releases and coordinating with media, analysts, and influencers.

✓ **Social media:** Make sure you are announcing your event presence on your social channels. Create a hashtag, custom imagery, and put paid promotions behind your efforts to get an extra lift. Take a look at Figure 14-18 for an example of social event promotions on Facebook.

Figure 14-18:
Social event promo-
tions on
Facebook.

Engaging during an event

Don't underestimate the importance of engaging with your audience *during* an event as part of your promotional plan. This works best if you are attending a full day event or a multi-day event because you will have plenty of time to craft messaging and reach out to your attendees.

Here are a few ways to leverage promotions during an event:

- ✔ **Be active on social channels:** Dedicate at least one person to monitor social media during an event. For sessions, your social media manager should be posting and tweeting out key takeaways. He should also be engaging attendees, posting photos, following the hashtag, and driving traffic to your booth.

- ✔ **Daily live blogs:** A great way to do a daily wrap-up is through live blogging. At the end of each day of a multi-day event, post a blog that sums up key takeaways and exciting moments.

- ✔ **Send out daily emails:** Send out daily emails to attendees letting them know about all of your activities throughout the event. This keeps them up-to-date and engaged.

Perfecting the follow-up

You can't just leave your leads hanging! You need to follow up with both attendees and no-shows so that you can continue the conversation after the event is over. An important detail to note is that you should plan your follow-ups *before* your event so you can get them out swiftly. Studies have shown that following up directly after an event gives you far more conversions than following up after a few days.

If you have a marketing automation tool, you can create your entire campaign and set it to go out immediately after the event comes to a close. If your event is a webinar, I recommend pre-loading the slides into the email and saying you will send out a recording in a few days. You always want to reach out to your leads immediately after an event ends.

Another suggestion if you have a multi-day event is to send out a follow-up email after each day. This can get tricky because you need to sync your lead scanner to your marketing automation platform each night to ensure you have the right list, but it works like a charm if you have the time and capabilities. Attendees are often impressed by a swift follow-up.

Pay special and close attention to your lead lists after an event and look to qualify that list — how good are the leads you collected? Your lists should be created immediately after an event is over. If you are attending a physical event, you will collect leads via a lead scanner or through business cards. Make sure you change the lead status depending on how they engaged with your company at an event. That way, you know what sort of follow-up you want to send.

Figure 14-19 shows an example of the lead qualification chart used to determine how a lead engages at a tradeshow.

Lead Status	Description
Pending	Leads have minimal engagement or no engagement at all (could've dropped their card in the fishbowl or got scanned passing by the booth).
Review	Leads have engaged with Marketo, and we have to identify if they fit our buyer profile.
Target	Leads have engaged with Marketo, and we know that they fit our buyer profile.
Lead	Sales-ready lead who we believe will be a potential opportunity.
Customer	A Marketo Customer; the list may have originated from a Marketo Customer-only event.

Figure 14-19:
A lead qualification chart.

Your main mode of follow-up communication is going to be via email because you can create personalized conversations with your attendees and send them relevant material from your event.

But follow-ups are tricky, so here are my top tips for successful email follow-ups:

- ✔ **Use pre-show testing to determine follow-up emails:** You most likely created a variety of invite emails to send out before the show. Pay attention to what sort of subject lines worked and what tone in your copy resonated with attendees.

- ✔ **Make your emails personal:** Send your leads emails that resonate with them and are applicable to what your lead did at the event. What sessions did she attend? Did he visit your booth? Is she from one of your target hot accounts? Think about creating multiple versions of a follow-up email so you can speak directly to the attendee.

- ✔ **Send valuable content from the event:** Send your session videos, presentation slides, or ebooks you offered at an event. The more high-quality content you can include, the more likely you will get engagement and conversion.

- ✔ **Include an offer:** Grab your lead's attention by giving him a special offer of some kind — entry into a contest, a follow-up download of a content piece, an invitation to another event, a discount on your product, and so on.

Figure 14-20 shows an example of an event follow-up email from a webinar. It has a big CTA of downloading the slides and also asks the lead to sign up for the next webinar in the series.

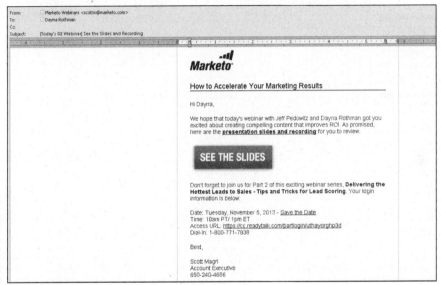

Figure 14-20:
A webinar
follow-up
email.

You also want to think about nurturing and scoring the leads you attract from your event. After someone attends an event, make sure she continues to be engaged.

Now that you have your event leads in your marketing automation system, add them to a lead nurture track. You can create an event-specific nurture track that, over time, sends leads correspondence relating to the event such as slide decks, blog posts, and any other content you created.

Lead scoring is also a critical piece to understanding interactions at an event. Marketo scores leads based on their engagement at an event. *Engagement* means that they spoke or interacted with someone at the Marketo booth. *No engagement* means that an attendee was merely scanned.

Just because someone visits your booth at an event does not mean she is a viable lead or that she has engaged with your company. Make sure you create that distinction in your follow-up and success metrics.

Figure 14-21 shows an example of a scoring matrix used for events.

Stage	Signed Up		Attended		Engaged at Show		Notes
	Lead Score	Behavior Score	Lead Score	Behavior Score	Lead Score	Behavior Score	
Early					5		
Late			5	5	10	10	Late stage means the conference is marketing automation focused.

Figure 14-21: An event lead scoring chart.

Chapter 15

Creating the Final Touch with Inside Sales

In This Chapter

▶ Combining your lead-generation efforts with sales follow-up

▶ Prioritizing hot leads for sales outreach

▶ Working with sales to outline the lead hand-off process to avoid a leaky sales funnel

▶ Training your sales teams to deliver your marketing messages and content to leads

*N*o lead can turn into a customer without the help of inside sales — they are your team on the front line and are often the first people to speak directly to a lead. What is an inside sales team? According to sales thought leader Ken Krogue, "Inside sales is remote sales, or sales in the cloud." Many B2B companies with longer sales cycles have both inside sales teams who qualify leads and set appointments (sometimes called sales development reps, or SDRs), and account executives who engage in a relationship-based in-person sell. (This is sometimes called *field sales* because those folks are out in the field.) Why does this approach work? You want to qualify your leads before you actually start selling them a product, so your inside sales teams qualify marketing's leads, and your account executives are the closers. Inside sales also provides a career path for those new to the world of sales who want to learn the ropes before getting into field sales.

An interesting aspect of an inside sales team is that many companies classify them as part of marketing because they help close the loop between sales and marketing. As a marketer, you need to be close to your sales team so that they can turn your leads into opportunities and qualify them to eventually be closed/won deals. By including inside sales as part of your marketing, you can cement the bond between the two teams.

And other companies include their inside sales function as part of their core sales team because the partnership between inside sales and field sales cements a solid sales process. How to structure your inside sales team may or may not be up to you, but you should know that there are options.

Marketo has done it both ways. Inside sales teams called sales development reps (SDRs) call marketing leads to get them ready for sales. They handle the sales and marketing handoff by either qualifying leads or sending them back to marketing for nurturing.

The inside sales function is a critical part to lead generation and ensuring that all of your effort as a marketer pays off in the end.

Forming an Inside Sales Team

I highly recommend that you consider forming an inside sales team to round out your lead-generation efforts, even if it is just one or two people. You don't want your account executives focusing on cold calling and qualifying leads, so with an inside sales team, your top sales executives can focus on what they do best — closing deals.

As thought leader Craig Rosenberg of Funnelholic says, "The most successful lead-generation programs have dedicated phone resources whose sole job in life is to take raw inquiries and qualify them before being sent to sales."

Hiring the best

Inside sales teams need to have sales acumen and be excellent communicators on the phone, which is a very specific and hard-to-find skill. Your sales reps need to be interesting, engaging, credible-sounding, and able to serve up a rebuttal for any form of rejection a lead gives them. Test their communication skills by doing extensive phone screens and role-playing.

LinkedIn is a great resource for good inside sales team candidates. Scout for people who have phone sales experience in high-volume businesses such as technology. You probably will find a lot of reps with phone sales experience within the technology sector.

Here are some other characteristics to look for when searching for your winning inside sales team:

- A college degree.
- Four to twelve months of experience on the phone or in a sales function.
- Leadership positions in college and high school, or involvement in competitive hobbies like sports.
- An outgoing personality: You don't want a shrinking violet as your sales front line.

✔ Excellent written skills: Your inside sales teams will be spending time creating emails, so make sure they know how to write one.

✔ A desire to succeed and move up: In many organizations, the inside sales team members get promoted to account executives.

Setting goals and quotas

You need to think about how your inside sales teams will be measured and what their daily activities consist of. A good rule of thumb is that an inside sales rep should spend about two-thirds of his time calling on inbound leads (sourced through marketing efforts) and the rest of the time cold calling and researching.

For example, Marketo wants their inside sales reps to have about 40–60 meaningful interactions with leads per day. This means a good phone call or email exchange. This does *not* include voicemails or hang-ups — these are not meaningful in any way.

When I first graduated from college, my first job was in sales. I had a call quota — I had to make 60 calls per day. But they didn't have to be meaningful interactions at all. I could leave voicemails and still get credit for the call. My phone had a counter and that was all. So I was able to successfully reach my call quota each month without actually having much interaction with my leads. You want to avoid this at all costs. Marketo insists that sales reps have meaningful conversations recorded in a customer relationship management system (CRM), with some sort of action being taken to qualify the lead or return the lead back to marketing for lead nurturing.

How do you come up with an inside sales quota? You take your number of daily meaningful interactions (say, 50 in this case), multiply that by 20 (because there are generally 20 business days in a month), and multiply again by two-thirds (because we know the reps are only spending two-thirds of their time qualifying leads). This gives you a target of interactions per month per inside sales person.

You can take this number, about 650 in this case, and divide that by 2.6 (which is the average number of calls it takes our inside sales reps to qualify a lead), and you can target your inside sales reps to work with about 250 quality leads per month.

Be sure to take into consideration your own sales cycle. Your inside sales reps may be qualifying more or fewer leads, depending on your sales cycle and how many leads your marketing team generates.

Syncing Your Marketing Automation Tool with Your CRM

To complete the lead handoff between sales and marketing, you need to have a good integration between your marketing automation tool and your CRM system. This ensures that all lead data, such as scoring and behavioral milestones (such as filling out a form), can be transferred directly to your CRM tool, where your sales teams live.

Why is this important? If you can communicate to sales what your hottest leads are at any given time so they can follow up right away, no leads fall through the cracks. Plus, your sales team can engage leads with relevant information because they have insight into where they have come thus far in their journey.

Many marketing automation systems, such as Marketo, provide sales intelligence in a simple dashboard format for applications made for CRM systems such as Salesforce and Microsoft Dynamics CRM.

Through these dashboards, as shown in Figure 15-1, sales can determine their hottest leads and opportunities so they can prioritize their time based on lead quality and urgency. Note the stars and flames indicate that the lead is urgent and timely.

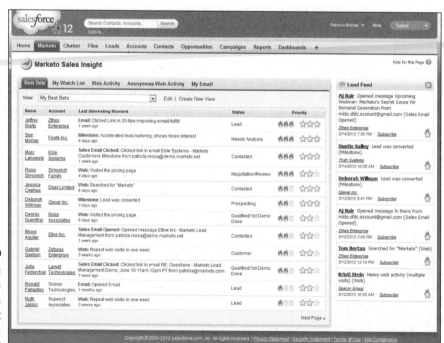

Figure 15-1:
A Marketo
Sales
Insight
dashboard.

Providing interesting moments to sales

Because leads do most of their research online before they speak to a sales rep, in order for your inside sales teams to truly have the knowledge they need to speak directly to a lead, they need in-depth information about lead activity.

Marketing automation tools can provide sales alerts when a lead has an "interesting moment," for example, when he downloads a pricing page or views a demo. Sales also can get detailed buying behavior such as email conversions, website pages visited, and behaviors that indicate strong buyer interest.

Figure 15-2 shows an example of what sort of behavior marketing automation can communicate to sales through a CRM in Marketo Sales Insight.

Figure 15-2: Marketo Sales Insight interesting moments.

Enabling sales to send trackable emails

Many CRM systems have the ability to send emails, but they simply don't have the type of functionality needed for detailed tracking. But with marketing automation integration, sales can track email performance and get alerts when a lead engages with an email. Inside sales teams can create their own text-based emails or use a variety of templates that marketing creates.

Figure 15-3 shows an example of what one of these trackable emails might look like in a system like Marketo.

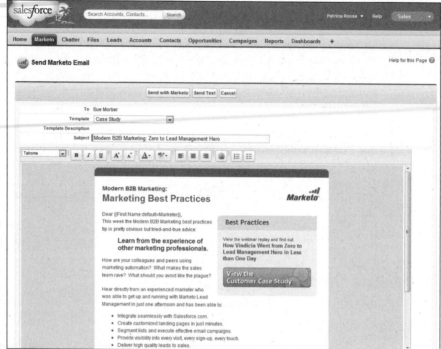

Figure 15-3:
Marketo
Sales
Insight
email tem-
plate in a
CRM.

Another great aspect about enabling sales to view data from a marketing automation tool within their CRM is that they can send leads directly back to marketing for lead nurturing. This is a huge part of the lead lifecycle process, and will be discussed at length in Chapter 17. Many times, a lead simply won't be ready to purchase yet — even if she has had an interesting moment. If a sales rep has the capability to send leads directly back to marketing or add them to a lead nurture flow, you can ensure that sales and marketing remain tightly aligned.

Defining the Lead Path

Sales and marketing need to agree upon a methodology to determine what leads are qualified and what leads aren't. This is a critical element to successful sales and marketing alignment. You need to come up with a *shared* sales and marketing definition for what a good lead means.

But what happens when a lead leaves marketing's hands and goes to sales? You need to have a concrete lead qualification path that inside sales reps can follow before they know whether to qualify them and send them onto an account executive, or send them back to marketing.

Marketing-qualified leads (MQLs)

A marketing-qualified lead can be defined as a lead that is defined as "good" by marketing. This means that the lead has hit a specific score or has had an interesting moment, indicating that an inside sales rep should call her.

These are the factors that should determine an MQL:

- ✔ **Fit:** These are mostly demographic criteria such as job title, industry, geography, and so on. These criteria should define what types of buyers typically purchase your product.

- ✔ **Behavior:** This indicates a lead's level of buying interest designated by his behavior. Maybe he has downloaded a late stage ebook or datasheet, or maybe he has attended a webinar.

Sales-accepted leads (SALs)

After a lead is sent to sales, your inside sales reps need to accept those leads. This step is often absent from many lead funnels, but it's an important step to pay attention to. Your sales teams need to take your MQL and make sure that the lead is close enough to purchasing to be qualified by sales and ultimately sent to one of your outside sale reps.

According to Sirius Decisions, there are specific reasons an inside sales rep might not qualify a lead. They include

- ✔ **Unable to reach:** A sales rep can only spend so much time trying to reach a lead by calling, emailing, and leaving messages. If the rep still can't reach a lead and she has met the Service Level Agreement (SLA), the lead can be recycled back to marketing.

- ✔ **Inaccurate data:** The lead data is not accurate — for example, it includes a wrong phone number, wrong email address, and so on.

- ✔ **No Budget, Authority, Need, and Time (BANT):** The lead has no budget, isn't the right person to speak with, doesn't have a need, or the timing doesn't quite work out.

- ✔ **No fit:** A lead's need does not line up with your product or service specifications.

If a lead is unable to be qualified by your inside sales rep, the lead should be recycled back to marketing so it can be nurtured again or removed from the mix.

Sales-qualified leads (SQL)

After a lead is accepted by sales, it needs to be qualified. SQLs are your golden tickets to be fast-tracked to your account executives to begin the sales process. Why is it important to truly qualify a lead? Well, if you send bad leads to sales, they won't close deals and then both you *and* sales look bad.

According to Salesforce, here is what you should look for when qualifying a lead to send to an account executive:

- ✔ **BANT:** The lead has the budget, authority, need, and the right timeline to make the right decision.

- ✔ **Shows interest:** The lead seems very interested in your product or service. She has downloaded a variety of assets, watched a demo, and had a positive interaction with your inside sales rep over the phone.

- ✔ **Fits your buyer profile:** The lead has many similarities to those that have purchased in the past.

- ✔ **Has a sense of urgency:** The lead is ready to purchase within a reasonable time frame. He has a sense of urgency about making a decision.

Enabling Your Sales Team with Content

Your sales teams need to supplement their selling skills with great content. This includes content in all stages of the funnel: TOFU, MOFU, and BOFU. Content types can include ebooks, webinar recordings, assessment sheets, ROI calculators, datasheets, and more. Your sales teams also need some professional-looking sales tools to showcase your product or service in a professional manner. That way, if a lead has a question during a call or needs a product or service explained, your sales team is armed and ready.

Make all of your sales collateral available to sales reps in one place — either directly in a CRM tool or through a cloud-based document hosting system such as Box or Dropbox. Also make sure you categorize your assets appropriately and in a way that sales can understand, so there is no guessing on what piece of content to use and when.

Developing sales presentations

Your sales teams need a professional-looking sales deck to present to leads through a virtual meeting using a tool like GotoMeeting or join.me or in person. It's my experience that if you leave each sales rep to create her own deck, you wind up with inconsistent branding and messaging. Plus, you can't ensure that each and every deck even looks professional.

In order for your sales teams to show a consistent brand experience, marketing should help create decks that include a company PowerPoint template, consistent product or service messaging, some professional screenshots (if applicable), and other nice-looking imagery.

I came across a great universal pitch deck on SlideShare created by Creative Aces, a company that makes sales decks for businesses. It has a great outline for what you should think about including when developing your master sales deck (note I removed slides that I thought weren't applicable):

✔ **Your title page: You** should include your company name, logo, stock ticker symbol (if your company is publicly traded), tagline, website, and nothing else. Take a look at the Creative Aces example slide in Figure 15-4. Note the deck includes images of the first slide for a few company decks as an example.

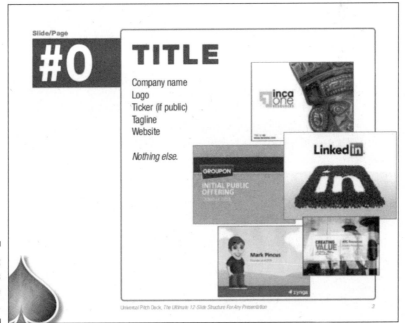

Figure 15-4: A sales deck title slide.

✓ **Overview:** This should contain your company tagline and why your company is awesome. This slide should really pop. Figure 15-5 shows the Creative Aces example page.

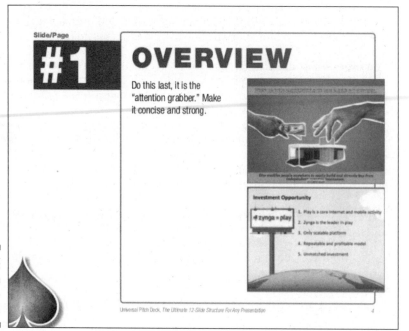

Figure 15-5:
A sales deck over-
view slide.

✓ **The problem:** What is the problem that your services can solve? I would encourage your sales reps to include their own copy here in addition to your main themes. Your reps should speak directly to the lead's personal problems. Figure 15-6 shows an example.

✓ **The solution:** Describe the key benefits your company has to offer. Figure 15-7 shows a few examples of what this slide might look like.

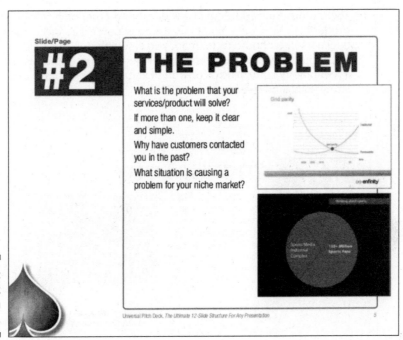

Figure 15-6:
A sales deck problem slide.

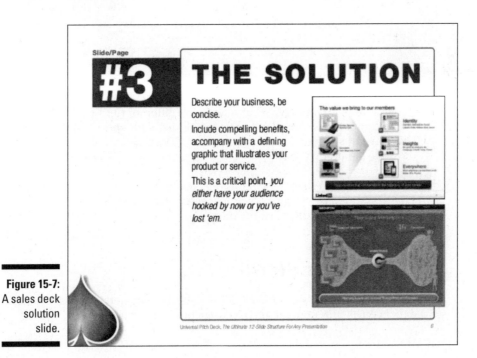

Figure 15-7:
A sales deck solution slide.

✔ **Technology/methodology:** How does your company deliver on the products or services? What can a lead expect? It's okay if your company doesn't sell technology. Instead, you can include your methodology or product development practices. Figure 15-8 shows an example of a technology slide. Notice how the examples have charts and graphs. Show your lead the *how*.

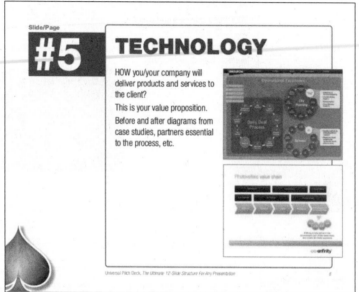

Figure 15-8:
A sales deck technology slide.

✔ **Competitive advantage:** What makes you different (and better) from your competitors? You don't have to call them out specifically, but talk about what sets you apart from the rest. Figure 15-9 shows different ways to set up this slide.

From there, you want to include additional customizable slides that pertain directly to your lead's unique issues. Consider creating slides to introduce the team or talk about the sales timeline.

Providing collateral

You want to give your sales reps all of the material they need to be successful. Brief them on all new content and tell them how they can use it.

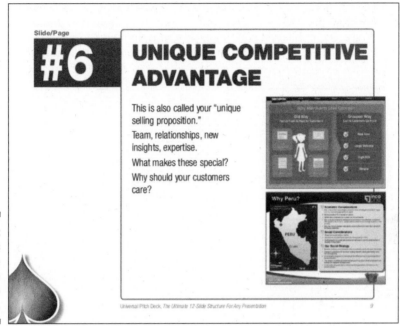

Initially, you should create a spreadsheet (preferably a shareable Google document) that contains the following information for each asset:

- Title
- URL
- Persona
- Buying stage
- Uses
- Industry
- Brief description

Having everything all in one place makes it easier for sales to access your content. You should provide sales training for new, larger content assets. I suggest personal training only for larger assets because if you are a company that creates multiple content pieces per month, you probably won't have the time to train each rep on every single ebook or infographic you come out with.

However, for your larger pieces, I highly recommend an in-person training that reviews your content and messaging. This makes it easier for sales to leverage your thought leadership.

For smaller assets, make sure they are aware of all the new pieces you create. For example, Marketo sends out a monthly content newsletter that includes blog stats, published content assets, and Coming Soon content assets. Take a look at Figure 15-10 to see an example from a content newsletter.

Hi All!
It's time for another content update! Lots of great new content came out in September and there is a lot of new content in the works for the coming months.

Blog Wars

- Rajiv Kapoor and Phillip Chen are neck and neck to almost hitting the next blog milestone of 7 posts!
- This month we got posts from Megan Ziman, Jon Miller, Glen Lipka, DJ Waldow, Greg Higham, Maggie Jones, and Phillip Chen
- **Would love to see more posts from sales, services, and engineering next month!!** Marketing is killing it with the most overall posts month over month
- **Top View Blog Wars Post for September**: Huge shout out to Greg Higham for the most viewed employee post for September with 10,661 views. Take a look at his post The CIO and Social Media: Embracing Change.
- **Top Shared Blog Wars Post for September**: Shout out to Maggie Jones for the most shared employee post with 1.6k shares. Check out her post Just In: The State of Content Marketing in 2014.

New Content in September

- Marketing Budgets: The Strategic Allocation Model: A Sirius Decisions report on budgeting best practices and the marketing budget allocation model.
- Based on DG2EEM:
  - How to Design Your Emails. Ebook to learn about email dimensions and size, responsive design, mobile email, images, and testing your designs.
  - Creating Your Email Subject Lines and From Names: Ebook that goes over how long your subject lines should be, how to build trust with your From name, and other best practices to follow.
  - Score Your Email Marketing Engagement: A quick cheatsheet survey to discover your company's level of email marketing engagement.
  - Conversations Not Campaigns: An ebook that discusses what engaging email conversations look like and how you can listen and adapt your email marketing strategy.
  - Graduating from an Email Service Provider to Marketing Automation: New and improved ebook! Learn why you need to graduate from email to marketing automation.
  - Email Deliverability: Ebook on why your reputation as a sender is crucial, legal issues around deliverability, and email deliverability best practices.

Coming Soon

- **Definitive Guide to Lead Generation: January**
- More DG2EEM Sub Assets:
  - Social Media and Email Marketing (ebook): October
  - Developing and Maintaining a Quality Email Marketing List (ebook): October
  - What is Engaging Email? (ebook): October
- State of Social Media and Healthcare (ebook): October
- Building a Budget Process that Works (ebook): October
- Marketing Budget Diaries: Making Life Easier with Marketo Financial Management (ebook): October
- Building a Facebook Editorial Calendar (ebook): October
- Program Planning Templates for Marketers (PPT Template): November
- 2014 Marketing Success Kit: November
- Social Media and Marketing Automation (ebook): November

Figure 15-10: A sample content newsletter.

Training your sales team

In addition to the training you provide for your content assets, you also want to provide overall product and messaging training for sales. Every time you launch a new product or service, or have a large lead generation effort planned (such as event), you should provide thorough training. This could include

- Messaging
- Call scripts
- Rebuttals
- New sales decks
- New assets

If you are doing a more in-depth training, like a demo training, consider offering a certification to your sales reps. For instance, teach and train your teams on how to give a demo of your solution, require them to learn the demo, and then test their knowledge by having your sales reps perform a demo. If they pass, they can get "demo-certified."

Overall, in order to have a seamless process between marketing and sales, you need consistency in definitions and consistency in messaging. If marketing leads the charge on this, your buyers will have great experiences and sales can close more deals.

Part IV
The Middle of the Funnel

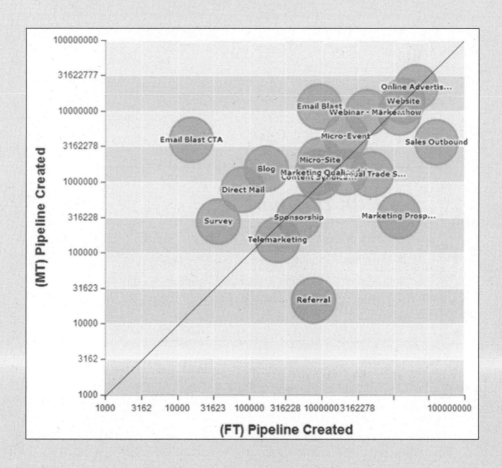

Visit www.dummies.com/extras/leadgeneration to find out how to make sure your emails hit the right inboxes.

In this part . . .

- ✔ Create well-designed emails that engage your audience
- ✔ Find out how to nurture leads until they are ready to buy
- ✔ Use multi-channel tactics in your lead nurture campaigns
- ✔ Learn scoring techniques that send purchase-ready leads to sales

Chapter 16

Communicating Through Email Marketing

*A*fter you have plenty of leads in your database, what do you do with them? Lead generation doesn't stop at acquisition. In fact, according to Marketo's data, 98 percent of their leads are *not* ready to buy when they come into their database. That sounds crazy, right? Well, if you are doing a ton of top-of-funnel lead-generation tactics, you are casting a wide net and introducing people to your company very early in the buying process.

Your leads have a buying journey to go through, and by engaging in middle-of-the-funnel marketing tactics such as email marketing, you can ensure that you are speaking to your leads in *all stages* of the buying journey. Email marketing helps create personalized relationships with buyers over time. Without a focus on a middle-of-the-funnel strategy, many of your leads dry up and never become customers. Email marketing is a great way to keep in touch with leads already in your database. Send emails to your leads when you are launching a new product or service, promoting a new content asset, attending an event, and so on. Email is as relevant as ever before, with 94 percent of Americans more than 12 years of age using it regularly. Fifty-eight percent of adults check email first thing in the morning. So, email should remain a large part of your holistic lead-generation strategy.

Your emails should serve one of the following purposes:

✔ **Transactional:** An operational email that could be related to a purchase or an event registration.

✔ **Promotional:** An email meant to promote an action — downloading an ebook, signing up for a demo, and so on.

- ✔ **Relationship development:** Meant to maintain your relationship with your leads.

- ✔ **Communication:** Update or communicate some sort of information, like a newsletter or product announcement.

- ✔ **Reminder:** A reminder that an event is approaching, such as a webinar or tradeshow.

Reaching the Right People

Hopefully you have a wide variety of leads in your database. You have leads that represent all of your different personas and more. An important part of effective email marketing is reaching the right people and segmenting your database appropriately. For instance, you wouldn't send a lead in Boston an invite to an event in San Francisco. By having clean data and understanding how you segment your database for an email send, you can have much better results.

Keeping your data clean

The first step to proper segmentation is a clean database. What does this mean? In short, it means making sure the data you have in your system is the *correct* data. This means incorrect phone numbers, email addresses, duplicate contacts, and other bad data can basically stop up your funnel. If you aren't sending the right emails to the right email addresses, you will have angry leads and lots of bounce-backs.

You can employ data cleaning services like LeanData and Talend, who fix your data by identifying and repairing incorrect, redundant, or non-conforming data. Here are also some best practices to keep in mind for clean data:

- ✔ **Collect the same data points on every form:** Identify the data you want to collect on a form and try to standardize the process. That means, if there are five things you want from a lead, try to keep that consistent. When you change one form, make sure the others are updated, too.

- ✔ **Clean duplicate data:** Duplicate data is often considered a low-hanging fruit because it is easier to find and fix than some other data problems. An example would be two of the same accounts belonging to the same rep or one lead with multiple different email addresses or spellings of her name. Many CRM and marketing automation tools enable you to clean out duplicate data.

- ✔ **Standardize fields in your CRM and marketing automation tool:** Make sure your fields are the same across the board. You can also easily bucket (or standardize) data to summarize all of the different answer possibilities. For instance, for someone's title, such as director of marketing, that data can be input in a ton of different ways: *director, marketing*; *marketing director*; and so on. Bucketing by common keywords and abbreviations helps you to standardize this process across your systems.

Segmenting and targeting

After you have determined how clean your data is (and hopefully it is fairly clean), start thinking about segmenting and targeting. By highly targeting your communications, you can have 30-percent higher rates of leads opening your messages than if you're sending undifferentiated messages, according to the Direct Marketing Associations National Client Email Report.

Small, segmented sends are more engaging than large, untargeted sends. Why? Because it's impossible to truly speak to a person in an engaging way with a generic message to a large group. Marketo has found segmentation to be the highest ROI impact tactic used by email marketers, as seen in Figure 16-1.

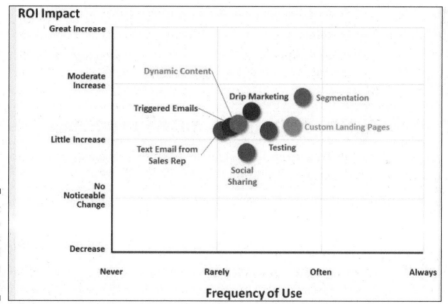

Figure 16-1:
Marketo benchmarks on email marketing ROI.

Here are two types of relevant segmentation techniques that you should be using:

- ✔ **Demographic:** Income, age, title, location, and so on
- ✔ **Behavioral:** What your lead has done and how she has behaved — online body language

Behavioral targeting and segmentation have the most effect on your leads because you can ensure you are remaining relevant. As an example, say you see a lead has downloaded three ebooks about email marketing. Why not send him a follow-up triggered email with more email marketing best practices? According to Jupiter Research, targeting emails based on behavior increases open rates by more than 50 percent and conversion rates by more than 350 percent.

Here is a list from Marketo of behavioral triggers to use when segmenting and targeting your emails:

- ✔ **Campaign response to prior email:** If a lead opened or clicked on a prior email campaign

- ✔ **Content interactions:** If a lead downloaded or shared a content asset

- ✔ **Social interactions:** If a lead commented on or shared a post on his social network

- ✔ **Buying stage:** What buying stage the lead is in, as determined by a lead score

- ✔ **One-time buyer versus repeat buyer:** How many times has a lead purchased from your company?

- ✔ **Transactional data:** What has the lead purchased over time?

- ✔ **Customer anniversary:** The date a lead became a customer

- ✔ **Cart abandonment:** If a lead added an item to her online shopping cart, but never purchased it

Considering paid email programs

Another way to reach the right people with your email campaigns is through paid email programs. A *paid email program* means you pay a vendor to send an email out for you. These programs are great if you want to reach a targeted group but don't have enough leads, or you want to increase the size of your database.

There are two main types of paid email programs you can participate in:

- ✔ **Sponsored emails:** You can work directly with a vendor to send an email campaign to their database on your behalf. Just be sure you choose a reputable vendor or organization that has a high-quality database.

- ✔ **List rentals:** You can purchase an email list through a list rental company based on various demographic criteria. List rental can be tricky, so do your research beforehand to make sure that the vendor updates their list regularly.

When creating your email for a paid program, make sure your branding and CTA (call-to-action) are very clear. Not everyone who receives your email will have heard of your company, so you want to make sure who you are and what you want the lead to do is as obvious as possible.

Engaging with Email

It is important to note that email marketing is no longer about email blasts. *Email blasts* are those old batch-and-blast spammy emails that marketers used to send to leads. Those just don't work anymore, particularly with new email advancements like the new tabbed inbox in Gmail that automatically puts promotional emails in a separate tab from the user's primary messages. Marketers have to *work* to get their email messages seen.

According to Jon Miller from Marketo, "Consumers are always on, always connected, and always overwhelmed. If you want to connect with them, you have to work hard to engage them. In order to be truly effective, email marketing must become trusted, relevant, personal, and strategic." In fact, *the best marketing shouldn't feel like marketing at all*.

Navigating the email opt-in

You want your leads to opt in to your communication — meaning, they are asking and agreeing to receive email communication from you. If they don't opt in, they will quickly perceive you as spam. If they do opt in, your leads can *expect* to receive your emails, and you become more trusted.

Here are some types of opt-ins to consider:

- ✔ **Single opt-in:** A lead enters his email address and other information into a form. He is immediately subscribed to your emails. *Implicit* opt-in is when your lead fills out a form to receive a content piece or offer, and *explicit* opt-in is when a lead signs up for your email marketing through a form on your website.

- ✔ **Single opt-in with a welcome email:** After a lead opts in implicitly or explicitly, she receives an auto-response email thanking her and welcoming her to your email correspondence. You can include messaging in this email about other offers and you should touch on what the lead can expect from your communications.

- ✔ **Confirmed opt-in:** After a lead enters his email address, a pop-up lets him know to expect another email with a link for confirmation. A few seconds later, a confirmation email is sent and the lead needs to click on the link to be confirmed.

As an example of a single explicit opt-in, take a look at Figure 16-2. Note that the CTA says Send Me Updates, so leads know that if they fill out this form, they will receive updates.

Figure 16-2:
A single
explicit
opt-in.

Keeping yourself out of the spam filter

Having opt-ins and providing the opportunity for leads to unsubscribe is one way to keep your messages out of the spam filter. But what is spam and why and when do leads decide an email is classified as spam?

A lead might consider the following spam:

✔ An email that is unexpected

✔ An email that is unwanted

✔ An email from an account that a lead has previously unsubscribed to

✔ Email copy that seems spammy — overuse of words like *free* and *deal,* for example, or the inclusion of a lot of exclamation points

✔ An email a lead no longer wants

Your best bet for keeping out of the spam filter is to create emails that are interesting, engaging, relevant, and that offer a WIIFM (What's In It For Me). Marketo has come up with a Subscriber Covenant that governs how we send emails to our own database:

Dear Subscriber,

We promise to

- ✔ Send emails you actually want
- ✔ Deliver those emails when you want them
- ✔ Use data we collect from you to send targeted, relevant information

Sincerely,

The Marketo Marketing Department

In 2003, an act called CAN-SPAM (Controlling the Assault of Non-Solicited Pornography and Marketing) was introduced to establish rules of engagement for commercial marketing messages and give recipients the right to enforce that a business stop emailing them. The act outlines numerous rules by which a commercial emailer must abide, including providing clear and easy ways to opt-out of communications and adding a physical postal address on every email sent out, and so on. As a marketer, be sure to check out the exact rules and regulations and meet with your legal or compliance team.

Listening to social cues

Another way to ensure that your emails are engaging is to integrate your email campaigns with your social marketing. Your leads and customers are living in a multichannel world, so be where they are. You can combine your social efforts and email marketing by

- ✔ Using your email list to grow your social followers through sharing buttons
- ✔ Using email to extend your social campaigns, and vice versa
- ✔ Using social media to grow your email list and promote your email content
- ✔ Always including a social icon on all of your emails so people can follow you and share your message
- ✔ Sending a dedicated email to your database and asking that they engage with you on social channels

Designing Emails

Now on to the fun part: making your emails eye-catching, appealing, and awesome! The design and how you present your emails are going to be what makes or breaks you in the world of email marketing. The more compelling and engaging your emails look, feel, and read, the more likely you are to delight your leads and keep them coming back for more.

Read on to find out how to create emails that convert.

Writing a compelling subject line

Your email subject line is what drives open rates, so this is one of the most important aspects of good email design. Feel free to play around with your subject lines a bit! You can be playful, humorous, mysterious, and intriguing. But make sure your subject line is clear and concise. The worst mistake an email marketer can make is to send out a subject line he thinks is clever, but is lost on everyone who opens it. So be creative, but also be clear. You can always A/B test your subject lines to see what works best (more on A/B testing in Chapter 19).

Here are some approaches to email subject lines that I have seen work very well:

- **Ask a question:** Create a subject line that includes a question. This type of subject line often compels your readers to open the email. It also forces your reader to pause and consider the answer to this question.

- **Make a list:** People love lists in blogs and content pieces, so why not try a list subject line in your emails? *Top 3*, *5 tips*, and so on do wonders for your open rates.

- **Surprise your readers:** Use a subject line that surprises your readers and makes them stop in their tracks. Recently, I got an email from one of my favorite sites, Copyblogger, with the heading *Why I Hate Copyblogger*. Of course, this piqued my attention and made me open the email.

- **Offer a discount:** Tons of discount emails hit my inbox, and I find that a deal is always likely to make me click. Start your subject line with *5% off*, or *Free Sample,* and you have someone's attention instantly.

- **Personalization:** With all of this talk about relevance, why not create a subject line that is personalized and speaks directly to the lead? If you are using marketing automation, you can create a personalized token, and you can trigger emails based off of behaviors. So if a person makes a purchase, send her an email saying, "Thanks for buying *X*, we know you will love *X*."

Crafting copy that converts

After you have your lead's attention, you have to *keep* that attention at least long enough for him to read your email and take an action. A good best practice is to make sure your copy is human. Have a little fun and don't be afraid to bring in some humor. You also want to educate and not sell. Show your leads why they should read your email and click through. No one wants to be bothered with an ad in the form of an email.

Take into consideration what function you intend your email to have. Is it promotional or relationship-building? The answer drives your copy and tone.

Just like any website or landing page, your copy should be clear and concise, address the pain point, and include bullets or lists for easy scanning. Don't forget to proofread! Spelling and grammar mistakes are a huge no-no.

Take a look at Figure 16-3 for an example of clear, concise copy. Note that Salesforce includes a couple of short paragraphs, followed by a clear CTA, and then a few bullet points on what you will learn by signing up for their webinar. What do I love about this? It's simple.

salesforce

Inside Salesforce.com's
Social Media Strategy

For businesses today, there is arguably nothing more important than defining your social strategy. Not only will an active presence bring you closer to your customers, but companies that invest in social are more profitable.

Join our Webinar to look inside our social playbook. You will find out what worked well and what pitfalls you should avoid when building your social strategy.

Webinar Details:
Inside Salesforce.com's Social Media Strategy
Hosted by the salesforce.com Social Team
Friday, January 25th, 11 am PST

REGISTER NOW >

During this 60-minute webinar, we'll give you insight into:

Salesforce Marketing Cloud is the World's Only Unified Social Marketing Suite

Learn More >

marketing cloud

Figure 16-3: An example of concise email copy.

- How salesforce.com is using social media to grow the business
- What programs are providing value and what tools salesforce.com is using group-by-group
- How salesforce.com coordinates social media

Including visual design

Visual design is an important component to creating an email that converts. What is good visual design? You want to not only include compelling images, but also make sure that your email is formatted properly.

When an email comes into an inbox, a subscriber has to turn on the images so that they come through. The good news is that 55 percent of consumers surveyed by The Relevancy Group say that they turn on images in the emails they receive. The bad news? Many consumers don't turn on their images.

Your email should *look* appealing. Don't use stock imagery if you can help it, and use imagery that is relevant to your audience.

Take a look at Figure 16-4 for an example of clean design with good use of imagery. This is an email from Apple about a recent product launch. The email has little copy and a very simple design. But the design and the small amount of copy included truly say it all and intrigue the reader.

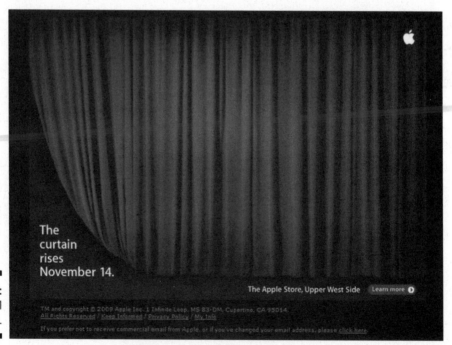

Figure 16-4:
Apple email
design.

Figure 16-5 is an email from Kiehl's. Note that they include copy asking the recipient to shop customer favorites with images of each product and Shop Now CTA buttons.

Figure 16-5: Kiehl's email design.

After you have your imagery in place, you need to make sure that you are optimizing your emails for those who do *not* have images turned on in their email program. A really cool way to do this is to create a download button that is not an image but is instead HTML code. Try using a button generator such as the Bulletproof Button Generator at `http://emailtransmit.com/bulletproof`.

You can go to the site, input your button text, format, button height, and width, and the site generates HTML code for you to input into your email. As you can see in Figure 16-6, the HTML looks like a button, so it really pops.

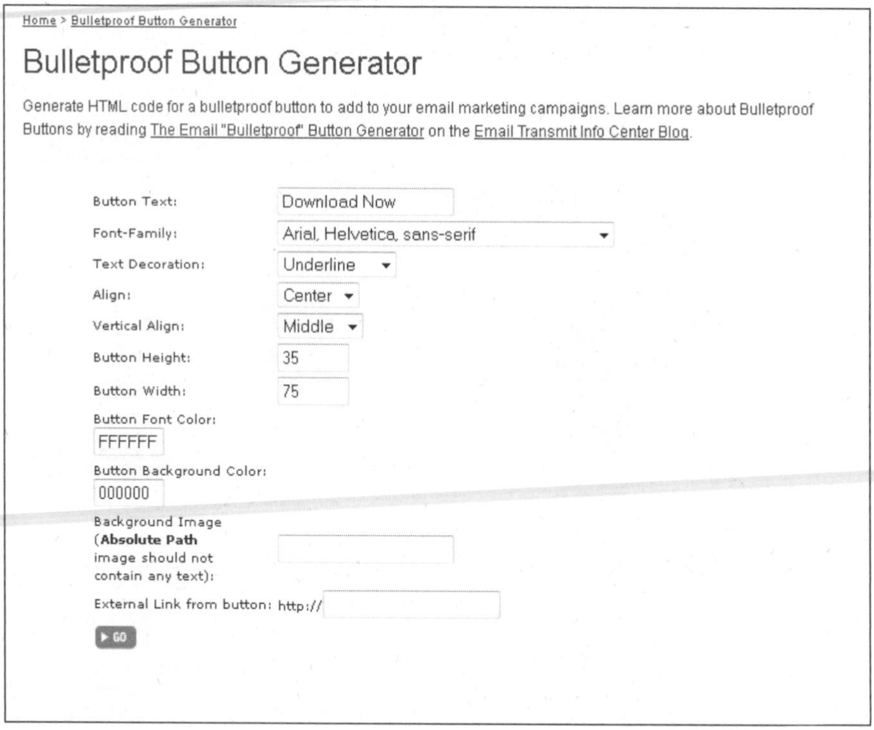

Home > Bulletproof Button Generator

Bulletproof Button Generator

Generate HTML code for a bulletproof button to add to your email marketing campaigns. Learn more about Bulletproof Buttons by reading The Email "Bulletproof" Button Generator on the Email Transmit Info Center Blog.

Button Text:	Download Now
Font-Family:	Arial, Helvetica, sans-serif
Text Decoration:	Underline
Align:	Center
Vertical Align:	Middle
Button Height:	35
Button Width:	75

Button Font Color:
FFFFFF

Button Background Color:
000000

Background Image
(**Absolute Path**
image should not
contain any text):

External Link from button: http://

▶ GO

Figure 16-6:
The
Bulletproof
Button
Generator
criteria
input.

And voilà! I have a text-based button and some code I can input to generate my button, as seen in Figure 16-7.

Bulletproof Button Generator

Generate HTML code for a bulletproof button to add to your email marketing campaigns. Learn more about Bulletproof Buttons by reading The Email "Bulletproof" Button Generator on the Email Transmit Info Center Blog.

Copy the code below

```
<table cellpadding="0" cellspacing="0" border="0"> <tr> <td
bgcolor="#000000" background="" height="35" width="75"
style="color:#FFFFFF; font-family:Arial, Helvetica, sans-serif;"
align="center" valign="middle"> <a href="http://" style="color:#FFFFFF;
text-decoration:underline;">Download Now</a> </td> </tr> </table>
```

Figure 16-7: A Bulletproof button.

Also make sure that you use image `alt` tags so that recipients who block images know what your email is about. For instance, if your email has a large image that reads *$50 Visa Gift Card for a Demo*, make sure your `alt` tag says `$50 Visa Gift Card for a Demo`. That way, even if your lead doesn't see your image, she knows what the image conveys.

Keeping it mobile-friendly

According to digital marketing agency Knotice, 81 percent of people read emails on their mobile devices. However, MarketingSherpa reports that 58 percent of marketers are *not* designing emails to be mobile-friendly. Yikes! That is a huge opportunity that we are missing to reach leads and customers where they are reading — their phones and tablets.

When designing emails to be read on mobile devices, keep the following design options in mind:

- ✔ **Responsive:** This is when the layout of your email responds and changes based on the proportions of the screen on which it is opened. Responsive design is a common technique for both email and website pages.

- ✔ **Scalable:** The layout of your email should be clickable and readable even when it is reduced to a very small size — that is, on a mobile phone or tablet.

Media Queries, a CSS3 module that allows for content to adapt to screen size and resolution, can help you control the way your emails display on mobile devices. Keep the following in mind:

- Mobile email is most often accessed on 320 px × 480 px screens.

- If a device does not support responsive design, your emails will be scaled.

- Your images should still be readable when resized, so check and see the minimum size for images allowed on various smartphones.

- Pay attention to the language you use in your *pre-header* — the preview that appears on most mobile devices. You want to make sure you convey the right message.

- Because most mobile readers tap items with their fingers, make your buttons large and easy to tap.

Placing your calls-to-action (CTAs)

Like any well-designed lead-generation campaign, your emails should have a clear and obvious CTA. And don't do too many things at once! Try to limit your email CTAs to one important item. For instance, you don't want to ask people to sign up for your webinar, download your ebook, *and* sign up for a demo. Ask them to do *one* of these things for maximum conversion. Make sure that your CTAs are bold and obvious. Many companies include their primary CTA at the top, in the middle of the text, and at the end.

Figure 16-8 shows an example of an email that provides a very clear call-to-action. Note how the CTA appears in the heading. There is a link within the text and a link at the end of the copy. All of these CTAs ask a lead to do the same thing — download an ebook.

The Definitive Guide to Lead Nurturing

The ultimate resource for lead nurturing, whether you're just starting to think about lead nurturing in your business or are looking for ways to enhance and optimize your existing programs.

Download Now!

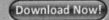

Your Ultimate Guide to Lead Nurturing

Hello Dayna,

When done well, lead nurturing plays a critical role in your organization. Up to 95% of qualified prospects on your website are there to research and are not ready to talk with a sales rep, but as many as 70% will eventually buy a product from you - or your competitors. On average, nurtured leads produce a 20% increase in sales opportunities versus non-nurtured leads. Are you ready to start nurturing yet?

The Definitive Guide to Lead Nurturing is packed with 40 pages of thought leadership, best practices, and actionable advice to jump-start your lead nurturing.

Inside, you'll learn:

- **What is Lead Nurturing?** Learn about building relationships and trust with your prospects in a way that is both consistent and relevant.
- **Lead Nurturing Basics.** Even if you are already using lead nurturing, these best practices can help augment your current initiatives.
- **Advanced Lead Nurturing.** Examine the nuances and winning strategies for advanced lead nurturing. Includes worksheets.
- **Calculating the ROI of Lead Nurturing.** Prove the ROI of lead nurturing in your own organization by comparing your results to industry averages. Includes worksheets.

Download your eBook now.

Figure 16-8:
An example of a clear email CTA.

Practicing Basic Email Metrics

Measuring your email campaign performance is a sure-fire way to look at program success so you can iterate and optimize emails going forward. Here are some basic metrics to keep in mind as you delve into email marketing feet first:

- ✔ **Sent:** The number of emails that actually moved through your sending email server.

- ✔ **Delivered:** The number of emails that were not rejected by the receiving server.

- ✔ **Bounced:** The number of emails that were bounced back and rejected. This includes both hard and soft bounces — a *hard bounce* being a permanent delivery failure, and a *soft bounce* indicating a temporary issue like a full mailbox.

- ✔ **Open Rate:** The number of recipients that opened and viewed your email.

- ✔ **Click Rate:** The number of recipients who clicked something in your email. Note this is only calculated once per recipient. The number of clicks is divided by the total number of emails delivered.

- ✔ **Unsubscribe Rate:** The number of recipients who unsubscribed to your communications.

Chapter 17

Learning the Basics of Lead Nurturing

In This Chapter

▶ Building relationships with leads that aren't ready to buy

▶ Driving leads through your sales funnel with lead nurturing

▶ Creating a variety of lead nurture campaigns

▶ Making sure your lead nurturing efforts are multichannel

*L*ead nurturing is the process of building relationships with qualified prospects regardless of their timing to buy, with the goal of earning their business when they *are* ready. Many of your lead-generation tactics will be very top-of-funnel, meaning you are hopefully casting a wide net and generating a lot of new leads. However, due to today's buying process, the majority of those leads are not ready to buy, since they are still researching options. Without a process like lead nurturing, your lead-generation efforts are dead in the water, meaning you are missing a *huge* opportunity for your lead-generation efforts to convert to revenue.

Through lead nurturing, you can provide relevant material that maps directly to each phase of the buying cycle, persona, and interests. Basically, lead nurturing plugs your leaky funnel!

Remember: You can't just send your leads a series of unrelated emails without context. You have to listen to signals across *all* of the channels they spend time on, and engage your leads based on their interests.

Setting Up a Basic Lead Nurturing Campaign

Focus your lead-nurturing efforts on your existing database of leads. Just think about how much untapped revenue is in there *right now*! And think about how much money you have spent to get those leads to your database in the first place. According to Marketo, "Despite the time and money invested, marketers often lack concrete processes for extracting value out of their existing database. At companies who are not investing in their current database, most leads come from new spending, there is no long-term benefit from marketing investments, and marketing is seen as a cost center."

That's not a good situation! So how do you get started with nurturing those high-quality leads into customers? One important step towards lead nurturing success is acquiring a marketing automation tool, and there are many great ones out there that can help make your nurturing a success. For more information on the different options available for marketing automation software, see Chapter 4 on choosing the right technology.

Incoming lead-processing campaigns

Think of lead nurturing as a way to build and cement a long-term relationship with your leads. An incoming lead-processing campaign is basically a welcome campaign that introduces your new leads to who your company is and what they can expect by opting-in to your communications. Understand where these leads are initially in your funnel, and create nurture tracks that address the buying process. Where they are in the buying journey can be determined by their initial lead score (more on lead scoring to come in Chapter 18).

Your incoming processing campaign is probably a good place to ask leads to opt-in to your nurturing program. This means giving a lead the opportunity to decline communication with you. Communication compliance could be a whole *For Dummies* book on its own, but know that all email marketers must comply with the CAN-SPAM Act, which means that all email marketing communication must provide a way for a lead to opt-out. You can read more about the CAN-SPAM Act in Chapter 16.

"Staying in touch" campaigns

After your incoming lead-processing campaign, most marketers will add their leads to a *stay in touch* campaign. These campaigns are exactly what they sound like — staying in touch — and are the bread and butter to most nurture programs. Basically, over time, you can send the lead relevant educational material that helps lead her down the funnel. A simple example of a stay in touch campaign might look like the following:

- ✔ Email 1: Welcome email
- ✔ Email 2: TOFU (top-of-funnel) asset 1
- ✔ Email 3: TOFU asset 2

- Email 4: TOFU blog post or infographic
- Email 5: MOFU (middle-of-funnel) asset 1
- Email 6: MOFU asset 2
- Email 7: MOFU blog post or infographic
- Email 8: Datasheet
- Email 9: Customer testimonials
- Email 10: Pricing sheet and demo request

Notice how each email drives your lead farther down your sales funnel — from early-stage assets, to mid-stage, and then finally, late-stage assets.

Accelerating leads down the funnel

Consider creating accelerator campaigns to move leads down the funnel at a faster rate. These nurturing campaigns are often triggered by specific behaviors, such as a lead downloading a specific type of content or visiting your pricing page. I have also seen accelerator campaigns implemented at the end of a month or at the end of the year, to drive sales.

Here are some elements to keep in mind when planning accelerator trigger campaigns:

- Know what behavior indicates a high level of interest.
- Develop multiple tracks that speak to different levels of interest — for example, someone downloading a mid-funnel asset versus downloading a pricing sheet.
- Use offers that spark immediate engagement — a $50 Visa card for a demo or sales meeting, a chance to win an iPad, and so on.

Using interest-based campaigns

Another type of nurturing track is the interest-based nurture track. Send the lead what you know he's interested in. If a lead comes to your site and downloads two ebooks on personal finance, continue sending him content on personal finance versus sending him content on small business finance. Through interest-based campaigns, you can move your leads down the funnel, but also make sure that he stays engaged with your content at the same time.

In fact, Marketo has seen a 57-percent increase in opens and a 59-percent increase in *click-to-opens* (the number of unique clicks divided by the number of unique opens) since they started doing interest-based nurture campaigns.

Recycling leads

Make sure you have nurture tracks created for recycled leads. A *recycled lead* is a lead that sales determines is not *sales-accepted* — that is, someone that doesn't fit the ideal lead profile or who isn't ready to talk to sales. For more detail on sales-accepted leads, refer to Chapter 15. Therefore, sales sends that lead back to nurturing. But just because a lead isn't ready to buy at the time she is contacted doesn't mean she will *never* be ready to buy. Create lead recycle tracks based on the data that a sales rep collected during the call, such as decision timeframe and interests. That way, you can make sure you communicate with your leads in an appropriate fashion post-sales.

Going Beyond Email to Multichannel Nurturing

Your buyers are in multiple different places. Whether they visit your website, go to one of your social channels, attend an event, or listen to a webinar, you need to be with them at every level. Imagine that a lead first enters your system by downloading an ebook about Twitter. Then imagine that you meet him at an in-person event where you conduct a demo and have an entire conversation with him. How would it look if the next week your company sent him an email asking if he would like a demo?

It doesn't look very good, and it makes the lead feel unimportant and like you weren't listening. A good lead-nurturing solution today includes capabilities to listen to your lead and respond across multiple different channels. By embracing engagement marketing through nurturing, you can know that your lead already viewed a demo at an event and send a more appropriate and *relevant* email triggered by an interaction.

New lead-nurturing modules such as Marketo's Customer Engagement engine enable you to send leads the best message and the right piece of content based on who the lead is and what she has done in the past. Examples of filters you might be able to apply in lead-nurturing programs can be seen in Figure 17-1, which shows a screenshot from Marketo that includes different triggers you can set up based on lead actions.

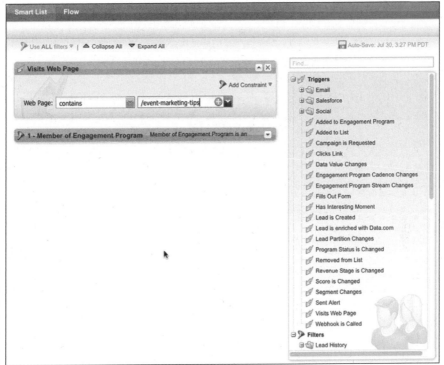

Figure 17-1:
Marketo
lead-
nurturing
triggers.

When thinking about multichannel engagement, consider the following:

- ✔ **Always listen and then respond:** Listen to and respond to leads both online and off in a consistent way.

- ✔ **Be aware of how often you communicate:** Many marketers have problems with lead nurturing because they don't have a holistic view of what they send and how often. Many advanced lead-nurturing solutions enable you to set communications limits so leads won't get blasted.

- ✔ **Know what content your lead has seen:** There is nothing worse than receiving duplicate content from a vendor. Leads easily get annoyed if you aren't listening. Make sure you have a lead-nurturing solution that lets you track and alerts you when you have already sent a particular piece of content to a lead.

- ✔ **Have an easy lead-nurture solution:** Don't lean on IT every time you need to set up a new lead-nurturing program. There are plenty of marketing automation solutions out there that offer ease of use and simplicity.

Chapter 18

Perfecting Your Lead-Generation Techniques with Lead Scoring

*H*ow do you know when a lead is ready to be contacted by sales? If you don't implement lead scoring, you will have no idea. *Lead scoring* is a shared sales and marketing methodology for ranking leads in order to determine their sales-readiness. Basically, lead scoring takes all of your lead-generation and nurturing campaigns and provides a methodology to determine how close a person is to purchasing and where she is on the buying journey. A lead score is created in your marketing automation tool.

Scoring should be determined based on the following overall factors:

> ✔ **Fit:** How does the lead fit in with your defined buyer persona?

> ✔ **Interest:** How interested is the lead in your products?

> ✔ **Buying stage:** How far along in the buying journey is the lead?

The score of your lead determines whether he will be fast-tracked to sales or sent back to nurturing. (Remember those recycled lead tracks I spoke about in Chapter 17?)

Establishing the Basics of Lead Scoring

Remember that shared sales and marketing definition of a good lead? Basically, lead scoring helps you drive towards that definition by giving a lead a positive or negative score in your marketing automation tool based on various demographics and behaviors. This means that you have to not only define what a good lead is, but you also have to determine how you score your assets and actions. For instance, you may give downloading a TOFU (top-of-funnel) ebook on a general topic a lower score than downloading a third-party analyst report that helps define purchasing behavior of a lead.

Knowing the difference between implicit and explicit scoring

Most marketers need to pay attention to two types of scoring: explicit (fit) and implicit (interest) scoring. *Explicit scoring data* is created from observable or collected information via an online form. This type of scoring takes into account demographic, firmographic, and BANT (budget, authority, need, and time) scoring criteria that you determined with sales early on in your lead-generation process. For a refresher on these definitions, be sure to re-read Chapter 2. Depending on the importance of each factor, you can establish varying scores for each criteria.

Here are some common explicit score changers to think about for a lead:

- Title and role
- Role in the decision process
- Years of experience
- Degrees received
- Company
- Number of employees
- Revenue growth
- Location
- Industry
- Budget
- Timeframe

Implicit scoring consists of tracking various behaviors to determine buying intent. Implicit scoring can also consist of inferred data such as IP addresses and so on. With implicit scores, you want to score the activity based on the value it has to purchasing.

Here are some common implicit score changers to think about for a lead:

- Attended a tradeshow
- Attended a webinar
- Downloaded an ebook or content asset
- Subscribed to the blog or email list

✔ Visited a product/service page

✔ Visited a pricing page

✔ Filled out a form

✔ Searched for company name

✔ Liked or followed your company on a social channel

Defining active versus latent buying behavior

When determining the numerical value behind each score, you need to understand the difference between active and latent buying behavior. Just because someone downloaded one of your ebooks doesn't mean that your sales team should pick up the phone and call her right away.

You need to determine what *defines* active buying behavior and score appropriately. *Active* behavior involves sales readiness and purchase intent. *Latent* behavior describes a behavior that shows less engagement and sales readiness.

For instance, take a look at Table 18-1.

Table 18-1	Active and Latent Buying Behaviors	
Behavior	*Latent Score*	*Active Score*
Downloads early stage content	+3	
Visits a web page or a blog	+1	
Watches a thought leadership webinar	+5	
Visits a pricing page		+10
Watches a detailed demo		+10
Downloads late-stage content		+12
Searches for branded keyword term		+8

The key here is that the follow-up for active versus latent leads is very different. For an active score, your sales reps should follow up immediately. For a latent score, trigger a personalized message instead.

You can also score leads negatively based on actions. For instance, a student might download a ton of early-, mid-, and late-stage content for a research paper. If that person fills out your form and indicates she is a student, you can give a negative score. They're most likely doing research and not actually interested in a purchase. The same is true for a person who visits your website's career page.

Creating a Scoring Model

After you have thought about scoring and how to best apply it to your own lead database, you need to create your scoring model. This is where you go through all of your implicit and explicit scoring criteria and determine how important each action or trait is to you and your business. Every business will be different. There is no right or wrong answer here, so score away!

Setting up your scoring matrix

I want to show a couple of examples of scoring explicit and implicit behaviors, and then I'll show you how to put it all together. Figure 18-1 shows an example of explicit demographic scoring from Marketo. Note how they break up scoring in terms of critical, important, influencing, and negatives. Then they assign a score value based on how important each criteria is to us.

Scoring Demographics – Our Example

Attribute	Value	Scores
Critical: (10-15 points)		
Title	Director or VP	+12
Industry	Healthcare, Financial, or High Tech Industry	+10
Purchase Authority	Decision Maker	+15
Company Revenue	Greater than 500 Million	+10
Product	Using competitive solution	+15
Timeline	Identified, less than 3 months	+12
Important: (5-9 points)		
Location	US	+8
Company Revenue	100 Million to 499 Million	+8
Title	Manager	+7
Timeline	Identified, more than 3 months, less than 8 months	+5
Influencing: (1-4 points)		
Location	English Speaking, Non US	+4
Timeline	Identified, more than 8 months	+3
Title	Analyst, Coordinator, or Specialist	+4
Company Revenue	Less than 100 million	+1
Negative:		
Title	Student	-15
Title	Consultant	-5
Industry	Services	-6
Industry	ecommerce	-10
Location	Non English Speaking Country	-10

Figure 18-1: An example of explicit scoring.

Figure 18-2 shows you an example of implicit scoring that scores behaviors based on buying intent.

Scoring Behaviors – Our Example

Behavior	Scores
Critical: (10-15 points)	
Visits pricing pages	+10
Downloads Marketo reviews	+12
Timeline < 3 months	+15
Watches demos	+5 overview demo
	+10 detailed demo
Important: (5-9 points)	
Downloads buyers guides	+8
Downloads data sheets	+8
Searches for "Marketo"	+8
Heavy web activity	+5
Influencing: (1-4 points)	
Watches any webinar	+4
Downloads any white paper	+2
Watches any video	+2
Visits any web page	+1
Bad Behavior: (negative points)	
Email unsubscribe	-10
No website activity for one month	-5
Added to "Do Not Call" list	-5
Negative social media comment	-4
Visits career page	-2
Visits investor page	-2

Figure 18-2:
An example of implicit scoring.

Next, take your chart for implicit and explicit scoring and create a matrix to determine when leads should be sent to sales. In Figure 18-3, you can see an example of a scoring matrix based on behavioral and demographic scoring. Use a similar chart to assign leads to sales.

			Behavior Score			
			50•	24-50	0-25	0
			1	2	3	4
Demographic Score	50+	A				
	24-50	B				
	0-25	C				
	0	D				

Figure 18-3:
A scoring matrix.

Prioritizing sales time

After you determine when a lead is sent to sales, it's important that sales understands what the score means and how "hot" that lead is. Consider creating a visual grading system to determine warm, hot, and super-hot leads so sales is aware of which ones to prioritize.

You can build these capabilities into your CRM or use a tool such as Marketo Sales Insight to determine urgency. Your sales teams also should understand how the lead was created and any interesting moments that a lead may have had — for example, attending a particularly interesting webinar.

Figure 18-4 shows an example of Marketo's Sales Insight dashboard, which integrates into Salesforce. The application tells you the lead name, the account, the last interesting moment, lead status, and priority. The flames indicate urgency and the stars indicate lead quality.

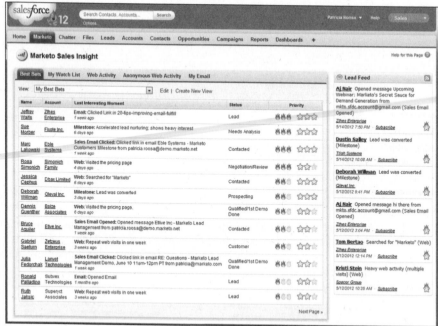

Figure 18-4:
The
Marketo
Sales
Insight
dashboard.

Part V

Measuring Your Lead Generation Efforts

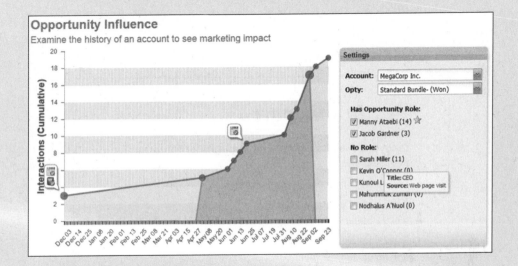

Visit www.dummies.com/extras/leadgeneration to discover the top social media metrics to watch.

In this part . . .

- ✔ Learn to test and optimize your campaigns for maximum performance
- ✔ Create an ideal testing process that works
- ✔ Design all of your lead-generation programs to be measureable
- ✔ Track your return on investment throughout the lead lifecycle and tie closed revenue to marketing programs

Chapter 19

Testing and Optimizing Your Campaigns

· ·

In This Chapter

▶ Learning about A/B testing and why it's important

▶ Understanding what multivariate testing is and how to use it

▶ Conducting your first test

▶ Knowing what to test

· ·

A ll lead-generation campaigns need to be tested. Why? You need to test in order to make your campaigns better over time! Personally, I find testing extremely interesting. Without it, I wouldn't have insight into my programs and I certainly wouldn't know what was working and what wasn't.

A marketing team that doesn't test often is a marketing team that is blind to what their leads are doing. So what do you do? Build testing into your campaign creation and measurement process, and make sure testing is ingrained in each and every team member's minds. Each of your marketers should test his campaigns on a regular basis, or you can even have someone on staff who specializes in (or who highly enjoys) testing.

Testing in lead generation and marketing is akin to the scientific method: communicate a question, hypothesize the answer, formulate your predictions, test those predictions, and analyze the results.

Understanding How to Test

Marketers typically use a few standard testing types to test their campaigns. Note that you can pretty much test any aspect of a campaign from channel used, to copy created, to subject line, time of day sent, and more. So get creative with what you are trying to find out. The more you know, the more you grow!

Depending on what you want to test, you can use your marketing automation platform, a solution that specializes in testing like Optimizely, or you can even use Google Analytics to track changes you have made. In some cases, you may not even need additional testing help. For instance, if you post two messages on a social channel, you can track yourself which post has more shares and engagement.

For more information on what product to use for what test, check out this chart that Conversion Rate Experts released on what solution to use for what test: `www.conversion-rate-experts.com/split-testing-software`. This covers a variety of testing options.

In the next few sections, I dig into some common testing types to set up the framework for success.

A/B testing

A/B tests are probably the most common type of test that a marketer runs. These are also called *split tests*, and they compare the conversion rates of two assets, such as an email or landing page, by changing one element at a time. You can also compare more than two assets by running an A/B/C test or an A/B/C/D test. However, when starting out, I recommend that you begin with a simple A/B test.

The key here is that you are changing only *one* variable at a time so you can pinpoint any change in conversion and attribute it to that changed variable. A/B tests are fantastic for testing things like CTA (call-to-action) buttons, copy, headlines, graphics, form length, and email time sent. You can even use A/B testing for social messaging, content format, or webinar frequency.

When using A/B testing, all you do is split your email send, PPC landing page traffic, or post your social messaging at two different times. You should see one asset performing better than the other.

Figure 19-1 illustrates the idea behind an A/B test from online testing vendor Maxymiser.

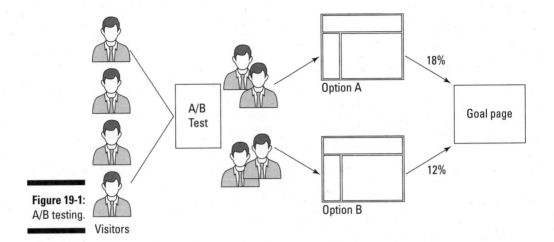

Figure 19-1:
A/B testing.

Visitors

A/B testing is perfect for testing small numbers of variables at a given time, is easy to grasp, and the data can be seen quickly and clearly. The disadvantage of an A/B test is that it is simplistic, so it can't handle multiple variable changes at a time.

Optimizing through multivariate testing

Enter multivariate testing, A/B testing's big (and more complicated) sister. A *multivariate test* can compare a much higher number of variables at one time. Generally, multivariate tests can also show more complex information, therefore telling you more about your campaign performance and testing results. Typically, when embarking on a multivariate test, you need a software solution like Monetate or Optimizely. What do you use multivariate testing for? Well, you can test a combination of design changes, CTA locations, copy choices, and more. However, this gets tricky because you have to ensure that your leads see all possible combinations of your asset to properly assign a winner.

This type of test is great for web and landing pages, and you can gain a lot of information on what the lead engages with. However, multivariate testing is not for everyone because you generally need a large database and a lot of traffic for it to be truly effective. Think of all the possible combinations if you have a landing page and are testing for copy, CTA location, headline, form length, and so on. You can literally vary thousands of things, and often more.

Figure 19-2 shows a multivariate test from HubSpot.

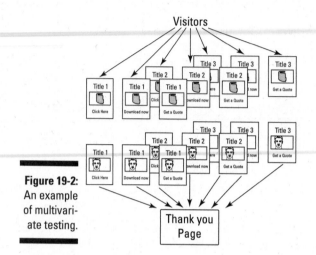

Figure 19-2:
An example
of multivari-
ate testing.

Creating Your Ideal Testing Process

Think of your lead-generation testing as a scientific process. It can be fun and
even exciting at times to test what really makes your audience tick. Everyone
eventually decides on a testing process that works for their own particular
needs, but I want to provide a framework for testing that I have seen work in
my experience.

Formulating your question

The first step in the process is formulating your question. *What* are you testing
and *why* are you testing it? An example would be, "What CTA works best in my
email campaign?" Or, "Which web page design generates the most clicks and
form fill-outs?" This stage can also involve looking at your previous campaigns
to determine what has worked in the past. That way, you can create an educated
hypothesis.

Defining success

Before you create your hypothesis, you also want to determine how you will define success and what your success metrics are. According to testing platform Optimizely, for lead generation, you want to look at macroconversion successes, primary conversions that turn into clicks, conversions, and ultimately leads. You also might want to think about other microconversion metrics, smaller scale conversions, in the form of steps that you want a lead to take, such as clicking a button, watching a video, or liking and sharing a blog post.

Constructing your hypothesis

A *hypothesis* is an educated guess based on the knowledge that you have obtained while thinking about both your question and your success metrics. Your hypothesis should determine what possible combination of variables might work best to achieve your ultimate success metrics. As stated by Optimizely, "Hypotheses make tests more informative because they provide a specific purpose by helping you hone in on what you are actually trying to determine." An example of a hypothesis might be that you believe a form with three fields might have a better conversion rate than a form with five, based on your research and previous campaign performances.

Conducting your test

Now on to the fun part: actually conducting your test. This is where you investigate your hypothesis so you can prove or disprove your theory. There are many best practices to testing and many elements to think about. The following list gives some easy-to-follow steps to conducting an A/B test:

1. **Isolate your variable.**

   For the sake of keeping it simple, I have chosen to use an A/B test as an example. Because it is an A/B test, we are going to focus on one variable that we are going to isolate. I'll use an example email A/B test conducted at Marketo using two different From names. The control email's From address, which Marketo had been using for some time, was Marketo Premium Content. The test email's From name was the personal email address of a sales rep.

2. **Use a large enough sample size.**

   It's tough to prove a hypothesis if your test sample size is small. The larger your sample size can be, the better your test results are. But you have to be careful. For our email example, if you use too large of a sample size, you risk having a large portion of your database receiving a less-effective email. You have to strike a balance right in the middle.

3. **Eliminate confounding variables.**

   Many factors can affect the results of your test, so try to eliminate variables that would render your test obsolete. For this example, you don't just need to leave your control unchanged, but you also need to send your emails at the same time and make sure your test is randomized. If you are using a marketing automation solution, you can usually conduct A/B testing quickly and efficiently by sending 50 percent of your emails to a random sample of your designated list.

4. **Look at the results.**

   After you have sent out your test, wait and examine your results to prove or disprove your hypothesis. First, you need to look to determine if a statistical significance, the probability that results are meaningful and not because of chance, exists between your two versions. A helpful hint here is to do an online search for *A/B testing significance calculator*. Figure 19-3 shows an example of a significance calculator from Visual Website Optimizer. You input the number of visitors for both the control and variation, as well as the number of conversions. And then you can calculate the significance.

   You can also use calculators to determine the confidence score, so you know just *how* significant your test is. A 95-percent or more confidence score is where you want to be to know your test is significant.

A/B Split Test Significance Calculator		
Are your results significant?		
	Control	Variation
Number of Visitors	600	700
Number of Conversions	100	150
P-value	0.014	
Significant?	Yes!	
	Calculate Significance	

Figure 19-3: An A/B testing significance calculator.

Back to the From name test. The personalized From name had 1,000 more opens and 500 more clicks than the control name. Our confidence level in our results was 99 percent. And because we only isolated *one* factor, it was clear why the email with the personalized From name received more clicks.

Next, of course, you want to optimize your campaigns based off of your test results. This should be fairly simple and straightforward if you are always testing as I suggest. Take your results and implement them!

Checking Your Tests off of the List

There are so many things you can test. Need some ideas? Take a look at this handy list courtesy of Dan Siroker, CEO and cofounder of Optimizely, and Pete Koomen, president and cofounder of Optimizely:

✔ **Calls-to-action**

- Change the CTA text on your buttons to see which word works to convert more visitors.

- Change the location of your CTA.

- Test different colors, shapes, and sizes for your CTA buttons.

✔ **Content**

- Try gated content versus ungated content. What is getting the most traffic and shares?

- Test different content types. Do your leads prefer visual assets like slide decks, or are they sticking to your ebooks?

- Test different ways of displaying your content on your website. Try a website resource center where all of your content lives, and test content displayed on product or service pages.

✔ **Copy**

- Change your headline text and try different tones and variations.

- Test paragraphs versus numbered or bulleted lists.

- Try different fonts and bold versus italics.

✔ **Imagery**

- Test different headers on your emails and landing pages.

- Test different graphic images on your website or on landing pages.

- Test a rotating carousel on your home page versus a static image or video.

✔ **Site navigation**

- Try out different menu navigations and determine what works best.

- Test fixed or scrolling navigation.

- Change your navigation titles to try out different copy.

✔ **Forms**

- Test the length of your forms.

- Try using drop-downs versus multiple choice fields.

- Test out offering coupons or promotions to try to get more leads to fill out your forms.

✔ **Social**

- Change the size and placement of your social sharing buttons to see what prompts more shares.

- Try different shapes and sizes of your social sharing buttons.

- Test social sign-on instead of having leads fill out a form.

✔ **Email**

- Test the length and copy of your emails.

- Test out different subject lines.

- Try different email send times to see when you get the most conversions.

✔ **Personalization**

- Test out sending personalized email correspondence on a lead's birthday.

- Create seasonal or holiday-specific promotions.

- Use personalization throughout your emails by calling out the lead's name and certain attributes.

Chapter 20

Developing Lead-Generation Metrics

As a marketer, you want a seat at the revenue table, right? I know I do! And if you have gotten this far in the book, I would say you probably do also. If marketing is seen as a viable part of the revenue team, you can be seen as a contributor to the company's bottom line, and not a cost center. This was difficult in the past because marketers did not have a clear way to measure ROI on campaigns. But luckily, this has all changed, for *smart* marketers anyways. Forget about those cute remarks from sales comparing marketing to "arts and crafts" that show they don't value your contribution to company growth. As a marketer in today's world, you need to get down to business and really measure the ROI of your campaigns.

After all, getting leads and *knowing* that they have contributed to revenue by becoming a customer is a critical element to successful lead generation. By thinking about metrics and designing your programs to be measureable, you can be on your way to that cushy seat in the board room.

Designing Programs to be Measurable

The best marketing plans are created with measurements in mind *before* the program has even been executed. And yes, *all* of your lead-generation programs are indeed measureable. Even the channels you might have a tough time measuring initially, like social, can be measured. For instance, want to beef up your Facebook presence? How about measuring shares or likes? No matter what your metrics are, know what they are early in the planning process. Ask yourself the following questions:

- *What* will you measure?
- *When* will you measure?
- *How* will you measure?

So how do you start thinking about making programs measureable? Read on to find out.

Creating obtainable goals

One of the first elements to keep in mind is to make your goals attainable. Start small, think big, and work quickly. This means don't overdo it. If your company has never created a Twitter account, gaining 100,000 followers in the first 6 months and tweeting 10 times a day might not be realistic. Think about the following items before you determine your goals:

- How much effort do I want to put into each channel/tactic?
- How many resources can I assign to making each channel/tactic a success?
- How much budget do I have to create programs this quarter/this year?
- How much time do I want to spend on each channel/tactic?

From there, you can determine how aggressive your goals are. Back to my Twitter example — if you decide that increasing Twitter follower count is a huge goal this quarter and you have one or two resources to put towards that goal, you can be more aggressive. Then commit to and forecast these metrics and report out on them.

Measuring in a marketing automation platform

You can track *some* metrics without a marketing automation platform. Your CRM (customer relationship management) tool probably has some basic metrics, your email service provider might have a few things, and you can do some calculations manually. However, to truly track your campaigns and tie them to revenue, you need a marketing automation platform that can tie programs to opportunities, pipeline created, and revenue. The more sophisticated your metrics are, the more marketing can be taken seriously, and the more budget you get for next year!

Here is a selection of the types of metrics you can measure with marketing automation. I go into more detail about many of these metrics in the coming pages:

- ✔ **Program analysis:** Proves the effectiveness of your programs and to see what delivers the most ROI (return on investment).

- ✔ **Reporting:** Create your own reports that can measure pipeline generated per program, ROI by channel, costs per new name per channel, revenue per program channel, and more.

- ✔ **Opportunity influence:** Know what programs affected which deals along the deal lifecycle.

- ✔ **Attribution:** See which campaigns generated the initial lead from a closed/won deal and see which campaigns influenced that deal over its lifecycle.

By leveraging the reporting functionality within your marketing automation tool, you can generate more accurate numbers and really show that program attribution that your execs crave.

Building a revenue modeler

You want an overall vision of your funnel, so you can map your buyer journey, define the stages of your company's sales funnel, and know where any given lead is at any given time. Programs like Marketo enable you to create a model of your revenue cycle directly in the application, so you can dig deep into each stage to determine how many leads live there, what the leads in each stage look like, how long a lead typically stays in each stage, and what the trends are over time. This type of insight gives you a true foundation for marketing analysis and forecasting because you are starting with a complete picture.

Figure 20-1 shows an example of Marketo's Revenue Cycle Modeler. This image is of our own revenue cycle, but you get the idea. The figure shows tracking your leads from anonymous status to won. You can also see that there are a variety of additional paths that include recycled, disqualified, and lost.

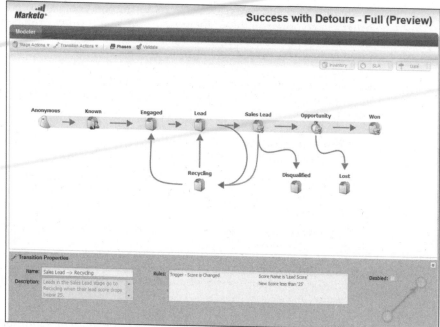

Figure 20-1:
Marketo's
Revenue
Cycle
Modeler.

Measuring and Optimizing Your Programs

After you have a good foundation for measurement, it's time to get to, well, measuring! You can use various different metrics from basic to advanced. I'm going to touch on some of the metrics I have used to have a clear picture of marketing contribution to pipeline and revenue.

Tracking investment

One of the first items you want to track and measure in your programs is your investment. You want to think of marketing as an *investment*, not a cost. You don't want to be seen as a *cost center*. When marketers talk about investment, they're indicating that marketing is a department companies invest *in*. It's an important distinction to make. So as I talk about tracking *investment*, I won't be using the term *cost*.

In order to determine how to track the ROI of your programs and investment, you need to have a pretty good view of *what* you are spending and *how* you are spending it, which is actually relatively difficult for many marketers.

Did you know that 89 percent of organizations use spreadsheets to track their spending? You are probably nodding your head and saying, "Yes Dayna, I use a spreadsheet to track my spending." This is a start, but let me talk a bit more about how different technology applications can really help you track your investment.

Spreadsheets create some problems. You can't track investment across different budgets and line items, and you don't get as much visibility as you need to accurately forecast. That's why many marketers do not have a clear picture on what they are investing.

There are many applications out there that can help you track spending to show what you are investing, budget versus actuals, and program alignment with investment. This means that with a budgeting application that syncs with your marketing automation tool, you can track important metrics like cost per lead and program ROI.

Figure 20-2 shows an example of an analytics dashboard in Marketo Financial Management, a budgeting tracking tool. Here you can keep track of forecasting, investments, and plan versus actual, which is a fantastic place to start with tracking ROI.

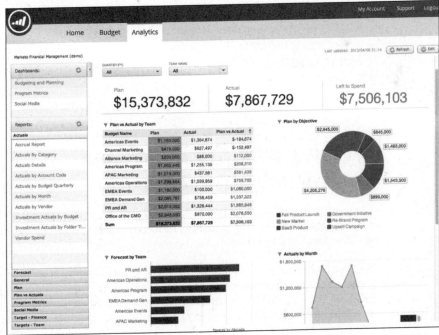

Figure 20-2:
The Marketo Financial Management analytics dashboard.

Knowing the most common metrics

Marketers track many common metrics. These metrics are a great start, and if you are taking baby steps to truly becoming a revenue marketer, make sure you at least have these measurements in place:

- **Marketing percentage of contribution to sales pipeline:** The percent of revenue in the sales pipeline (opportunities) that originated from marketing efforts
- **Marketing percentage of contribution to closed revenue:** The percentage of revenue in closed, won deals that originated from marketing efforts
- **Quantity of sales-qualified leads (SQLs):** The number of SQLs sent to your sales teams
- **Quality of SQLs:** The percentage of SQLs not rejected by sales
- **Investment per inquiry:** Total lead acquisition investment/the total number of inquiries
- **Cost per lead:** Total campaign costs/quantity of leads
- **Inquiry to marketing-qualified lead (MQL):** Conversion of initial inquiry to marketing-qualified lead
- **MQL to sales-accepted lead (SAL):** Conversion from MQL to sales-accepted lead
- **SAL to sales-qualified lead (SQL):** Conversion from SAL to sales-qualified lead
- **SQL to opportunity:** Conversion from SQL to opportunity

Working with first-touch and multi-touch attribution

The basics measurements are a great place to start, but they don't give you a complete picture. The next few, more advanced, measurements are my all-time favorites to attribute lead-generation efforts to revenue.

Single-attribution measurements help you give credit for a deal to marketing programs that originally created or that closed the deal, known as first-touch (FT) and last-touch (LT) attribution. Because many of your lead-generation programs are TOFU (top-of-funnel), you will have a lot of FT attribution in your measurements.

Multi-touch (MT) attribution tracks how each marketing program touches a deal throughout the lead lifecycle. It essentially spreads the value of the deal over all marketing interactions with the lead to see how your programs work together to create opportunities and drive closed/won deals.

Many marketers don't track MT attribution, so they don't get credit for how they *influenced* a deal over time. But because marketing is multichanneled and today's buyer self-educates, marketing most likely touches a deal many times before that deal is closed.

By using FT, LT, and MT attribution in your marketing automation tool, you can pinpoint marketing's influence granularly versus relying on sales to mark something in their CRM tool that indicates marketing found a lead. Figure 20-3 shows a screenshot from Marketo's Revenue Cycle Analytics that shows which programs typically create more MT pipeline, and which programs create more FT pipeline.

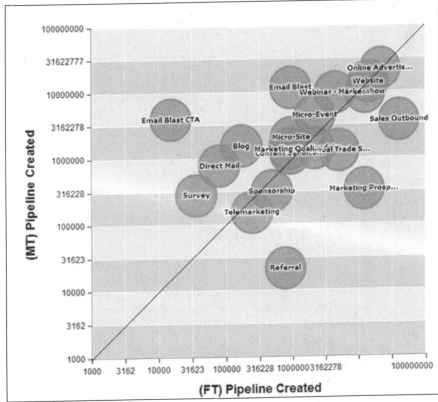

Figure 20-3: Marketo Revenue Cycle Analytics FT and MT attribution.

In addition to each of these basic FT and MT attributions, also consider tracking MT ratio, which can be defined as pipeline/investment, for a more in-depth look at program performance. This tells you in more detail what works and what doesn't. At Marketo, for example, MT ratios higher than 10 indicate good programs, ratios around 7 are OK, and lower than 5 is not good enough.

Figure 20-4 shows a real screenshot of Marketo's metrics. This figure shows the program channel, the investment in each channel, FT opportunities created, MT opportunities created, and the MT ratio.

Program Channel	Investment	(FT) Opportunities	(MT) Opportunities	(MT) Ratio	% Above Min*
Website	$0	2,448	4,255	N/A	N/A
Paid Online (PPC+Email)	$4,020,328	2,195	3,035	22.6	52%
Webinar - Marketo	$687,898	907	1,815	79.2	79%
Nurture Email	$15,750	37	1,515	2,886.6	
Tradeshow	$1,338,339	1,684	1,296	29.1	46%
Nurture Email - CTA	$26,665	25	516	580.3	
Blog	$0	47	475	N/A	N/A
Event - Roadshow	$470,119	305	427	27.3	39%
Micro-Event	$722,041	390	414	17.2	38%
Sales Outbound	$0	2,877	377	N/A	N/A
Virtual Trade Show	$368,325	404	232	18.9	38%
Content Syndication	$605,091	140	202	10.0	29%
Micro-Site	$0	63	164	N/A	N/A
Source: Marketo Revenue Cycle Analytics, Oct 2013					
Percentage of all programs in channel that achieve MT Ratio > 5				7.6	52%

Figure 20-4: A Marketo pipeline generation report.

Tracking influence

Many sales cycles, particularly in the B2B world, involve more than one decision-maker. In fact, these days, there are usually buying teams that include multiple decision-influencers. To fully track lead-generation program FT and MT attribution to deals, you need to look at how marketing affects *all* of the influencers in a design process.

Say your team is purchasing a community platform so you can engage your customers in a community environment. You have a team of about seven people who are involved in the decision process, but you are the named decision-maker. Particularly if you are an executive, you might task your team to do research — download ebooks, attend webinars, and check out different websites of solutions that fit your criteria. Your teams do their research and come back to you with their suggestions. You take those suggestions, make a decision, and engage with the sales team. In a CRM tool, it would show that you were the only decision-maker and marketing had very little contact with you before you spoke to sales. CRM systems don't track how many touches marketing has made with your influencer team. Marketing automation typically has the functionality to track influencers and tie them to closed deals.

Figure 20-5 shows an example of opportunity influence, a depiction of how marketing touched every influencer in a deal cycle. You can see that there are two named decision-makers who have an opportunity role. The lighter part on the left indicates that a customer was a lead, and the darker shading on the right shows when that lead turned into a customer. Looking at this, you probably would think marketing didn't do much to turn that lead into a customer.

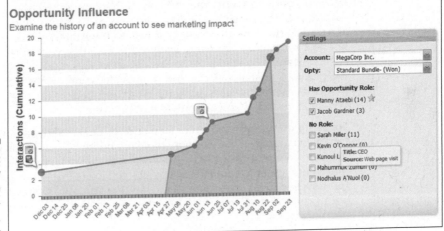

Figure 20-5: Opportunity Influence decision-makers.

But if you hover your mouse pointer over the associated influencers that are tagged with no role, you can see that Sarah Miller, who is the CEO, has had many interactions with marketing over the lifecycle of the deal, as shown in Figure 20-6. This indicates that there has in fact been marketing influence on this account. Most likely, Sarah told a team member to contact sales to start a discussion after she did a fair amount of research.

Figure 20-6: The Opportunity Influence buying team.

Knowing the Challenges of Lead-Generation Metrics

To really be on your game, you should be aware of the common pitfalls that marketers often fall victim to when measuring their program efforts:

✔ **Focusing only on vanity metrics:** Many marketers track things like Facebook Likes, blog post shares, and how many names were gathered at a tradeshow. Now, these are all things to track internally on your teams, but be aware that your C-suite likely won't care that your most recent Facebook post received 500 Likes. Instead of focusing only on empty metrics, look at analytics that focus on business outcomes and revenue. Remember your goal as a marketer is to contribute to the bottomline, and you can't do that if you are only counting Likes.

✔ **Focusing on quantity:** A ton of leads doesn't necessarily amount to a ton of *good* leads. If you are only focusing on how many leads you can get from an ebook download, you are not focusing on the lead quality. It may sound great to report that you got 400 leads from your new ebook, but how *good* are those leads? Are they 400 students who will never buy your product? If so, you need to work on targeting and optimizing your campaigns.

✔ **Sticking to the easy measurements:** Metrics are hard, I get that. But if you are taking the easy way out and not measuring based on some of the more advanced metrics I cover in this chapter, you are not proving your value in a way that ties your team to financial outcomes.

✔ **Looking only at activity:** It's great that you publish a blog each day, and you can certainly report on that, but how is that affecting the business's bottom line? How many leads are those blogs generating, and how much revenue can you attribute to those blogs? Focus on outcomes rather than activities.

Part VI

The Part of Tens

Visit www.dummies.com/extras/leadgeneration to find out what the top ten lead generation blogs are.

In this part . . .

- Learn the top ten most common lead-generation pitfalls
- Meet ten lead-generation influencers to watch
- Discover ten additional lead-generation tactics that can take your programs from blah to wow

Chapter 21

Ten Common Lead-Generation Pitfalls

I am sure your head is swimming with a ton of great information after reading this book. And I'm sure you can't *wait* to go out there and implement these tactics in your own business. But first, a few warnings about common pitfalls I see marketers make time and time again.

Measuring Quantity over Quality

This is a big one. Many marketers, especially those just starting out with lead generation, get excited by the *number* of leads they can generate. However, remember that it isn't about the number of leads you throw at sales that makes a good program. Instead, it is the number of *quality* leads that sales can actually close. Don't be the marketer who throws leads at the wall like spaghetti to see what sticks. By following the rules in this book and testing, optimizing, and measuring your programs, you will have better luck at sending warm and qualified leads to sales.

Not Understanding Your Audience

The buyer persona exercise I discussed in Chapter 6 is one of the most important initial steps to a solid lead-generation program. You need to understand in detail who your buyer is and his buyer journey. Without this in-depth understanding, you are setting yourself up for failure. How can you speak directly to someone you barely know?

The key to lead-generation success is sending relevant messages to your audience and creating a relationship. Take the time to understand who they are and what makes them tick.

Not Paying Attention to Buying Stage

Your leads go through a buying journey. Respect that process and present your leads with the right offers at the right time. A lead who is just researching what your solution is all about isn't ready to be sold, so don't put her in that situation. Match your offers to what she is seeking. Marketers who don't do this will likely see leads going dark. By understanding where a lead is on his journey, you can provide helpful information that moves the lead through the sales cycle over time.

Serving Up Only Promotional Content

This is another biggie, and one that I see time and time again, especially for companies just starting out with lead generation and content marketing. Instead of building a solid foundation of educational thought leadership, these companies fill their funnel with promotional papers and demos. These types of assets won't resonate with buyers until they are ready to buy. Don't be afraid to push out content that doesn't beat your own chest. The soft, relationship sell of educational content will reel your lead in over time. Plus, you can quickly become a leader in your space, which helps your trust and credibility.

Including too Many Calls-to-Action

If a lead doesn't know what to do, he will most likely not do anything. Don't clutter your program collateral with too many CTAs. It's tempting to cram in every last thing into an email when you are trying to promote a new ebook, a webinar, and a tradeshow at the same time, but remember K.I.S.S: Keep It Simple, Stupid. Highlight one main CTA so your leads know exactly what to do.

Don't Rely Only on Inbound Marketing for Lead Generation

Inbound marketing has all the buzz, but you need to combine it with outbound marketing tactics in order to have an effective lead-generation strategy. According to VP of Content at Hubspot, Joe Chernov, "There's this dirty little secret: inbound is ineffective for landing those super-critical first 30 customers (for a new company, product, or division). It just takes *time* to build out the machinery, generate the traffic, convert the visitors, and then move leads through the funnel." You need to combine those efforts with a solid outbound plan that includes sales, networking, and just plain hustling to grow your business. Joe continues by stating that "[inbound] needs to be built and refined in parallel with your [outbound efforts] so that when product and market fit is achieved, inbound can scale growth." That's why both inbound *and* outbound techniques are discussed at length in this book. Despite how popular inbound marketing has become, don't forget about the power of outbound.

Not Aligning Sales and Marketing

I see many companies where sales and marketing exist in separate silos. This is a very hard habit to break. Sales thinks marketing is "arts and crafts" and marketing thinks sales doesn't understand what they do on a day-to-day basis and the value they bring. As a result, leads fall through the cracks. Good sales and marketing alignment accomplishes many objectives — most importantly, closing more leads to grow your business.

Failing to Nurture Leads after Acquisition

I know I have a whole chapter devoted to lead nurturing, but the concept is so important it begs to be repeated. Most of your leads are not ready to buy when you get their names, especially if you are rocking out your lead generation with a lot of top-of-the-funnel campaigns. You have to build relationships with your leads over time through lead nurturing. That way, you can stay top of mind so that when your lead is ready to buy, she will consider your company first.

Not Testing Your Campaigns

You can test almost everything in your lead-generation plan. Test campaigns, copy, subject lines, times of day, design, and so on. You know how in the movie *Glengarry Glen Ross*, the sales reps live by ABC (Always Be Closing)? Well, as a marketer you should ABT (Always Be Testing), because that is the only way you can know what works and what doesn't work. Testing also helps you learn more about your target buyer and his behaviors and actions.

Being Boring

Finally, don't be boring! I don't care if you are a B2B start-up company or a large enterprise. You are still selling to *people*. People like to be entertained. People like to be educated. People want to be spoken to as though they are humans and not drones. No matter what industry you are in, all of your lead-generation campaigns can use some spicing up. If you are interesting and creative, you will be heard through all of that noise out there.

Chapter 22

Ten Lead-Generation Influencers to Watch

....

In This Chapter

▶ Learning about permission marketing through Seth Godin

▶ Perfecting your social strategy with the help of Jay Baer

▶ Automating your marketing with Jon Miller

▶ Rocking your content strategy with Ann Handley

....

*T*here is a lot of thought leadership out there in the lead-generation space, so make sure you pay attention. By following interesting thought leaders through their blogs, on Twitter, and on LinkedIn, you can always have your finger on the pulse, and gain additional knowledge to help you grow. Many of these folks are also published authors, so be sure to check out their books.

Here is my list of the top 10 lead-generation influencers to watch!

Seth Godin

Seth Godin is a bestselling author and blogger. He has written 17 titles, including well-known marketing books such as *Linchpin: Are You Indispensable?* and *Purple Cow: Transform Your Business by Being Remarkable*. Seth is a speaker and founder of www.squidoo.com, and has also been inducted into the Marketing Hall of Fame. Prior to being a blogger and author, Seth was VP of direct marketing at Yahoo!.

What I love about Seth Godin is his blog, which is certainly easy to get lost in. Godin coined the term *interruption marketing* to describe tactics that work only if they interrupt you to get your attention. Instead, Godin promotes *permission marketing*, where a business provides relevant information to buyers.

Seth writes about all things marketing and more. Check out his website at www.sethgodin.com/sg and follow him on Twitter (@ThisisSethsBlog).

Guy Kawasaki

Guy Kawasaki is a Silicon Valley legend. Previously chief evangelist at Apple, Guy now focuses his energy on being a special advisor to the Motorola business unit at Google and writing bestselling books like *APE: Author, Publisher, Entrepreneur; What the Plus!: Google+ for the Rest of Us*; and *Enchantment: The Art of Changing Hearts, Minds, and Actions*. He has a BA from Stanford University and an MBA from UCLA. He also has an honorary doctorate from Babson College. Currently, he is partner at Garage Technology Ventures and a cofounder at Alltop.

Kawasaki has almost 1.5 million Twitter followers (@GuyKawasaki), an active blog, `http://blog.guykawasaki.com`, and many speaking engagements all over the world. One of his recent works, *APE*, discusses self-publishing and the rise of content marketing.

Jay Baer

Jay Baer is a keynote speaker, author, entrepreneur, and social media and digital marketing consultant. In fact, Jay was named one of America's top three social media consultants. He runs one of the top marketing blogs out there, `www.convinceandconvert.com`. Jay has written the *New York Times* bestsellers *The NOW Revolution: 7 Shifts to Make Your Business Faster, Smarter, and More Social* and *Youtility: Why Smart Marketing is About Help and Not Hype*.

Jay blogs about all things marketing from social media to content marketing and everything in between. His blog is a great source of information to jumpstart your lead-generation programs, and be sure to follow him on Twitter, @jaybaer.

Chris Brogan

Chris Brogan is publisher of *Owner* magazine and president and CEO of Human Business Works, a publishing and media company. Brogan is an accomplished speaker and an active blogger on `www.chrisbrogan.com`. Brogan also does consulting with companies like Disney, Microsoft, Coke, Google, and so on. And if that's not enough, he's a *New York Times* bestselling author with books like *The Impact Equation: Are You Making Things Happen or Just Making Noise?* and *Trust Agents: Using the Web to Build Influence, Improve Reputation, and Earn Trust* under his belt.

Chris has 13 years of experience in online networks, social communities, and other areas of digital business. Follow him on Twitter (@chrisbrogan). He also has a very active blog that you can check out: www.chrisbrogan.com/blog.

Jon Miller

Not only is Jon Miller the VP of Marketing at Marketo (and in the interests of full disclosure, he's also my boss), he is also one of the best minds in digital marketing. Jon runs all areas of product marketing and content at Marketo. In 2010, the CMO Institute named Jon one of the Top 10 CMOs for companies under $250 million. Jon holds a bachelor's degree in physics from Harvard and an MBA from Stanford Business School.

Jon is an active speaker and blogger for Marketo's blog (blog.marketo.com), where he blogs about all things marketing (and has a particular love for the analytical side). Also be sure to check out Jon on Twitter (@jonmiller).

Gary Vaynerchuk

Gary Vaynerchuk is an entrepreneur, speaker, and social media evangelist. Gary is cofounder of VaynerMedia, an agency that works with Fortune 500 companies like GE, Pepsi, and the New York Jets. Gary helps companies build their digital brands. Vaynerchuk is an investor who has helped companies like Tumblr, Path, and Uber get off the ground. He is also a bestselling author of three books, including *Jab, Jab, Jab, Right Hook: How to Tell Your Story in a Noisy Social World; The Thank You Economy;* and *Crush It!: Why Now Is the Time to Cash in on Your Passion.*

Be sure to follow him on Twitter (@garyvee). About once a week, Gary asks his followers, "What can I do for you?" He invites his followers to ask him for requests or favors.

Mari Smith

Mari Smith is the premiere leader for social media, particularly Facebook. She is a social media strategist and author of *The New Relationship Marketing: How to Build a Large, Loyal, Profitable Network Using the Social Web* and coauthor with Chris Treadway of *Facebook Marketing: An Hour a Day*. Mari does speaking engagements, offers an online course specializing in Facebook marketing, and consults with companies on social media strategy.

Follow Mari on Twitter (@MariSmith) and be sure to read her blog at `www.marismith.com/mari-smith-blog/`.

Ardath Albee

Ardath Albee is CEO of Marketing Interactions, where she specializes in B2B marketing strategy. She has 25 years of business management under her belt and was recently selected as one of the 2011 Top 20 Women to Watch in sales lead management and one of the 50 Most Influential People in sales and lead management.

Follow Ardath on Twitter (@ardath421) and be sure to check out her blog at `http://marketinginteractions.typepad.com/` to learn about all things B2B marketing.

Ann Handley

Ann Handley is the chief content officer at Marketing Profs and is a veteran of creating and managing digital content. Ann is the coauthor of *Content Rules: How to Create Killer Blogs, Podcasts, Videos, Ebooks, Webinars (and More) that Engage Customers and Ignite Your Business.* Ann is a fantastic speaker and has a great blog about content marketing — `www.annhandley.com/blog/`. Be sure to also follow her on Twitter (@annhandley).

Robert Scoble

Robert Scoble, tech evangelist and startup liaison officer at Rackspace, is best known for his blog, `http://scobleizer.com`. Robert writes about all things tech, and also spends a good deal of time discussing how blogs are changing the ways companies interact with customers. Check out his book, *Naked Conversations: How Blogs Are Changing the Way Businesses Talk with Customers,* to learn more about Scoble's views on blogging.

If you have a startup or work in tech, Robert is one to watch. Follow him on Twitter (@Scobleizer).

Chapter 23

Ten Powerful Lead-Generation Tactics

. . . .

In This Chapter

▶ Creating an impact with guerilla marketing

▶ Engaging with thought leaders through influencer marketing

▶ Making an impact with a jingle or a song

▶ Using visuals like infographics and photo memes in your content strategy

. . . .

I've talked about many innovative lead-generation strategies in this book, but there are a few more that I wanted to draw your attention to. If you integrate these additional tactics into your holistic lead-generation plan, you can give your campaigns that extra *oomph* they need to stand out.

Going Guerilla

Guerilla marketing is a strategy that uses unconventional methods, at often low cost, to get your message across. This could be as simple as putting stickers or posters up around your neighborhood, or could be something more robust like organizing a flash mob. In my experience, guerilla marketing techniques work particularly well around an event.

For instance, at Salesforce's Dreamforce 2013 conference, a competitor, SugarCRM, created a guerilla campaign called Escape Dreamforce. Outside of the conference, they gave attendees a chance to win a trip to Hawaii by putting on a SugarCRM T-shirt and taking a "selfie" photo and tweeting the picture with the hashtag #DF13 #SugarSelfie. Because guerilla marketing is disruptive, this campaign got a ton of discussion among attendees and journalists alike.

Making Viral Videos

In a similar vein as a guerilla campaign, a viral video generates a lot of buzz. You can either create a viral video on your own, or consider newsjacking a video that is already popular. Obviously of the two, creating your own viral video can be trickier because you never really know what people will latch on to. However, many companies have great success by using a video that is already viral and creating a parody. HubSpot does a great job with this. They have created videos that emulate viral sensations such as *Gangnam Style* or *The Fox (What Does the Fox Say?),* and geared them towards marketers.

After you have created a video, use it in your lead-generation campaigns, particularly on your social channels.

Delving into Influencer Marketing

I didn't include a chapter on this, and honestly it could be a whole *For Dummies* book in and of itself. Influencer marketing is akin to relationship marketing. Every industry has a set of people who are deemed influential: Maybe they are the CEO of a leading company, an author, a blogger, or a speaker. Create a list of at *least* ten people (sometimes there can be hundreds) you would love to have on your side. Then create relationships and network with those people. Swap blogs, links, and invite them to speak on a webinar.

Generally, if you help them with additional exposure to your audience, they will also help you.

Using Memes

Marketo uses memes all of the time in social campaigns to generate additional engagement. What is a meme? Simply put, an *internet meme* is an idea that spreads virally online. Memes are often funny, include a simple statement or popular phrase, and can take the form of a video, photo, image, microsite, or hashtag. For example, you can use memes in the form of photographs with funny phrases or quotes. You can be super-creative with memes. Using a pop culture icon and creating copy that relates to who that person is often results in a ton of engagement on Facebook and Twitter.

Creating Campaigns Around Current Events

A technique I love to use is newsjacking. Basically, *newsjacking* is taking a popular current event and creating a marketing campaign, blog, or ebook that speaks directly to that event. Consider using a television show or movie as inspiration for your next infographic. In fact, I'm working right now on an infographic that references the popular show *The Walking Dead*. I'll relate this to marketing and launch it during the television show's mid-season finale for extra lift. I'll post the infographic on Twitter using the show's hashtag so that everyone who follows that hashtag will see the infographic. That is just one example, but there are tons of ways to use current events or pop culture as part of your marketing strategy.

Engaging with Infographics

An *infographic* is a piece of content that conveys a story or data in a highly visual way. This could be your product story or usage stats, or maybe even an infographic focusing on something hot in your industry.

At Marketo, I try to create two infographics per month, and I work with a design team at Column Five to make sure that each infographic not only speaks to our audience, but is also buzzworthy for the press. Your infographic design firm should also do media outreach for you to pitch the infographic so that it can be seen on other industry sites. Sites like Mashable and TechCrunch have picked up our infographics.

Trying a Jingle or a Song

Another fun tactic is to create a jingle or a song to go along with a product launch or new content asset. These can be pretty simple to create if you contact the right people. I've seen people hire vendors from the website Fiverr (www.fiverr.com) to create short jingles about new content pieces or products. Typically, you can give the songwriter some messaging bullet points and she comes up with a song. Consider putting some animation behind it, if possible. When it's finished, you have a catchy tune to put on social media, in emails, and in other lead-generation campaigns.

Introducing a Google Hangout Series

Google+ is great for SEO, and another standout feature is the Google Hangout. Basically, a Google Hangout is similar to video conferencing. Have a Google Hangout with an influencer in your space or a thought leader at your company. Just as with a webinar, send email invitations and post on social channels. Invitees can go to your Google+ page to view the hangout, which you can also record for later viewing sessions. The pros of Google Hangout are that is pretty easy to set one up, it has a simple interface, and audience members can ask questions directly on your G+ account. The con is that as of this writing, you can't collect lead information for who attended your hangout. Therefore, although it can be a good TOFU (top-of-funnel) lead-generation channel, you might want to hold off on a hangout if you are trying to promote mid-funnel content.

Creating "Chocolate Cake" Content Pieces

Every company should have a mix of content that they are creating. Your mix should range from the more serious industry reports to the fun stuff. Marketo thinks of the fun stuff as *chocolate cake content*. This could be a fun infographic, a visual slide deck, or simply a few fun blog posts.

For instance, Marketo often creates infographics that are created as "link bait" and for social sharing. These infographics are meant to appeal to the masses and are generally fun in nature. We recently published an infographic called Kittens and Bacon, where we compared how often bacon was referenced on social sites compared to how often kittens were mentioned. This obviously has nothing to do with marketing automation specifically, but it was about digital culture and social media in general, which works for our audience. It was fun and viral, and we got a ton of shares.

Using an Automated Voicemail in a Campaign

Many services, such as Boxpilot, specialize in automated voicemails. These are fantastic to use before events to ramp up attendance, and you won't be wasting the time of your inside sales reps calling to promote your event. Automated voicemail services allow you to create your own script and use your own voice talent. Think of using your CEO's voice, or even that of a famous person, if you can afford it! The service calls your potential registrants during off-hours and leaves your voicemail on their machine. Voilà! While you're asleep, you get tons of new registrants for your event.

Index

• D •

About the Author

Dayna Rothman is the senior content marketing manager at Marketo, a leading marketing automation software maker and a thought leader in the lead generation space. Dayna has been in the trenches at a fast-paced technology company and has seen first-hand how to run a lead-generation machine. Prior to Marketo, Dayna spent time developing lead generation strategies for a variety of start-ups in the Silicon Valley. Dayna has an undergraduate degree in Technical writing and English from Southern Connecticut State University, and an MBA from Golden Gate University. You can find some of Dayna's writing at Marketo's blog (http://blog.marketo.com) and her ebooks at www.marketo.com/resources.

Growing up, Dayna always loved to write. At college in Connecticut, she found a knack for non-fiction writing and aspired to write technical manuals for businesses. As luck would have it, her first job offer was in sales, where she worked for quite a few years. She then ventured to Oakland, California and landed a marketing job in the bustling world of technology. A lot of hard work, an MBA, and a few marketing jobs later, she found herself at Marketo, where she finally found the perfect intersection of the business world she had grown to love, and the writing that she had always longed to get back into. Since then, she has authored a number of blogs, ebooks, and some of Marketo's *Definitive Guide* series. Additionally, Dayna has spoken at numerous industry events and webinars.

Dedication

I dedicate this book to my fabulous husband, Gabriel Rothman. Without your loving support, this book would not have been possible. You have stuck by me through thick and thin, richer and poorer, in sickness and in health. You have endured long nights and weekends of writing, in addition to my already demanding job. You have been my saving grace and driving force.

Author's Acknowledgments

This project couldn't have succeeded without the help and support of many people.

I want to thank Jon Miller, VP of marketing and cofounder of Marketo. He has been a great mentor to me and without his support and guidance, this book wouldn't have been possible. I want to thank Marketo's CMO Sanjay Dholakia for his continued support of this project. I also want to thank my co-workers and the lead generation team at Marketo, including Maggie Jones, Carra Manahan, Heidi Bullock, Amy Palmer, Jessica Langensand, Miles Gotcher, Lauren Moskowitz, Phillip Chen, and D.J. Waldow.

I want to thank the folks at Wiley for taking a chance on an unknown author, and I want to thank my technical editor and friend, Liz Kao, for her guidance on writing a *For Dummies* book.

Also, special thanks to my family — my husband Gabriel Rothman, my mother Michele Garber, my father Jeffrey Racow, my stepmother Sue Racow, and my stepfather Alan Garber. I also want to thank my sister Kim Racow — even though she is so far away in Africa, she is always in my heart. Thanks also go to my extended family, Jeff and Kathy Rothman, Stacey Rothman, Loren Rothman, and Toni Sicola.

Publisher's Acknowledgments

Acquisitions Editor: Amy Fandrei

Project Editor: Linda Morris

Copy Editor: Linda Morris

Technical Editor: Liz Kao

Editorial Assistant: Annie Sullivan

Sr. Editorial Assistant: Cherie Case

Project Coordinator: Phil Midkiff

Cover Image: © iStockphoto.com/3dts